To Dad,
For a
Christmas 2001.
With love,
John.

GW01417842

THE

BOOK OF SUN-DIALS.

COLLECTED BY

MRS. ALFRED GATTY,

AUTHOR OF "PARABLES FROM NATURE," ETC.

NEW AND ENLARGED EDITION,

EDITED BY

H. K. F. GATTY AND ELEANOR LLOYD,

WITH AN APPENDIX ON THE CONSTRUCTION

OF DIALS BY

W. RICHARDSON.

LONDON:

GEORGE BELL AND SONS, YORK STREET,

COVENT GARDEN.

1889.

PORTABLE DIAL AND COMPASS IN THE ANTIQUARIAN
MUSEUM, EDINBURGH.   SEE NO. 30.

THE BOOK OF SUN-DIALS.

DIAL AT CAWSTON LODGE, NEAR RUGBY.
See No. 660.

PREFACE.

" IF anyone should open these pages expecting to find in
them an astronomically scientific account of sun-dials,
from their first simple origin to the complicated and even
confused perfection at which they arrived, just before they
were superseded by clocks in the beginning of the eighteenth
century, he will be disappointed."

This sentence formed the opening paragraph of my mother's
Preface to her "Book of Sun-dials;" and it is repeated here,
because, though a considerable amount of scientific and
archæological information has been added to the book, its
main intention remains the same—namely, that of treating
sun-dials chiefly from their moral and poetical aspect.

In the brief Memoir of Mrs. Gatty, which was written by
my sister, Juliana Horatia Ewing, she said, with reference to
our mother's interest in sun-dials: "As a girl she began a
collection of mottoes to be found on sun-dials, the collection
being illustrated by drawings of the sun-dials themselves.
Possessed—when they have mottoes, as all sun-dials should
have—of both 'body and soul,' these primitive and picturesque registers of the 'fleeting hours' of successive generations had a natural charm for her taste, which must have

---

[1] "Parables from Nature," in two series, 1s. each (paper), p. xviii.

been increased by the attractions they offer to the sketcher's eye. At one place half buried in the rank grass of a neglected lawn, with unclipt yews threatening to part the dial from the sun; at another preaching tombstone morality from a moss-grown motto among equally forgotten graves; here a picturesque patch upon whitewash at the sunny corner of some street in France or Italy; there, gleaming more with gold than sunshine, high up upon the weather-stained brickwork of a civic building in Old England: an ugly sun-dial or a senseless dial motto are alike rare."

One of the first dials which attracted my mother's attention was that which hung over the porch of Catterick Church, where her father, the Rev. A. J. Scott, D.D., was vicar (see No. 161). The sketch she made of it stands on the first page of her album; and I learnt with great regret, soon after her death, that the dial had been removed during the restoration of the church, and was lying broken in the churchyard. It was injured beyond repair. But let me here gratefully record that, owing to the kindness and energy of William Booth, Esq., of Oran, an exact copy of the old face has been made and erected over the porch. Would that an equally good friend could be found for each dial which is mentioned here as having been misplaced! I hope that the treatise in our Appendix which Mr. Richardson has written on "The Construction of Sun-dials," will be found useful in cases where a vicar or his churchwardens are willing to restore an old relic, but do not know how to make the calculations necessary for doing so.

This treatise is the most important scientific addition which this volume contains. Mr. Wigham Richardson has written it specially for us; but it will be published separately, in a cheap form, so as to be within reach of purchasers who are interested in dialling from its practical side only. Mr.

Richardson sympathises with both its poetical and its practical
aspects. He put a motto on the dial which adorns his Neptune Works, at Newcastle-on-Tyne (see No. 177), and was
interested to find how many of his own and of other workmen wished to learn the art of mechanical dialling.

For the additional archæological information in this edition
I am almost entirely indebted to the unwearied diligence of
my fellow-editor, Miss Eleanor Lloyd, but, indeed, she has
contributed the chief part of all the additions to the book, and
has also drawn the illustrations. She helped my mother
greatly in compiling the original edition, and it has been a
great advantage, as well as pleasure, to labour with so true a
friend and accurate a worker during the preparation of this
second issue of the volume.

The only helpers whose names my mother recorded in her
Preface were Miss Eleanor Lloyd and my father, the Rev.
Alfred Gatty, D.D., and to the latter the book was dedicated
in the following words:—

" TO THE DEAR HUSBAND,
TO WHOM I AM INDEBTED FOR THE BEST HAPPINESS OF
THE HOURS OF EARTHLY LIFE,
AND WITH WHOM I HOPE TO SHARE THE EXISTENCE
IN WHICH
TIME SHALL BE NO MORE,
I DEDICATE THIS VOLUME,
IN THE COMPILATION OF WHICH HE HAS TAKEN SO GREAT
A PART AND INTEREST.

M. G."

It is not easy to discriminate amongst the correspondents
who have all been generously ready to help me by supplying
information for this second edition ; but though I am sorry

to pass over any names in silence, yet I feel bound to select the following as belonging to those who have had special opportunities of aiding me :—A. A. Armstrong, Esq., Rev. E. Askew, Rev. S. Bennett, Robert Blair, Esq., Rev. W. S. Calverley, Lewis Evans, Esq., Rev. J. T. Fowler, Dr. George Frank, J. Park Harrison, Esq., Albert Hartshorne, Esq., Miss Salwey, Rev. W. H. Sharpe, Rev. D. Smith, Rev. W. D. Sweeting, Rev. R. V. Taylor, Rev. E. Templeman, Miss Trollope, and Rev. J. Evelyn White. To Miss A. M. Crellin I am indebted for notes on Manx dials taken from a paper which she is preparing to be read before the Natural History and Antiquarian Society of the Isle of Man ; and from Thomas Ross, Esq., of Edinburgh, I have received very valuable notes and drawings of Scotch dials which he collected whilst writing his work on "The Castellated and Domestic Architecture of Scotland." [1] I am sorry to be unable to reproduce Mr. Ross's drawings in this book—but hope they will appear in a book of his own on ancient Scotch dials. To the Rev. Dr. Littledale and to Reginald J. Smith, Esq., I owe especial thanks for the trouble they have taken in translating the dial mottoes, many of which were very difficult, owing to their condensed phraseology.

In conclusion I would say that my gratitude to all who have helped me is the same whether their names are recorded or not ; for in a work of this kind the accuracy of even the smallest detail is essential to the value of the book, and without the aid of my correspondents, I could not possibly have verified the facts contained in this volume.

HORATIA K. F. GATTY.

December, 1888.

[1] By David McGibbon and Thomas Ross, architects. (Douglas, Edinburgh.)

INTRODUCTION.

THERE is no human invention more ancient, or more interesting, than that of the sun-dial: so ancient that the exquisite essayist, Charles Lamb, says, "Adam could scarce have missed it in Paradise;" and so interesting that we may be sure that man's first want, after supplying the cravings of hunger, would be to invent some instrument by which he could measure the day-time into portions, to be allotted to his several vocations.

"Please, sir, what's o'clock?" is the child's enquiry, as he "tents" his mother's cow in the lane pastures; and the hardy backwoodsman, hewing out a settlement for himself in the primeval forest, leans on his axe, and looks to the sun's position in the heavens for information how soon he may retire to his hut for food and sleep. Time is a blank if we cannot mark the stages of its progress; and it has been found that the human mind is incapable of sustaining itself against the burden of solitary confinement in a dark room, where you can take no note of time. The great Creator, who made the sun to rule the day and the moon and the stars to govern the night, has adapted our nature to these intermitting changes, and implanted in us an immediate desire to count how, drop by drop, or grain by grain, time and life are passing away.

Edgar Poe sings, in melancholy strain, as he stands in imagination on the sea-shore—

B

> " I hold within my hand
> Grains of the golden sand ;
> How few, yet how they creep
> Through my fingers to the deep,
> While I weep ! "

The first motion of dissecting time would of course be suggested by a tree, or a pole stuck in the soil, the shadow of
which moving from west to east as the sun rose or declined
in the sky, would lead men to indicate by strokes on the
ground the gradual progression of the hours during which the
daylight lasted.   Further observation would discover that if
the pole slanted so as to point to the north star, and run
parallel with the earth's axis, a sun-dial was constructed that
would measure the day.   But the fixing of a complete instrument, varying in its lines and numbers, according to the
locality, and whether horizontally or vertically placed, would
be a matter of progressive astronomical and mathematical
calculation, which only the scientific could accomplish, long
after the rude art of uncivilized man had discovered the
means of ascertaining midday, and dividing into spaces the
morning and afternoon.

Herodotus (*flor.* 443 B.C.) says, " It was from the Babylonians that the Greeks learned concerning the pole, the
gnomon and the twelve parts of the day." (B. ii. cap. 109.)[1]

---

[1] "The Greeks of later times had a double mode of reckoning the
hours. According to the popular method, they divided the period from
sunrise to sunset into twelve equal parts. The hours reckoned upon this
principle varied in length with the season. According to the more
scientific method, the day and night at the equinox were severally
divided into twelve equal parts, and each of these was reckoned as an
hour. The division of the day into twelve parts, which Herodotus describes, ... was doubtless reckoned according to the former method.
Πόλος signified a hollow hemisphere ; and hence came to signify the
basin or bowl of a sun-dial in which the hour lines were marked. In

These twelve parts, however, would always differ in length according to the season, except at the equinox, because the ancients always reckoned their day from sun-rise to sun-set. The word "hour" therefore, as they used it, must be regarded as an uncertain space of time, until it was accurately defined by astronomical investigation.

The Jewish Scriptures, our oldest literature, give us no clear information as to how time was reckoned in the ancient world. "The evening and the morning were the first day" (Gen. i. 5) is the earliest description of a period of time whose duration we cannot precisely estimate. A week is also thus defined : "On the seventh day God ended His work which He had made, and He rested on the seventh day from all His work which He had made." (Gen. ii. 2.)

Farther on in the Jewish history we find the day divided into four parts : in Nehemiah ix. 3, we read, "They stood up in their place, and read in the book of the law of the Lord their God one-fourth part of the day ; and another fourth part they confessed, and worshipped the Lord their God." This mode of computation appears to have lasted until our Saviour's time ; the householder in the parable, hiring servants, is described as going out at the third, sixth, and ninth hours to engage additional labourers, and afterwards at the eleventh hour before the day closed. (Matthew xx. 1—8.) The night was not divided into hours, but into military watches ; the Jews recognized three such divisions, the "beginning of the watches" (Lam. ii. 19), the "middle watch" (Judges vii. 19), and the "morning watch" (Ex. xiv. 24 ; 1 Sam. xi. 11) ; "the second watch, . . . or the third watch" (Luke xii. 37, 38). The Greeks and Romans had four of these night watches, this sense it is used by Herodotus."—Adapted from SIR G. C. LEWIS, "Astronomy of the Ancients."

and after the establishment of the Roman supremacy in Judæa it is evident that the division of the Jewish night was altered. In Acts xii. 4, four relays of soldiers are spoken of; and in Matt. xiv. the "fourth watch;" whilst in Mark xiii. 35, the four watches are described as "even, midnight, cockcrowing, and morning."

The mention of the hour as a distinct space of time occurs first in the book of Daniel;[1] it is probable therefore that after the Captivity, the Babylonian division of day and night into twelve parts was adopted by the Jews and amalgamated with their own system. This was also the case with the Assyrians, amongst whom the calendar of their Accadian neighbours was in use as early as the reign of Tiglath Pileser I. "Along with the establishment of a settled calendar," writes Professor Sayce, "came the settled division of day and night. The old rough division of the night into three watches, which we find in the Old Testament, remained long in use, but although the astrological works of Sargon's library do not know of any other reckoning of time, it was gradually superseded by a more accurate system."[2]

The Egyptians divided their day and night into twenty-four parts at a very early period.

But our business is with sun-dials, and the first on historical record is that of Ahaz, who reigned over Judah 742 B.C. It has been observed that the Babylonians or Chaldaeans were the first people who seem to have divided time by any systematic mechanical contrivance. A lucid atmosphere is favourable to celestial contemplation, of which the people of the East have always fully availed themselves; and even now those

---

[1] Daniel iii. 6; iv. 19.
[2] "On the Astronomy and Astrology of the Babylonians," by Rev. A. H. Sayce, "Transactions of the Society of Biblical Archæology," vol. iii. 1874.

countries most abound in sun-dials which have the clearest skies. The Rev. S. C. Malan thus speaks of a visit to Ur of the Chaldees, and the landscape of serene beauty presented to him on the site of Rebekah's well : " As the shadows of the grass and of the low shrubs around the well lengthened and grew dim, and the sun sank below the horizon, the women left in small groups ; the shepherds followed them, and I was left in this vast solitude, yet not alone ; the bright evening star in the glowing sky to westward seemed to point to the promised land, as when Abraham took it for his guide."

From this people of Chaldaea, these star-searchers of the old world, we may conclude that Ahaz got his dial, and we read in the history of the unfortunate reign of this king a possible, nay a likely, cause of his introduction of Babylonish customs. Being pressed in war by the kings of Israel and Syria, Ahaz sought alliance and rescue from Tiglath Pileser, king of Assyria, who indeed released him in his emergency, but made him pay heavy tribute, and conform his worship to that of the Assyrians. "The altars at the top of the upper chamber of Ahaz " (2 Kings xxiii. 12) which Josiah removed, were probably connected with the worship of the stars, and they prove the adoption of Babylonian usages. Amongst these we may imagine that " the dial of Ahaz " (2 Kings xx. 9-11) held a conspicuous place ; but what its actual form was, still remains a matter of conjecture.

The word " degrees " in our translation of the Bible has been in the margin and the Revised Version rendered " steps ;" and this reading has given rise to various suppositions. Some writers have thought that a pillar outside the king's palace threw a shadow on the terraced walk, which indicated the time of day. The Rev. J. W. Bosanquet [1] considers that

[1] " Transactions of the Society of Biblical Archæology," vol. iii, 1874.

" the invention of the pole and gnomon combined, producing an instrument perfect in itself for all observations, was probably connected with the rectification of the Babylonian calendar in B C. 747, nineteen years before the accession of Ahaz," and that the dial was therefore a scientific instrument, the shadow being cast on steps in the open air, " or more probably within a closed chamber, in which a ray of light was admitted from above, which passed from winter to summer up and down an apparatus in the form of steps. Such chambers were in use in Eastern observatories till the middle of the last century." On the other-hand, one of the explanations which the Rabbins give of the dial of Ahaz is, that it was " a concave hemisphere, in the middle of which was a globe, the shadow of which fell upon diverse lines engraved on the concavity. They add that these lines were twenty-eight in number." [1] This description is not unlike the dial attributed to Berosus.

It is remarkable that no sun-dials of the Egyptian period are known. Those which have been found associated with Egyptian monuments, such as the one discovered at the base of Cleopatra's Needle, were additions of more recent date. Professor Rénouf, writing in 1887, says :—" We are at a loss as to the method used by the Egyptians for measuring time. They certainly had some method, for we have copies of a very ancient calendar, giving the hours of the night at which certain stars culminated. Of course this could not have been a dial, and it must have been an instrument by which *equal* intervals of time were measured. It may have been an hour-glass or a water-clock, but no such instruments have been found. There is an Egyptian word signifying a clock, but the picture of the hieroglyph looks to me like a meridian instrument. There is no reason for supposing that the

[1] Kitto's " Pictorial Bible," notes, vol. i.

obelisks were intended for gnomons, though they might possibly have been utilized for the purpose. We know that at a later time they actually served as lightning conductors."

Whether obelisks or pillars were formerly used as time-tellers in Egypt or not, we are told that a primitive mode of computing time is still practised in Upper Egypt: the natives plant a palm-rod in the open ground, and arrange a circle of stones round it—forming a sort of clock face—and on this the shadow of the palm falls and marks the time of day. The plougher will leave his buffalo standing in the furrow to consult this rude horologe, and learn how soon he may cease from his work—illustrating the words of Job (vii. 2) " as a servant earnestly desireth the shadow."

A learned friend offers the following remarks : " The shadow of a tree or vertical pillar cannot permanently indicate the time of day, because its motion is not uniform. The sun's motion in his diurnal track is uniform ; he always describes the same angle in the same time; but the angular velocity of the shadow of a tree or pillar is greater at noon than it is at sunrise or sunset ; it also varies with the time of year. The gnomon that indicates the time of day must slope to the horizontal plane at an angle equal to the latitude of the place, and must also lie due north and south. This may be illustrated by the blunder the Romans made in bringing a Sicilian sun-dial to Rome." (Plin. H. N. vii. 214, Censorin. de D. N. 23.) The same authority proceeds to say, " The proper slope of the gnomon may be obtained without a knowledge of the latitude ; and the Babylonians probably did obtain this, and from it determined the latitude, and ascertained that the earth is spherical ; so also the Greeks. (Strab. ii. pp. 125-136.) A vertical gnomon may be used to determine, not the time of day, but its length and variation of length in terms of equinoctial hours ; and thus the

Egyptian obelisk brought to Rome by Augustus was used. (Plin. H. N. xxxvi. 72.) Though from causes which Pliny conjectures, the inferences they drew were subsequently found to be erroneous. During the Attic period, the Greeks of that city ascertained the time of day by measuring a shadow; but it is difficult to determine how they did this. They talk of a six-foot shadow or mark, a ten-foot shadow or mark, &c. Expressions of this kind are very frequent, and yet they give little or nothing whereby to show the particulars of the measurement—whether it was the length of the shadow that was measured, or its angular distance from a given line, or even what the thing was that gave the shadow." [In Aristophanes (Eccl. 652) is found the expression στοιχεῖον δεκάπουν, *a gnomon ten feet long*, probably meaning "supper time;" and in other Greek writers of a later period the same word is used, with epithets signifying six, twelve, and seven feet. There also occurs the word ἡ σκιὰ, *the shadow*, to which the same epithets are applied.] "There is little in any of these writers to suggest even a conjecture, still less to support a probable one, respecting the mode of measuring the shadow. The shadow was thrown on the ground; it was twenty feet long in the morning, about six at noon, and ten or twelve in the afternoon. Salmasius conjectures that it was each man's own shadow which he measured with his own foot. This is really ingenious; but all that is certain is, that the method was far from exact, very imperfect, and required altering several times in the year."

Such is the conclusion at which our learned friend has arrived; but one more quotation must be given from his kindly comments: "There certainly is a considerable probability that what is called poetic astronomy is as old as human nature itself; and it is a very perfect system. Without any instrumental aid the first occupiers of Arabia could determine the time of year and the time of day with as much accuracy as they had any occasion for. The loss of this science, and the causes, moral and historical, that produced it, are curious, and as connected with the Holy Bible, they are important; but all these matters require leisure, long life, and patience—things which few possess, and still fewer wish for."

It is time that we descended from the heights of conjecture to the plain level of facts; remarking, by the way, that the studious contemplation of the heavenly bodies led to the worship of them, and also to astrology, which was a base corruption of the highest science known to men.

Anaximander of Miletus, who placed gnomons in the sciothera of Lacedaemon for the purpose of indicating the solstices and equinoxes, is said to have introduced sun-dials into Greece about the year 560 B.C. The Greeks may also have obtained their knowledge through the Phoenicians, to whom, the art which had reached Jerusalem two hundred years before, could not long remain unknown. If, as Vitruvius says,[1] Berosus the Chaldaean, who lived in the third century B.C., was the inventor of the "hemicycle hollowed in a square, and inclined according to the climate," there must have been earlier forms in Greece. Meton, the celebrated astronomer, is said to have set up a sun-dial against the wall of the Pnyx at Athens in 433 B.C. Alciphron[2] makes mention of a hollow basin, in the midst of which a perpendicular staff was erected, the twelve parts of the day being marked by lines; and the comic poet Baton, who lived in the first half of the third century B.C., also speaks of a horologium or sun-dial as a means for determining the time of day. A dial of the form ascribed to Berosus, with the hours marked in Greek letters, is now in the British Museum, having been

[1] Lib. ix. cap. 9.   [2] Epist. iii. 4.

found at the base of Cleopatra's Needle, near Alexandria.
Another of the same kind was fixed on the point of a rock
on the right of the monument of Thrasyllus at Athens.   A
drawing of this is given by M. Le Roy in his work, " Sur les
Ruines des plus Beaux Monuments de la Grèce."

There was a dial at Achradina, near Syracuse, in the time
of Archimedes, a copy of which was placed upon the deck of
the great ship of Hiero, and dials of various kinds are named
by Vitruvius, including those which were portable or suspen-
sory, and used by travellers.

As the Greek numerals are represented by the letters of the
alphabet, it is curious that those letters which express the
hours six, seven, eight, nine (from noon till four o'clock)
should spell the word ζῆθι, " live." An epigram, attributed to
Lucian, notices this in the lines :—

> ἓξ ὧραι μόχθοις ἱκανώταται, αἱ δὲ μετ' αὐτὰς
> γράμμασι δεικνύμεναι ΖΗΘΙ λέγουσι βροτοῖς.

> " Six hours are quite enough for toil, and those that are shown
> by the letters after them say to mortals, ' Live.' "

The Romans adopted dials from the Greeks, and the first
erected in Rome was placed by Papirius Cursor in the court
of the Temple of Quirinus, 293 B.C.   At this time the astronomical year of twelve months was introduced instead of the
old Roman year of ten months ; and, perhaps, says Mr.
Dyer,[1] " with a sly innuendo on the part of its dedicator, this
dial was placed in front of the Temple of Quirinus, or
Romulus, who was reputed to have established the year of ten
months." Before this time noon was proclaimed by a crier—
the Consul's marshal—from the front of the Curia, when the
sun appeared between the Rostra and a spot called the

---

[1] " City of Rome," Introd., p. lvi.   See also Pliny, H. N., vii. 60.

"station of the Greeks." About thirty years afterwards, in 263 B.C., during the first Punic War, Valerius Messala, having taken the town of Catania in Sicily, brought a sun-dial from that place. This was placed on a pillar near the Rostra, but not being calculated for the latitude of Rome, it told the time inaccurately enough. It remained, however, without a rival for ninety-nine years, until, in 164 B.C., Marcius Philippus, then Censor, put up a more carefully designed dial beside it. Another sun-dial was subsequently placed in the Forum, on the Basilica Aemilia, and was probably drawn upon a plane surface. That of Marcius Philippus seems to have been a concave spherical dial.

The obelisk which is now to be seen in the Piazza Monte Citorio, Rome, was brought from Egypt by the Emperor Augustus, and set up as a gnomon in the Campus Martius (Pliny, H. N. xxxvi. 9, § 71, 72), under the direction of the mathematician Facundus Novus, to show the hours of the day, and also the day of the month. The pavement around it was marked out with lines in bronze, which were sunk as deeply in the ground as the height of the obelisk itself. The obelisk seems to have kept its place for some centuries, but was ultimately thrown down, and disappeared from view. It was found in 1463 with part of the figures of the dial, but again suffered neglect, and was not placed in its present position until 1792.[1]

That dials were of frequent occurrence in ancient Rome is obvious from the lines attributed to Plautus, who died about 184 B.C.; and it is probable that their existence, or rather information, was noisily announced at stated intervals by trumpeter or crier.

---

[1] Authorities: "Astronomy of the Ancients," by Sir G. Cornewall Lewis; "Encyc. Brit.," 8th edition; "Rome and the Campagna," by R. Burn.

"The gods confound the man who first found out
How to distinguish hours—confound him, too,
Who in this place set up a sun-dial,
To cut and hack my days so wretchedly
Into small pieces! When I was a boy,
My belly was my sun-dial—one more sure,
Truer, and more exact than any of them.
The Dial told me when 'twas proper time
To go to dinner, when I had aught to eat;
But, now-a-days, why even when I have,
I can't fall to, unless the sun gives leave.
The town's so full of these confounded dials,
The greatest part of its inhabitants,
Shrunk up with hunger, creep along the street."

(*Quoted by* AULUS GELLIUS, B. 3. *c.* 3.)

Cicero, in the year B.C. 48 (Epist. ad Fam., xvi. 18), writes to Tiro about a sun-dial which he desired to put up at his villa at Tusculum, possibly the very dial which was found in the same neighbourhood, in the place which some have supposed to be the site of his house.   This is now in the Museum of the Collegio Romano at Rome.   Cicero's death is said to have been foretold by the omen of a raven striking off the gnomon of a dial (Lewis, "Astronomy of the Ancients," Val. Max., 1, 5, 5).

An epigram attributed to the Emperor Trajan (Anthol. Pal. xi. 418) refers to the art of dialling :—

ΤΡΑΙΑΝΟΥ ΒΑΣΙΛΕΩΣ.

Ἀντίον ἠελίου στήσας ῥίνα καὶ στόμα χάσκον,
δείξεις τὰς ὥρας πᾶσι παρερχομένοις.

"Set your nose and wide mouth to the sun, and you will tell
the hours to every passer by."

He was ridiculing a man who had a long nose and a wide mouth, very much curved and grinning, whilst his many teeth, all visible, resembled the characters that denote the hours, and their double line.

If sun-dials came, in spite of the rivalry of the more accurate clepsydrae, into common use in Rome, and (to judge by
the remains which have been found of late years) in many
parts of the Roman empire as well as in the imperial city,—
it is not to be supposed that Greece would be behindhand.
Most of those which have been preserved were evidently the
work of Greek artists. The beautiful marble dial with four
faces which Lord Elgin brought from Athens, with the name
of Phaedrus upon it, has been assigned to the second or third
century A.D., and the Tower of the Winds at Athens had a
dial on each of its eight sides. The date of these is uncertain—some attributing them to the time of Hipparchus, others
to a later period. The first mention of them is made by
Varro, B.C. 35. In the sixth century we find a notice of a
dial at Constantinople, existing in the reign of Justin II.,
A.D. 565-578, from which Sir George Lewis quotes the following couplet :—

> ὡράων σκοπίαζε σοφὸν σημάντορα χαλκὸν
> αὐτῆς ἐκ μονάδος μέχρι δυωδεκάδος.

> " Watch the wise brazen index of the hours
> From very unity until the twelfth."

The Arabs adopted and simplified the Greek constructions,
and studied deeply the science of gnomonics, which came to
them from Greece. Abul Hassan, a noted writer of the
thirteenth century, taught the construction of dials on cylindrical and other surfaces, making one himself in the shape of
a horse's hoof, and introduced the equal hours. The invention of clocks, which was due to the Arabians, had also the
effect of compelling the dial-makers gradually to adopt this
more exact method of dividing time; but although we are
told that during the next two centuries the science of
gnomonics made considerable advances, there are, so far as we

know, scarcely any existing remains of the actual dials of this period.

It is probably owing to the interest which was taken in this study by the Arabs that even at the present day sun-dials are common in Mohammedan countries.

As prayer is ordered to be observed five times in every twenty-four hours, all the principal mosques in Constantinople are provided with a dial, in order that the people may ascertain the exact times of worship. The sun-dials on the mosques of S. Sophia, Muhammed, and Sulimania, have no motto or inscription, except what expresses the course of the shadow and the name of the maker. But on some, in addition to the lines which mark the solar movement, there is a line drawn which points to the sacred town of Mecca, towards which the faces of the faithful must be turned during the performance of their religious offices. It is said that the Turks erect a sun-dial whenever they build a mosque.

The dial in our figure is painted on the wall of the Kassim Pasha barracks, where the marines are quartered who work in the Arsenal. The inscription in the right-hand corner means: " The engraver Essüd Osman. At the Arsenal Hidjrà one thousand one hundred and ninety-seven. 1197."

" Sun-dials," writes a correspondent of the highest authority, " are the commonest things possible in China. You cannot get into your chair, or palanquin, but a flat board, with a dial fixed in the centre, is put before you to keep you in. They are on the sides of houses, and on boxes—indeed, they are most common, but none of us recollect any mottoes under them: though the Chinese have such a habit of putting mottoes to everything, that it is more than likely that sun-dials are no exception. They are probably ancient. There are sun-dials in Japan, for I had one in my garden."

Touching Japanese dials, one who was long resident in
Japan, writes: "In regard to sun-dials, I can only say that
there are sun-dials in Japan, but not as fixtures; and that they
are not provided with mottoes, as is the case on old sun-dials in
Europe. You will probably remember the small bronze portable sun-dials every Japanese carries about with him; but I
never saw a large fixed sun-dial anywhere, except at a watch-

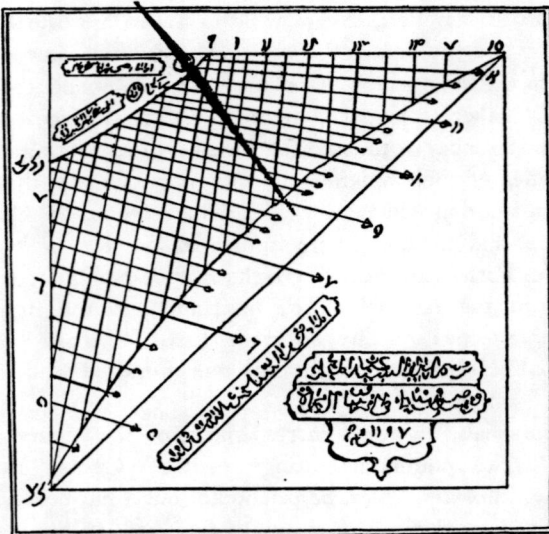

maker's shop in Yokohama, who had made use of the railing
round his shop as a kind of dial, according to which he
adjusted his watches. The shadow of the railing had been
previously adjusted, and was marked off after the Saturday gun
from the flagship."

We may here remark that at Paris, and we believe also at
Edinburgh and elsewhere, a cannon has been used for pro-
claiming the hour of noon, which was fired by the rays of the

sun being concentrated on a magnifying glass so placed as to ignite the powder in the touchhole, when the sun reached its meridian height. Moreover, the gun stood on a platform which was marked as a sun-dial, and, therefore, simultaneously with the explosion, the gnomon cast its shadow exactly on the figure xii. We hardly need add that this mode of ascertaining twelve o'clock is not pursued at Greenwich or any scientific observatory.

Small portable dials made of boxwood, and shaped like boxes, are commonly sold in Chinese towns. They have silken string gnomons, and are sun-dials and moon-dials combined; the sun-dial faces are marked inside the box, the moon-dial ones on the interior of the lid. They include a compass, and closely resemble the portaria made at Nuremberg in the sixteenth and seventeenth centuries. A family in the province of Ngáuhwni is said [1] " to have had from remote antiquity the monopoly of this manufacture. But though the Chinese are known to have been able to determine the obliquity of the ecliptic by means of the gnomon as early as B.C. 1100,[2] we cannot yet tell when they became acquainted with the use of the pole. Possibly this discovery may have come to them, as to the Greeks, from Babylon. Their daynight, like that of the Chaldaeans, is divided into twelve parts, and begins at what with us is eleven p.m. These spaces, which are marked by signs, are subdivided into eight *kih*, answering to our quarters of an hour. This system is of later date than Confucius, in whose time the ten-hour division was in use.

Passing from Asia to America, we meet with traces of sundials which existed before the Spanish conquest. Prescott [3]

[1] Macgowan, Timekeeping: "Chinese Repository," vol. xx.
[2] "Transactions of Society of Biblical Archæology," vol. iii. Pt. i.
[3] Prescott, "Conquest of Mexico," Lond. 1850, vol. i. p. 103.

tells us of the immense circular block of carved porphyry, disinterred in 1790 in the Great Square of the City of Mexico, on which the calendar was engraved, and which is declared by Gama to have been a vertical sun-dial. The Peruvians [1] also had erected pillars of curious and costly workmanship, serving as dials, and from these they learned to determine the time of the equinox. When the shadow was scarcely visible under the noontide rays, they said that " the god sat with all his light upon the column." Their Spanish conquerors threw down these pillars, as savouring of idolatry.

We shall not expect to find amongst the northern nations that understanding of the art of dialling which was carried to such ingenious perfection by the Greeks. We have, however, some records of the manner in which our Teutonic forefathers measured time, in the dials which are here and there found built into the walls of old churches. These stones, roughly engraved with lines placed at varying intervals and radiating from a common centre where once was placed the gnomon, upright or horizontal, according to the position of the dial, were the time-tellers of Englishmen before the Norman conquest, and show from a very early period the manner in which the tribes by whom Britain was settled used to divide their day.

The Greek and Latin method of dividing day and night into twenty-four hours, which now prevails over Europe, made its way slowly in England. It is clear that it was not adopted by the invading tribes for a long time after their settlement in Britain. If the Britons, as is probable, learned it from the Romans, they kept their knowledge to themselves, and this time-division must have been re-introduced into the country by St. Augustine and his companions, and was

[1] Ibid., "Conquest of Peru," vol. i. p. 120.

gradually adopted by the inhabitants. The Rev. D. H. Haigh, from whose exhaustive paper in the "Yorkshire Archæological Society's Journal" (vol. v. pt. 17) these facts are mainly drawn, finds in the early sun-dials of the Teutonic settlers evidence of four different ways of dividing the day-night, viz. :—

I. The octaval system, or division of day-night into eight, and subdivision into sixteen and thirty-two parts, customary amongst the Norsemen and Angles.[1]

II. The duodecimal, or Chaldaean division of day-night into twelve portions, still in use in China.

III. The decimal, or division into ten, a system followed by the Jutes and early Danes, as also by the Chinese in the time of Confucius, and even now amongst the Hindus.

IV. The twenty-four hour system, adopted by the Egyptians, Greeks, and Romans.

V. The combination of the Greek and Latin hours with the octaval division.

The octaval system is of very ancient origin. We find in Job xxiii. 8, 9 allusion made to a man with his face toward the sunrising, looking before, behind, to the right hand, and to the left, or as it is rendered by the Targum, "rising, setting, glowing, hiding," corresponding with the four cardinal points ; and the course of day and night was similarly divided into four parts. This the Chaldaeans subdivided by three. The four in their hands became twelve ; in those of the Egyptians, Greeks, and Romans, twenty-four. But the Northmen—nor they alone, for the same practice has been found to exist in parts of Hindustan and in Burmah—held to the four great divisions of time, dividing and subdividing them as follows :—

[1] The Mexicans also divided their day-night into sixteen parts.— PRESCOTT, "Conquest of Mexico."

2 Dagr, sun E.S.E. to W.S.W. = 3 eikts, or tides = 6 stundr = $7\frac{1}{2}$ a.m. to $4\frac{1}{2}$ p.m.

3 Aftan, sun W.S.W. to W.N.W. = 1 eikt, or tide = 2 stundr = $4\frac{1}{2}$ p.m. to $7\frac{1}{2}$ p.m.

4 Nott, sun W.N.W. to E.N.E. = 3 eikts, or tides = 6 stundr = $7\frac{1}{2}$ p.m. to $4\frac{1}{2}$ a.m.

"From the hours allotted to Morgan and Nott, it would seem," says Mr. Haigh, "that this system took its rise in Lat. 42° N., the Caucasian home of the Aryan race, light and darkness being at the summer solstice about fifteen and nine hours respectively."

1 Morgan, sun E.N.E. to E.S.E. = 1 eikt, or tide (old English) = 2 stundr = $4\frac{1}{2}$ a.m. to $7\frac{1}{2}$ a.m.

In Iceland and the Faroe Islands the octaval division of time still exists. Sir Richard Burton, in his "Ultima Thule," written in 1878, tells us that day-night is divided by the Faroese into eight, and by the Icelanders into nine watches. Seven of the latter number three hours in each, and the remaining two an hour and a half, which practically corresponds with the eight tides of the Norsemen, if the subdivision of one portion be allowed for, while the names of three divisions agree with those of the ancient days. In Iceland also the primitive mode of measuring time by the sun's passage over natural objects was still in vogue as late as 1813-14, when Dr. Henderson visited that country. "He found that very few persons owned a clock, and that the only dial in use was the natural horizon of each township, divided into eight equal parts by mountain peaks, when such were situated conveniently, and by pyramids of stone when natural marks were wanting. These marks, natural or artificial, had been fixed by the first colonists, and the latter had been renewed and kept in repair from generation to generation. Twelve years before Dr. Henderson's journey, an indefatigable antiquarian wanderer, Arentz, visited the district of Sondfjord (in Norway), and has left a record of the eight tides of day-night, which were in use amongst the people there, and of the regulation thereof, by marks on hill and valley, so accurate that midday was seldom at variance with clock time."

A device of the same kind existed up to the end of the last century at Settle, in Yorkshire. A hill called Castle-

berg, which rises at the back of the town, is crowned by a pile of rock which cast a shadow upon large slabs of stone placed at regular intervals, and marked with Roman numerals, telling the hour of the day from eight to twelve. These stones have long disappeared.[1]

Another gigantic dial might be seen on the Mull mountain in the parish of Rushen, Isle of Man. It consists, we are told, "of a ring mound, about forty-five feet in diameter,

[1] The illustration is reproduced from a pen-and-ink sketch in the Warburton Collection of MSS. British Museum. It was probably drawn by one of the brothers Buck, other sketches in the same volume, and

with short radiations to the eight points of the horizon. On each of these radiations were set parallel rows of stones about fourteen inches apart, consisting of three stones each. On the circle between each pair of three radiations were two parallelograms, each separated by an interval of little more than a foot, about eight feet long, consisting of four stones. Nothing is wanting but a pole in the centre of the circle to constitute a dial. The eight divisions of the day-night are marked by the eight radiations, and the subdivisions by the intervals between the kists.''

It is conjectured that upright solitary stones, such as the Rudstone pillar in Yorkshire, may have formed gnomons to dials of the above description.

The smaller English examples of these octaval dials are now generally seen in the walls of old churches, though very rarely in the position they once occupied, and they probably belonged to earlier buildings. The Irish dials described or figured by Mr. Du Noyer,[1] were chiefly found on upright stones in ancient graveyards. They belong to Christian times, and two of them (at Inniscaltra and Kilcummin), may, it is thought, be dated before A.D. 661. The dial on the cross at Bewcastle, Cumberland, on which the Roman hours

---

apparently by the same hand, being signed S. Buck. It does not appear to have been engraved, and is most likely to have been drawn in the early part of the eighteenth century. Samuel Buck died in 1779, aged eighty-five; his brother Nathaniel some years before. In 1778 a larger engraving of the "very extraordinary sundial facing the Market place at Settle in the West Riding of Yorkshire," drawn and engraved by S. Buck, was published, and has been photographed and included by Mr. Eckroyd Smith in his " Illustrations of Old Yorkshire." He adds that the late Dean Howson, who was educated at Giggleswick School, and died in 1885, aged 69, remembered old people who had heard of, if they had not seen the dial. The hour-slabs had probably been destroyed before Mr. Buck's engraving was published.

[1] " Archæological Journal," No. 99.

are combined with the octaval system, belongs to the first year
of King Ecgferth, 670 ; and two in Hampshire to the time of
Wilfrith, A.D. 681 ; while a portable dial found in 1816 at
Cleobury-Mortimer in Shropshire, marked with lines according to the decimal system, is assigned to the fifth or sixth
century.

Besides certain small dials which show the division of day-
night into twelve parts, according to the Chaldaean method,
we have one of considerable size in the stone circle at Wallsend, co. Durham. A Roman altar thrown on its side served
as a base for the gnomon, and stood in the midst of a circle
of twelve stones, each twelve inches in height, and nine in
thickness. Twelve rudely-cut lines radiated from the hole
in the centre of the altar, and Roman coins were found
buried beneath it. Evidently this money was still in circula-
tion when the dial was made. It is thought to have been
constructed by Danish settlers as early as the fourth century.
It is worthy of note that this division of day-night into
twelve, was the method followed by Alfred the Great
in his contrivance for measuring time by the burning of
candles.

That the octaval system was still in vogue at the time of
the Norman Conquest is shown by the Kirkdale dial, the
most interesting and complete of all the early specimens.
This dial and its brethren are also standing witnesses of the
long and intimate association of sun-dials with churches.
In ancient days they had been connected with public buildings and places of worship, as an inscription, " Horologiare
templum," dedicated " Jovi optimo maximo et Junoni
Reginae," records : and from the time when Pope Sabinianus,
the successor of Gregory the Great, commanded that dials
and clocks (clepsydrae) should be placed on churches to distinguish the hour of the day, down to the present age, the

union has been maintained. To the monasteries, sun-dials
must—before the invention of clocks, which were early
adopted by the monks—have been almost indispensable.
Cassiodorus in the sixth century gave one to a monastery in
Languedoc, and in like manner Herebert of Winton, who
founded the monastery of Weaverthorpe, placed on his
church a dial which still, though feebly, records his name.
Sometimes it was given by a layman, a nobleman, as that Ulf
who " bade arrear " Aldbrough Church, " for the poor and
for Gunware her soul," or by a faithful retainer, as at Byland,
where it is written " Svmarledan hvscarl me fecit," " Sumarlethi's house-carl made me."

Portable dials were probably a luxury of the great; whilst
people who lived in remote places would find the hour of
noon much in the same way as a certain farmer's wife on
the Yorkshire Moors, who to this day sets her clock according to the moment when the sun strikes along a groove in
the stone floor, just within the house door, and at an angle
with the threshold! Men who were fortunate enough to
dwell near a church or monastery consulted the shadow on
the dial, and this in its turn regulated the bell which the
" tide-shower " rang out from time to time to tell how the
hours passed away, a sound still familiar to those who live
beside some of the older parish churches, where the custom of
ringing a bell at six in the morning, at noon, and at curfew
is even yet maintained.

From the latest Saxon dial to the earliest dated specimen
on which time is measured according to the system of twenty-
four equal-hours, there is a wide interval. It is, however,
probable that the church dials which still remain, dating from
the sixteenth and seventeenth centuries, in many cases replace predecessors worn out by wind and weather, and that in
former days almost every church had its sun-dial as now it

has its clock. Some of those which have been cut on the stones of old churches may be nearly as old as the buildings themselves. We are told that Gerbert of Auvergne, afterwards Pope Sylvester II., who died in 1003, placed a horologium in Magdeburg for the Emperor Otho, after observing through a tube the star which guides the seaman. But after this time, between the thirteenth and sixteenth centuries, we are assured that "the history of gnomonics is a blank." A dial on the south side of the Minster at Freiburg-in-Breisgau is thought to belong to the end of the thirteenth, or beginning of the fourteenth, century. There can be little doubt that many more were made in the middle ages, but excepting some rough remains on English parish churches, we have no known specimens.

When, however, learning began to revive in that period which is justly called the Renaissance, dialling again took a place amongst the subjects which occupied the minds of the mathematicians. The works of some of the earliest authors have never been printed, but in the sixteenth century both writers on gnomonics and constructors of dials came fast into favour. The book of disbursements of Sir Thomas Lucas, solicitor-general to Henry VII., who built the hall at Little Saxham, in Suffolk, in the twentieth year of that king's reign (1505), records an item of " xx^d " as paid " for a dial set on my bruge ; " and the church of Rouelles, in Normandy,[1] still shows two picturesque dials, with the hours marked in Arabic numerals, which are placed at right angles to each other beneath a beautiful projecting window, and were probably set up but a few years earlier than the example just given. From that time forward the art advanced rapidly. Pocket dials, as Shakespeare reminds us, were in ordinary use,

[1] Figured in the "Journal of the British Archæological Institute," Sept. 1873.

pillar dials were the natural luxury of a nobleman's or gentleman's house, vertical dials adorned the churches, and dials of
curious and elaborate construction were the delight of artists
and mathematicians, of learned, rich, or understanding men.
Albert Durer, who died in 1528, introduces a dial into his
engraving of the Melancholia, placing it above the hour-glass,
and near the bell which tolls for the passing hour.   Tun-
stall, writing to Cardinal Wolsey from Lucca in 1520, tells
how he had met with one Nicholas Cratzer, " an Allemagne,
deviser of the King's horologies," who showed him how the
king had licensed him to be absent for a season, and he was now
ready to go to England.   He came, and was made a Fellow
of Corpus Christi College, Oxford, by Fox, Bishop of Winchester, and by command of Henry VIII. he read astronomy
at Oxford.   His friend, Hans Holbein, was also a designer, if
not a maker, of dials ; he introduced one into his illustrations
of the Old Testament with reference to the history of Heze-
kiah ;[1] and designed an elaborate timekeeper which united the
functions of sun-dial, clock, and clepsydra, for Sir Antony
Denny to present as a new year's gift to Henry VIII.

Not only were sun-dials thought suitable offerings from a
subject to a king, they were also worthy gifts from a prince
to his people.   The white marble slab which projects from
the façade of Sta. Maria Novella in Florence bears, besides the
hour-lines and the armillary sphere of Ptolemy, an inscription
to the effect that it was given by the Grand Duke Cosmo de'
Medici to the students of astronomy, A.D. 1572.   The date
of 1537 on the dial on Schaffhausen church, and 1579 on
that of the cathedral of Chartres, are proofs of their wide-
spread use in Europe ; and, indeed, an ardent writer on the
subject in 1562, Andrew Schoner, gave it as his opinion that
they could no more be dispensed with than meat and drink.

[1] Published London, 1547.

The first English work on dialling was published in 1593. It is a small black-letter quarto, entitled " Horologiographia ; the Art of dialling, teaching an easie and perfect way to make all kinds of dials on any plaine plat howsoever placed ; with the drawing of the twelve signes, and houres unequall in them all. At London. Printed by Thomas Orwin, dwelling in Paternoster Row over against the signe of the Checker 1593." The author, Thomas Fale, writes in his preface that " many have promised (but none as yet performed) to write of this science in our English tongue, which hath been published in other languages, as D. Recorde long since. M. Digges, M. Blagrave, with others, who if they would take the paines, I knowe could doe it with great commendation."

Mr. Blagrave seems to have responded to this appeal, for in 1609 he also published a book on the art of dialling. The work of the mathematician Clavius, which appeared in 1612, is said to have exhausted the subject, but he was, notwithstanding, followed by many writers, both English and foreign, up to the middle of the last century. So highly esteemed were the dials set up in the king's privy garden at Whitehall, that in 1624 Mr. Edmund Gunter, Professor of Astronomy at Gresham College, wrote a full description of them by the special direction " of the Prince his Highness," and dedicated it to King James I. The interest of Charles I. in the subject never flagged. He constantly carried about with him a small silver mathematical ring, a dial, though not a *sun*-dial ; and gave it to his attendant, Herbert, in charge for the Duke of York, shortly before his execution. Probably to his fine taste, the beautiful dial called " Queen Mary's," at Holyrood House, is due. It was made in 1633, the year in which the king visited Scotland and was crowned in Edinburgh. He is said to have presented it to Queen Henrietta Maria. Several other dials, similar in character to " Queen Mary's," are still to be seen in Scotland. These also date from the seventeenth century, and will bear comparison in elegance and beauty with the crosses of the middle ages. -

About this period, or a little later, it also became the custom to make use of the shafts of the defaced and destroyed crosses, to which we have just referred, as supports for sundials. The destruction of the crosses was begun in Queen Elizabeth's reign, as is shown by the following entry in the parish books of Prestbury, Lancashire : " 1577. Item for cuttynge the cross in the Churchyard, and for charge of one with a certificate thereof to Manchester, xij^d." ; and the practice was continued during the civil wars. The old cross of Ote de Tilli at Doncaster, broken down by the Earl of Manchester's army in 1644, was afterwards repaired and crowned with dials ; several of the fine crosses in Somersetshire have been treated in a like manner, while in many churchyards the pillar, which now bears a plain horizontal dial plate, may be readily recognized as the shaft which was allowed to remain after the cutting or "stumping" of the cross had taken place.

Several existing entries in the household books, or churchwarden's accounts, of this period, refer to the cost of putting up dials. In 1620 "two sundials were got" for Naworth Castle, after its rebuilding by Lord William Howard ; in 1608 the churchwardens of Hartland, in Devon, paid " for the diall on the church wall iii^s ;" in 1624, " for a diall for the church 12^s ;" while in 1651 those of Maresfield, Sussex, note that the " brazen sundyal" cost " on shilling, $\overset{s}{1}$." The Company of Clockmakers, incorporated in 1631, were given jurisdiction not only over clocks and watches, but over dials also, and were authorized " to search for and break up all bad and deceitful works."

The pillars mounted on steps and crowned by a square

block of stone, with a dial on each face, which were not unfrequently erected at this period, were often of fine and
simple proportions, and adorned the streets or squares where
they were placed. Such an one was in 1668 subscribed for by
some inhabitants of Covent Garden, and set up in the centre
of the square. Another, designed by Inigo Jones, stood in
the middle of the New Square at Lincoln's Inn. Sir John
Dethick, Lord Mayor of London in 1655, placed a very
handsome pillar with a dial and fountain at Leadenhall
Corner; and the Seven Dials owes its name to the solid
erection which once adorned that now singularly unadorned
locality. These are all gone; and gone, too, are the curious
inventions of Father Lyne, alias Francis Hall, one specimen
of which stood in the Privy Garden at Whitehall, but whose
works at Liège were sought for in 1703 by the Rev. Charles
Ellis, and found even then to be " shamefully gone to decay."

Many of the London churches once bore dials. Mr.
Collins, writing in 1659, speaks of his friend, "Mr. Thomas
Rice, one of the gunners of the Tower, much exercised in the
making of dyals in many eminent places of the city." The
subject was pursued with interest by various writers in the early
part of the eighteenth century, and the setting up of dials still
went on. Mr. Thomas Wright, a distinguished mathematician and astronomer, received a gratuity of twenty guineas
from the Commissioners and Conservators of the river Wear for
a composition of dials which he invented, setting up the model
on the pier at Sunderland in 1733; and a small cylindrical
dial was presented by him to the Earl of Pembroke. Perhaps
the last work of note on dialling was that of James Fergusson,
re-edited by Sir David Brewster, from which Robert Stephenson constructed the dial which is still to be seen on his father's
old cottage at Killingworth. Since that time the subject has
been relegated to the encyclopædias, which usually give

elementary, and not very clear, directions for the construction of the simpler forms of dials only.

The practice of inscribing mottoes on sun-dials seems to have gone hand in hand with the art of making them, since the beginning of the sixteenth century, the earliest specimen in our collection dating from 1556. What could be more natural to a scholarly and reflecting mind than to point the moral of passing time in the brief sentence which arouses thought? The very presence of the clock on the church tower teaches us, as it has been said, that " Time is a sacred thing ; " but the passing of the shadow on the dial is more suggestive and more poetical than the sound of the pendulum, and for upwards of two centuries it has spoken by word as well as by deed to many generations of inquirers.

> " With still more joy to thee I turn,
>   Meet horologe for Bard to love,
> Time's sweetest flight from thee I learn,
>   Whose lore is borrowed from above.

> " I love in some sequestered nook
>   Of antique garden to behold
> The page of thy sunlighted book
>   Its touching homily unfold.

> " On some old terrace wall to greet
>   Thy form and sight which never cloys,
> 'Tis more to thought than drink and meat,
>   To feeling than Art's costliest toys.

> " These seem to track the path of time
>   By vulgar means which man has given,
> Thou, simple, silent, and sublime,
>   But show'st thy shadowy sign from Heaven ! " [1]

But time and the changes of weather have dealt hardly with the sun-dials. On churches and public buildings they

[1] Bernard Barton.

have been to a great degree superseded by clocks, and dials removed at the "restoration" of old buildings have not always been replaced. They were often painted on wood, and the board has rotted and fallen to pieces, and even when carved in stone, the material, if at all soft, has crumbled away. Many a mark on a church wall shows where a dial has once been, in a place which now knows it no more. Decay is also overtaking the sun-dials, with their graceful inscriptions, which have abounded on the plastered walls of Italian and Provençal villages. The suppression of the monasteries has influenced their fate. Many of the mottoes in this book have been copied from convent walls, and are now fast becoming obliterated, for the hands which repaired them are gone. "Tempora mutantur, nos et mutamur in illis."

There have been many quaint devices connected with dials. For instance, in the garden of Wentworth Castle, near Barnsley, the property of F. Vernon Wentworth, Esq., a dial was formed of box-edgings cut into the proper numerals, whilst a clipped yew-tree in the centre acted as the gnomon. Floral dials have also been invented, being composed of flowers that bloomed in succession during the months of sunshine. These, however, are conceits which hardly come within the compass of our subject.

As clocks were erected in the church towers, or showed their faces in the market-places, the vocation of the learned dialler gradually ceased. The old dial may still retain its footing in the quaint yew-tree'd garden, or may stand conspicuously in the churchyard; but few consult it as an oracle, and it rather lingers superfluously amongst us as a memento of the past. It has nevertheless to many minds a touching interest; it has drawn forth maxims in the form of mottoes, and it would be like discarding wisdom were we not to preserve and cherish them.

" But if these dials tell us after all
We are but shadows on Life's sunny wall :
They not less point us, with a hope as bright,
To that good land above where all is light."

H. V. T.

Howard the philanthropist is said to have thus spoken on
his death-bed :—" There is a spot near the village of Dauphigny where I should like to be buried. Suffer no pomp to
be used at my funeral ; no monument to mark the spot
where I am laid, but put me quietly in the earth, place a sun-
dial over my grave, and let me be forgotten." Sir William
Temple ordered that his heart should be placed in a silver
case, and deposited under the sun-dial in his garden at Moor
Park. So tender have been the uses to which the dial has
been applied, so striking is the thought that the eyes of succeeding generations look in its time-telling face only to read
their own *memento mori*, that we are ready to fall into David
Copperfield's vein of meditation, as we see it ever cheerfully
return with sunlight to the performance of its duties, and
ask, " Is the sun-dial glad ?—I wonder, that it can tell the
time again."

*   *   *   *   *   *

The present collection of dials, with their mottoes, was
begun about the year 1835. Perhaps the presence of a
curious old dial over our church porch (Catterick), with
something like a punning motto, " Fugit hora, ora," may have
had somewhat to do with originating the idea. Also at the
home of some dear friends, a few miles off, the porch of their
picturesque little church (Wycliffe), on the banks of the
Tees, bore another inscription, " Man fleeth as a shadow."
A third motto surmounted an archway in a stable-yard
(Kiplin), " Mors de die accelerat." A fourth was over the
door of a cottage in a village (Brompton-on-Swale), bearing

the warning words, "Vestigia nulla retrorsum," which shone out in gold and colour amidst evergreens. Here lived the venerable sister of a canon of Lincoln, which may perhaps account for the presence of the dial. A fifth looked out from the depths of pyracanthus on a house at Middleton-Tyas, hinting to callers not to waste the precious hour, with its "Maneo nemini;" while last, and not least in our esteem, stood the touching inscription, "Eheu, fugaces!" on a pillar-dial outside the drawing-room at Sedbury Hall, Yorkshire, where it betokened the scholarly character of the hospitable owner. These six mottoes (all, somewhat remarkably, in one neighbourhood), made an admirable beginning of a list which soon swelled to twenty or thirty pages by taking a wider circuit, and with the assistance of the contributions of friends. And thus the matter went on from more to more; but the great impulse was given when the friend, alluded to in the Preface, undertook to collect in the south of France and the north of Italy—a fair field indeed, and one even yet imperfectly explored. As to these dial mottoes, there are perhaps as many differences of opinion, as there are differences of character in those who read them. We, who have studied them for so many years, feel with Charles Lamb that they are often "more touching than tombstones," while to other people they seem flat, stale, and unprofitable. One correspondent describes them as "a compendium of all the lazy, hazy, sunshiny thoughts of men past, present, and in posse;" and says, "The burden of all their songs is a play upon sunshine and shadow." But this is no fair description. The poet's words,

> "Liberal applications lie
> In art as nature,"

have never been more fully realized than in the teachings

which have arisen from dials, as we trust the following pages will prove beyond a doubt. So far from the burden of all their songs being a play upon sunshine and shadow, one of the most fertile subjects of thought is the sun's power, as being his own time-keeper, which he certainly is, whilst the mottoes constantly assert the fact.

The sun describes his own progress on the dial-plate as clearly as he paints pictures on the photographer's glass— human art assisting in both cases. " Solis et artis opus," says the dial in a street at Grasse, near Cannes—somewhat baldly, perhaps. More refined is the " Non sine lumine " of Leaden- hall Street; and perhaps higher still the " Non nisi coelesti radio " of Haydon Bridge. " Non rego, nisi regar " is the modest avowal of another dial in a street at Uppingham, acknowledging itself to be but an instrument governed by an overruling power. And these are but a few of the many " applications " the poet speaks of. The reader will find all these mottoes in their proper places in the list, on which our first happens to be a foreigner.

SUN-DIALS.

I.

A LUMINE MOTUS.

Moved by the light.

ON a dial at Sestri Ponente, on the Riviera, a few miles to the west of Genoa. This, the first motto on our list, suggests some fanciful thoughts. Light moving a shadow —one intangible thing acting on another, and the result becoming visible. It can be explained, of course, in the most matter-of-fact manner; but this need not hinder our casting a fleeting glance at the idea. A curious list might be made of things most familiar to us, such as wind, thunder, &c., with the view of ascertaining by how few or how many of our senses they are cognizable.

2.

A ME TOCCA POI LA SORTE
DI SEGUIRTI FINO A MORTE.

That to which fate urges me
Is unto death to follow thee.

At Graglia in Piedmont.
The motto

"*A me poi tocca la sorte*
Di seguirlo sino alla morte"

is said to be on a dial in "a village between Graglia and Oropa." Probably this is only another copy of the motto at Graglia : travellers passing rapidly from one place to another are liable to make inaccurate notes of what they see.

3.
A SOLIS ORTU USQUE AD OCCASUM.

From the rising up of the sun unto the going down of the same.

On the cemetery wall at St. Gervais in Savoy. This motto is taken from Psalm cxiii. 3, and a slightly different form of it was once on the dials which formed the uppermost division of the Queen's Cross, Northampton. There were four dials, one facing each point of the compass : on the east were the words AB ORTU SOLIS, on the south LAUDATVR DOMINUS, on the west VSQVE AD OCCASVM, and on the north AMEN . MDCCXIII. The cross itself was erected by Edward I. in memory of his wife, Eleanor of Castille, who died 21 Nov., 1291, and in 1713 the cross was repaired by order of the Justices of Northampton, and the dials and mottoes added ; but in 1762 the latter were omitted when the faces of the dials were repainted, and the cross again repaired. The text "A solis ortu usque ad occasum," with the additional words "Laudate Domine, Domine alleluia," has lately been inscribed under the clock which stands beside the north aisle of the choir in York Minster. This clock used to be outside the building, above the entrance to the south transept, but it was taken inside when that part of the cathedral was restored. In Dugdale's "Monasticon," there is a plate of the exterior of the transept, showing that a sun-dial formerly stood over the entrance, and this was no doubt removed to make way for the clock.

4.

A SPAN IS ALL THAT WE CAN BOAST,
AN INCH OR SO OF TIME:
MAN IS BUT VANITY AND DUST
IN ALL HIS FLOWER AND PRIME.

On an erect stone dial, south declining east, which was placed, in the year 1862, over the barn door of East Lodge Farm, near Carthorpe, Yorkshire, by G. J. Serjeantson, Esq., whose initials, with the date, are engraved on the stone.

5.

A STITCH IN TIME SAVES NINE.

At Camphill, Yorkshire. (See No. 625.)

6.

AB HOC MOMENTO PENDET AETERNITAS.

On this moment hangs eternity.

This favourite motto may be seen on dials at the following places :—at Sprawley, in Worcestershire; on a house at Offerton, between Stockport and Marple; in a private garden at Northampton; on the pedestal of a dial in St. John the Baptist's Churchyard, Margate (see No. 737); on the parish church, Great Sankey, near Warrington, Lancashire, with the name and date "J. Simkin 1781;" in the Frankfort Museum; over the porch of St. Andrew's Church, Auckland, co. Durham, with the date 1749; over the door of a house at Wentworth, Yorks, with the date "Dec. 26,

1765," and " Delineavit Johan Metcalfe ; " and in the
churchyard of Childwall, near Liverpool, where the words
" I. Simkin, Burtonwood, 1791," are engraved above the
motto, and " Wᵐ Spencer, and Wᵐ Owen, churchwardens,
1791," below it.

7.

AB ORIGINE VIRTUS.
AD SUBLIMA CURSU(S).

From the source is (my) goodness
To the heights (my) course.

In Nuremburg Museum there is a large plate, made of
some fine kind of composition, on which two dial faces are
carved in low relief, the lines of numerals being concentric.
At the top of the plate there is an armorial shield with a
coronet ; the mottoes are inscribed on scrolls below the
gnomon. Between the two lines of numerals verse 3 from
Psalm cxiii. is written " Sic nomen Domini benedictum,
ex hoc nunc, et usque in saeculum : a solis ortu, usque ad
occasum, laudabile Nomen Domini."   At the corners of the
plate there are the following designs and inscriptions :—

(1.) Sun and bird. " Aspicit unum."

(2.) Sun and bird. " Gaudet superis."

(3.) Lily, lion, and sun. " Quo altior utilior."

(4.) Tree, lion, and star. " Jam sunt insignia sidus."

The signs of the Zodiac, and names of the months also
appear on the plate, and amongst the foliated ornamentations
down the sides are the words " Sequar, Ortus, Suprema, Ex-
specto, Occasus, Supernas ; " but the concords of them fairly
baffle our comprehension.

The name of " Philippo Antonio Libero Baroni de Reinach," is inscribed on the dial ; probably it belonged to him, and the coat of arms was the one he bore ; at the base of the plate is the name of the maker, "Devot^mo Franc : Xav : Josephus Bovius. SS. Can. Exam. approb. presbyter Eystet-tensis invenit fecit et demississime dedicavit." There are three more mottoes on the dial plate. (1.) "Phoebus semper serenus niteat," *May Phœbus ever brightly shine.* (2) "Candore omnia vincit," *In whiteness it surpasseth all things.* (3.) "Recta se tollit in altum," *Straight it rises to the height.*

8.

AB ULTIMA CAVE. 1838.

Of the last (hour) beware.

Painted, with the date, 1838, on a dial over the door of a house which stands surrounded by trees near the edge of a cliff, facing the rocky headland of Porto Fino, in the Gulf of Genoa. There is a local tradition that an English queen was buried here. Berengaria, queen of Richard I., suffered shipwreck in the Mediterranean ; which was perhaps enough to give rise to a legend for which there seems to be no historical evidence.

9.

ABOUT YOUR BUSINESS.

On a dial at the Nursery, West Felton, Salop, erected by the owner, John Devaston, an intimate friend of the poet Shenstone. Recorded in the "Gent. Mag.," 1815. (See Nos. 41, 174 and 475.)

10.

ABSQUE SOLE, ABSQUE USU.

Without sun, without use.

Roger Hargreaves and Richard Whittle, chapel-wardens.
A. Dom. 1826.

On a stone dial over the south doorway of Heapey Church,
Lancashire.

11.

ABUSE ME NOT, I DO NO ILL:
I STAND TO SERVE THEE WITH GOOD WILL;
AS CAREFUL THEN BE SURE THOU BE
TO SERVE THY GOD, AS I SERVE THEE.

This inscription used to be on a copper horizontal dial in
Shaw churchyard, in the parish of Oldham ; the cross on
which it was erected remains, but the dial-plate was stolen,
and a new plate and a different motto have been substituted
for the old ones. (See No. 367). Three mottoes somewhat resembling the above have been noted as occurring on clocks.
The first was supplied to Mrs. Gatty some years ago, and
found in her common-place book :—

"I labour here with all my might
To tell the hour by day and night,
If thou wilt be advised by me
Thou'lt serve thy God as I serve thee."

The second, which differs very slightly from this version, is
on the Town Hall of Bala, Merionethshire. The third
version was kindly sent to us by the Rev. H. Maclean,
Vicar of Lanteglos-by-Fowey, Cornwall, who while visiting

a parishioner noticed the following lines placed under an ancient timepiece, neatly written and framed in coloured paper :—

> " Here my M^rs bids me stand
> And mark the time with faithful hand,
> What is her will is my delight,
> To tell the hours by day by night.
> M^rs be wise and learn of me
> To serve thy God as I serve thee."

12.

AD OGNI ORA CHE IO SEGNO, TU RAMMENTA CHE ALTRO CERCAR NON DEVI CHE DIO SOLO. MDCCCLXVI.

At every hour which I mark, remember that thou oughtest to seek after none but God only.

Dial on the garden front of the Instituto delle Suore della Carità di San Vicenzo di Paolo, in Rome.

13.

ADVENIET ILLA DIES: SEMPER PARATUM.

That day will come : (be thou) always ready.

UT UMBRA SIC VITA.

As a shadow, so is life.

On the terrace at Derwent Hall, Derbyshire, now the property of the Duke of Norfolk. Some such words as *decet esse* or *habe te* must be understood.

14.

AETAS CITO PEDE PRAETERIT, 1787.

The age passes with swift foot.

On the porch of the church of St. Hilary, near Marazion,
Cornwall.

15.

AETAS RAPIET DIEM.   1783.

Time will hurry away the day.

At Sally Hill, near Gosforth, Cumberland.

16.

AFFLICTIS LENTAE CELERES GAUDENTIBUS HORAE.

To them that mourn the hours are slow,
But with the joyful swiftly go.

At Courmayeur, in the valley of Aosta; at Hyères; on
the Municipio of Rusigione, near Voltri; and at the Sacro
Monte, near Varese, with No. 19 and the date 26th Feb-
ruary, 1857. Dean Alford met with the motto between
Bordighera and the river Nervia, and he rendered the
meaning as above. A similar idea is expressed in Nos. 143,
291. The sentiment is a favourite theme with poets. W. H.
Spencer's song, "Too late I stayed," is a good instance of
this, and two lines from it have been adapted as a dial motto.
See No. 340. Lamartine's poem "Le Lac," is a still more
graceful expression of the idea :—

" O temps, suspend ton vol ! et vous, heures propices,
    Suspendez votre cours !
Laissez-nous savourer les rapides délices
    Des plus beaux de nos jours !

" Assez de malheureux ici-bas vous implorent :
    Coulez, coulez pour eux ;
Prenez avec leurs jours les soins qui les dévorent ;
    Oubliez les heureux.

" Mais je demande en vain quelques moments encore,
    Le temps m'échappe et fuit ;
Je dis à cette nuit : ' Sois plus lente,' et l'aurore
    Va dissiper la nuit.

" Aimons donc ! aimons donc ! de l'heure fugitive
    Hâtons-nous, jouissons !
L'homme n'a point de port, le temps n'a point de rive ;
    Il coule, et nous passons ! "

17.

AH, WHAT IS HUMAN LIFE !
HOW LIKE THE DIAL'S TARDY MOVING SHADE :
DAY AFTER DAY GLIDES BY US UNPERCEIVED,
YET SOON MAN'S LIFE IS UP, AND WE ARE GONE.

On a dial at Hesketh, in Lancashire, with a second motto
(No. 620). The idea contained in this stanza is finely
expressed in a sentence from the Talmud, translated by
the late Emmanuel Deutsch : " Life is a passing shadow,
says the Scripture. Is it the shadow of a tower, of a tree ?
a shadow that prevails for a while ? No, it is the shadow of
a bird in his flight—away flies the bird, and there is neither
bird nor shadow." For analogous teaching see also Wisdom
v., 11, 12, 13.

18.

ALLEZ VOUS.

Pass on.

Some years ago, a Dutch vessel came into port at Dartmouth, and brought a Dutch sun-dial of singular workmanship which bore this motto. The dial came into the possession of the Vicar of St. Petrox, Dartmouth, and was placed at the time in the garden of the vicarage ; but it is no longer there.

19.

AMICIS QUAELIBET HORA.

To friends—any hour they please.

At Grasse, in the south of France, on a house which is situated in one of the small old-fashioned squares of the town ; on the Sacro Monte, Varese (No. 16) ; at the Etablissement at Oropa ; and at Chatillon, Val d'Aosta. (See No. 440.) It is also inscribed on a dial that is sketched out on the yellow wall of a house in Murano, which stands in a garden beside one of the canals that intersect the island (see No. 274). The shape of this dial is oval, and it is dated 1862 ; the hour xii is marked by the figure of a bell.

In addition to the Latin inscription, there is the following Italian motto written below :—

L'ORA CHE L'OMBRA MIA FEDEL TI ADDITA,
PENSA CHE FU SOTTRATTA DALLA TUA VITA.

The hour which my faithful shadow points out to thee,
Remember, has been taken from thy life.

The dial is placed between the upper windows, and just escapes the shadow cast by the low roof; but occasionally it

is eclipsed, even on the brightest day, when the west wind
blows the smoke across it from the famous glass works of
Murano.

20.

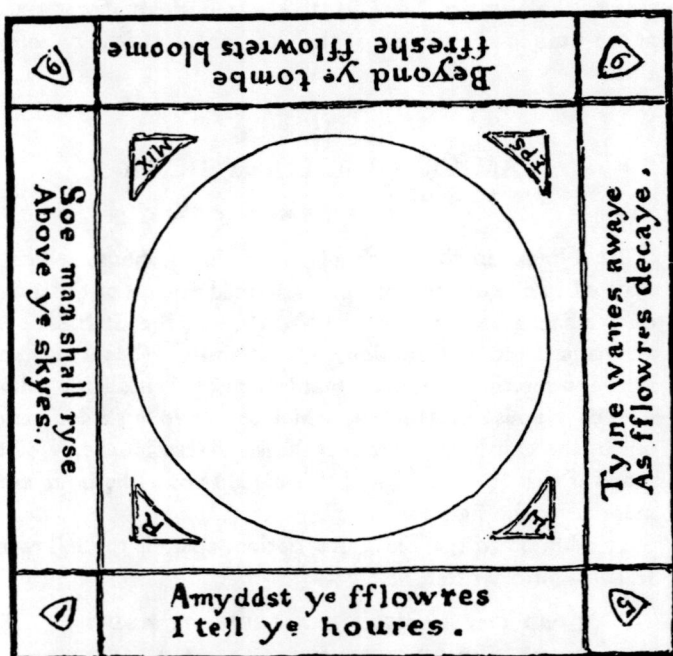

This design, with the following description, is taken from
" Aurelia," by Greville J. Chester, pp. 160, 161. " * *
inside the old espaliers, drooping with russet apples and jargo-
nelle pears, a double row of Hollyhock-spires of flame, and
rose-colour, and primrose, and white, and crimson, each as
big almost as the spire of a modern 'district' church ; and

within these again white lilies—worthy, methinks, of the Virgin Mother of God, the meek maid Mary—and bunches of golden Aaron's rod, and Canterbury bells, brought from my Lord Archbishop's garden at Addington in flowery Kent, and Bee larkspurs, and Prince's feathers, and later on in the year, tufts of purple, golden-eyed Michaelmas daisies ; and at the end of all, upon a lump of turf, stood a grey time-tinged sun-dial, inscribed on its four sides with the quaint distiches devised by Bishop Edmund Redyngton who set it up A.D. 1665."

21.

ARRIPE HORAM, ULTIMAMQUE TIMEAS.
8BRE 1812.

Snatch the (present) hour, and fear the last.

Is on a house at Tours. The dial is more fanciful than useful. It is square in shape, and at the two upper corners the sun and moon are figured. On the dial-face there is no numeral but xii., which is at the bottom, and the gnomon is formed by two arms projecting from a crescent : they are centrally placed, and lay hold of the sun.

22.

ARS LONGA VITA BREVIS.
Art is long, life is short.

QUALIS VITA FINIS ITA.
As the life, so the end.

BAASE JIU BIOYS MAIRAGH.
Death to-day, life to-morrow.

On a pedestal dial at Ballafreer Farm, Braddan, Isle of

Man. The inscriptions are on the north, south, and west sides of the pedestal. This dial was made by John Kewley, who also constructed No. 331.

23.

AS A SHADOW, SUCH IS LIFE.

Is on a dial placed immediately over the entrance of the south porch of Wensley Church in Wensley-dale, Yorkshire, with the date 1848, Lat. 52.20.

24.

AS O'ER THE DIAL FLITS THE RAPID SHADE,
SO SPEED THE HOURS OF LIFE'S EVENTFUL DAY:
AS FROM THE PLATE THOU SEE'ST THE SHADOWS
    FADE,
TIME UNIMPROVED FLEETS TRACELESSLY AWAY.
LET THY BRIGHT HOURS, LIKE SUNBEAMS, CALL
    FORTH FLOWERS:
TRUTH, MERCY, JUSTICE, HOLINESS, AND LOVE;
HERE THEY MAY DROOP BENEATH AFFLICTION'S
    SHOWERS—
DOUBT NOT THEIR FRAGRANCE SHALL ASCEND
    ABOVE.

These lines, under the title " Inscription for a Sun-dial," are in " Poems " by Lady Flora Hastings, p. 71.

25.

AS SHADOWE SO MAN SPEEDETH.
1613.

Dial on Church Farm House, Marston Magna, county Somerset.

26.

AS THE SHADE IS SO IS LIFE.
Lat. 53.15. J. Smurthwaite. 1804.

On a wooden sun-dial, which till lately was placed on the Red-house farm, near Kirklington, Yorkshire, where the Smurthwaite family had lived as tenants for several generations. The dial is now in possession of G. J. Serjeantson, Esq., and was much praised by its former owner as being " a good 'un to go by, better nor any clock."

27.

AS THE SVNE RVNES
SO DEATH COMES
W.L. 1683.

On the two faces of a dial at the corner of Liberton House, near Edinburgh. The initials W. L. were those of William Little, the proprietor of the Liberton estate; and between the letters there is a shield bearing his coat of arms.

28.

AS THESE HOURS DOTH PASS AWAY
SO DOTH THE LIFE OF MEN DECAY.
MEMENTO MORI.

1731.

On the plate of a pillar dial in Wetherall churchyard, Cumberland. The pillar is of old red stone, and stands picturesquely amongst the gravestones, on the banks of the river Eden. The church contains some fine monuments of the Howards of Corby Castle, and also a tomb bearing the effigies of Sir Richard de Salkeld and "his lady Dame Jane," from whose descendants Lord William Howard bought the Manor of Corby.

"Pray for their souls for charitie:
For as they are now—so must we all be."
Epitaph on Sir Richard de Salkeld.

29.

AS TIME AND HOURS PASSETH AWAY
SO DOUTH THE LIFE OF MAN DECAY

1694.

This motto is almost identical with that at Wetherall; it occurs on an old slate sun-dial, placed over the porch of Diptford Church, Devon. In the corners are the initials $_E^P$ W $_K^T$ W evidently those of the wardens for the year 1694, their office being signified by the letter W.

It is also on the dial on Brent Church, South Devon, with initials and date E. M. 1685.

E

A notice in the " Gentlemen's Magazine," quoted by Mr. Suckling in the " History of Suffolk," says that in Blytheborough Church, at the west end of the middle aisle, there was a clock with the figure of a man who used to strike the hours on a bell (after the manner of the figures at old St. Dunstan's in Fleet Street) ; and under the clock the following lines were painted on wood :—

> " As the hours pass away
> So doth the life of men decay."
> 1682.

30.

AS TIME AND HOVRES PASETH AWAYE
SO DOETH THE LIFE OF MAN DECAYE
AS TIME CAN BE REDEEMED WITH NO COST
BESTOW IT WELL AND LET NO HOWRE BE LOST.

These lines are engraved round the outer edge of an elaborate brass portarium the size of an old-fashioned watch, which is preserved in the Antiquarian Museum in Edinburgh. When opened it is seen to contain a dial and compass, and on the opposite face the meridians " of all the principall townes and cities of Europe " are inscribed, with the words " This table beginneth at 1572 and so on for ever." The name of the maker, " Humfrey Cole," and the date 1575, are also given.

Humfrey Cole is noticed in the " Archæologia " (Vol. XL. 1865), as having been, in the reigns of Edward VI. and Queen Elizabeth, the leading English maker of astrolabes and similar instruments, some of which are now in Greenwich Hospital.

31.

ASPICE IN HORAM, ET MEMENTO MORI.

Look upon the hour, and remember death.

R. E.

1775.

Over the door of an old house in Thomas Street North, Monkwearmouth, which was formerly the town house of the Barons of Hylton, and afterwards inhabited by the father of the noted northern antiquary, George Cooper Abbs. The initials R. E. are those of Robert Emerson, who was parish clerk and schoolmaster of Boldon from 1770 to 1805. He possessed considerable mathematical knowledge, and constructed two dials in his own village, one of which he placed over his house, and the motto of this is now (1888) illegible. The other remains over the church porch.

32.

ASPICE, RESPICE, PROSPICE.

Look, look back, look forward.

At Tornaveen, Torphius, Aberdeen. See No. 52.

33.

ASPICE UT ASPICIAR.

Look on me that I may be looked on.

This graceful appeal from the Dial to the Sun was inscribed upon a device belonging to Queen Louise de Vaudemont, the wife of Henry III. of France.

34.

ASPICE UT ASPICIAS.

See that thou mayest see.

This motto is engraved on the south side of a pillar-dial in the churchyard of Areley Kings, Worcestershire. Below the motto is a figure of Time, with an hourglass and spade, and the lines :—

TIME'S GLASS AND SCYTHE
THY LIFE AND DEATH DECLARE,
SPEND WELL THY TIME, AND
FOR THY END PREPARE.

CONSIDER

O MAN, NOW OR NEVER,
WHILE THERE IS TIME TURN UNTO THE LORD
AND PUT NOT OFF FROM DAY TO DAY.

On the north side of the pillar is inscribed :—

THREE THINGS THERE BE IN VERY DEEDE,
WHICH MAKE MY HEART IN GRIEF TO BLEEDE :
THE FIRST DOTH VEX MY VERY HEART,
IN THAT FROM HENCE I MUST DEPARTE ;
THE SECOND GRIEVES ME NOW AND THEN,
THAT I MUST DYE BUT KNOW NOT WHEN ;
THE THIRD WITH TEARS BEDEWS MY FACE,
THAT I MUST LODGE NOR KNOW THE PLACE.

I. W.
fecit, anno Dm̃i
1687.

Under the date is a figure of Death standing on a human body, holding a dart and spade, and with a fallen hour-glass beside him :—

BEHOLD MY KILLING DART AND DELVING SPADE,
PREPARE FOR DEATH BEFORE THY GRAVE BE MADE;
FOR
AFTER DEATH THERE'S NO HOPE.

IF A MAN DIE, SHALL HE LIVE AGAIN?

ALL THE DAYS OF MY APPOINTED TIME
WILL I WAIT TILL MY CHANGE COME. Job xiv. 14.

THE DEATH OF SAINTS IS PRECIOUS,
AND MISERABLE IS THE DEATH OF SINNERS.

On the east side there is :—

SI VIS INGREDI IN VITAM,
SERVA MANDATA.

If thou wouldst enter into life, keep the commandments.

JUDGMENTS ARE PREPARED FOR SINNERS. Prov. xix. 29.

And on the west :

SOL NON OCCIDAT
SUPER IRACUNDIAM VESTRAM.

Let not the sun go down upon your wrath.

WHATSOEVER YE WOULD THAT MEN
SHOULD DO UNTO YOU,
DO YE EVEN SO UNTO THEM.

This dial formerly stood in a private garden at Norchard, in the parish of Hartlebury. The house was a white one, timbered, and the dial was behind it, surrounded by a yew hedge. According to tradition it was erected, or at any rate inscribed, by an occupant of the house, who was a student and recluse, and went by the title of "the wizard." The present rector of Tedstone Delamere, Rev. F. Simcox Lea, recollects "the wizard's pillar" as being one of the sights of

Hartlebury in 1834, and he believes that the somewhat morbid tone of all the inscriptions arose from the introversial character of the inscriber's mind, who seems to have held much solitary communion with himself, and to have had a great dread of the future life. Queen Louise's *Aspice ut aspicias* was an address, as most dial mottoes are, from the dial to the sun; but all the Wizard's inscriptions are admonitions to himself, "*Aspice ut aspicias* being a kind of 'conceit,' or play on words, very probable in the scholarship of the last century—' *Look, that thou mayest consider* '—the first in the literal or bodily, the second in the figurative or mental use of the word."

The house at Norchard was pulled down about the year 1837, and the dial was bought to save it from destruction. The purchaser was a surgeon in Stourport named Watson, and he gave it to the Rev. H. J. Hastings, rector of Areley Kings, who put it into the churchyard where it still stands. All the inscriptions are now (1888) illegible except the date. There were vertical dials on the south, east, and west sides of the pillar; traces of the numerals, and the places in which the gnomons were fixed, can be seen. The pillar is about seven feet high, including the square capital at the top, on which the dials were placed. The sides of this are sixteen inches square.

In "The Rambler in Worcestershire," by John Noake, published 1851, there is a paragraph about the house at Norchard which contains an allusion to the "Wizard:" "Upon a stone built into a wall of the house where the pillar was originally erected, are the initials E. W. and the date 1692. It is generally understood that the initials refer to the mason employed, and not to the owner of the property. A friend of mine was assured by an old man, several years ago, that his father had been in the service of "Master Fidkin," a most singular character, who owned the estate, erected the dial, lived, died, and desired to be buried there ; that he could "cast a spell," and sometimes kept persons wandering round about the village all night, until sun-rise, after which 'Master Fidkin' had no power."

35.
ASPICIENDO SENESCIS.
Thou growest old in beholding.

This motto is painted on the south wall of a house in the Place Bellevue, Nice, near the old port. It is close under the roof, much wider than long in shape, and has a red border. The words are underneath the dial in capitals. Part of the plaster having fallen off, the date has been left imperfect : "26 Giugno 182—." The same inscription is on an upright dial on a house wall in one of the squares at Aix-les-Bains, Savoy, dated 1853, and the maker's name " A. F. Arsenio Capucinorum " below.

36.
AUJOURD'HUI A MOI,
DEMAIN A TOI.
To-day for me, to-morrow for thee.
In the cemetery of Courmayeur.

37.
AURORA HORA AUREA.
Dawn the golden hour.
Engraved on the index of an old pillar dial, standing on the lawn at Mountains, near Hildenborough, Kent.

38.

AUT DISCE, AUT DISCEDE.

Either learn or go.

On a dial at the Royal Military Academy, Woolwich.
The same motto, with the addition MANET SORS
TERTIA CAEDI (*A third choice remains, to be flogged.*) is
preserved on a tablet at the end of the schoolroom of Winchester College, being characteristic of the hardy discipline of
that ancient public school.

39.

AUT LAUDA, VEL EMENDA 1738, R. Nellson, Fecit.

Either commend, or amend.

The note respecting this dial has been imperfectly filled
up; and the collector has lost all recollection of the locality.
Its application is dubious.

40.

BAASE JIU BIOYS MAIRAGH.

Death to-day, life to-morrow.

At Ballafreer Farm, I. of Man.   See No. 22.

41.

BEGONE ABOUT YOUR BUSINESS.

Is inscribed on a wooden dial of a house at High Lane,
near Disley, in Cheshire.   Mr. Timbs records that it was on
the dial of the old brick house which stood at the east end of

the Inner Temple terrace, and was removed in 1828. The brusqueness of the advice is accounted for by the following pleasant legend given in "Notes and Queries," 2nd S. v. ix. p. 279. "When the dial was put up, the artist enquired whether he should (as was customary) paint a motto under it? The Benchers assented, and appointed him to call at the Library on a certain day and hour, at which time they would have agreed upon the motto. It appears, however, that they had totally forgotten this; and when the artist or his messenger, called at the Library at the time appointed, he found no one but a cross-looking old gentleman poring over some musty book. 'Please, sir, I am come for the motto for the sun-dial.' 'What do you want?' was the pettish answer: 'why do you disturb me?' 'Please, sir, the gentleman told me I was to call at this hour for a motto for the sun-dial.' '*Begone about your business!*' was the testy reply. The man, either by design or mistake, chose to take this as an answer to his enquiry, and accordingly painted in large letters under the dial, BEGONE ABOUT YOUR BUSINESS. The Benchers when they saw it decided that it was very appropriate, and that they would let it stand— chance having done their work for them as well as they could have done it for themselves. Anything which reminds us of the lapse of time should remind us also of the right employment of time in doing whatever business is required to be done." The idea is repeated on the gable of a cottage between Stockport and New Mills, and on the church of Bury St. Edmunds. (See Nos. 9, 174, and 475).

42.

BEHOLD, AND APPLY YOURSELF TO DUTY,
CONSUME NOT YOUR TIME IN IDLENESS.
1839.   Lat. 53° 30'.

On an octagonal dial at Upper Mill, Saddleworth, Yorks.
The plate is elaborately engraved, eight points of the compass
being indicated.

43.

BLESSED ARE THE DEAD WHICH DIE IN
THE LORD.

These words, from Rev. xiv. 13, have been inscribed at
the base of a pillar dial in the churchyard of St. Botolph
Without, Aldersgate Street, London.   The plate is adorned
with an engraving of the old Aldersgate; and the following
inscriptions are cut on three sides of the pillar: "This
ancient burial-ground, converted into a garden by vote of the
parish, and with the concurrence of the vicar, was opened to
the parishioners by John Staples, Esq., F.S.A., Alderman,
on Thursday, 28 October, 1880.   S. Flood Jones, M.A.,
Vicar.   George Sims, C.C.   John Hutchinson, Churchwardens.   1881."   This marks the date of the dial.

44.

BOAST NOT THYSELF OF TOMORROW, FOR
ON THINE EYELIDS IS THE SHADOW OF
DEATH.

In the Albert Park, Middlesbrough.   See No. 613.

45.

BREVIS SUNT DIES HOMINIS.

Short are the days of man.

On the church, Niederwald, Haute Valais, Switzerland.

46.

BREVIS AETAS VITA FUGAX.

Time is short, life is fleeting.

DEUS ADEST LABORANTIBUS.

GOD stands by those who labour.

DUM SPECTAS FUGIT.

Whilst thou art looking, (the hour) is flying.

VIGILA ORAQUE.

Watch and pray.

TEMPUS FUGIT.

Time flies.

On the south transept of Leighton Buzzard Church. There are five sun-dials on this church.

47.

BREVIS HOMINUM VITA.

Man's life is short.

On the dial which was formerly on the porch of Aberford Church, Yorkshire. It was removed when the church was rebuilt, and is now laid aside.

" Hic breve vivitur, hic breve plangitur, hic breve fletur ;
Non breve vivere, non breve plangere, retribuetur."

Bernard de Morlaix.

48.

BULLA EST VITA HUMANA.
The life of man is a bubble.

FUGIO, FUGE.
I fly—fly thou.

NOSCE TEIPSUM.
Know thyself.

NULLA DIES SINE LINEA.
No day without its mark.

PEREUNT ET IMPUTANTUR.
They perish, and are reckoned.

QUID CELERIUS TEMPORE?
What is swifter than time?

SIC TRANSIT GLORIA MUNDI.
So passes the glory of the world.

UMBRA DEI.
The shadow of GOD.

UT VITA SIC UMBRA.
As life so is a shadow.

VIA VITAE.
The way of life.

All the above mottoes are on a cross-dial at Elleslie, near
Chichester.

Thus writes Bishop Henry King :

> " Like to the falling of a star
> Or as the flights of Eagles are,
> Or like the fresh spring's gaudy hue
> Or silver drops of morning dew,
> Or like a wind that chafes the flood,
> Or bubbles which on water stood,
> E'en such is man whose borrow'd light
> Is straight called in and paid to-night.
> The wind blows out, the bubble dies,
> The spring entombed in autumn lies ;
> The dew dries up, the star is shot ;
> The flight is past,—and man forgot."

49.

BY LIGHT FROM HEAVEN I MARK HOW DAYS DO DIE ;
HOW RISE AGAIN AT MORNING-TIDE I MARK.
WHEN CLOUDS OBSCURE THAT LIGHT, I PATIENTLY
STRETCH MY DUMB GNOMON, HOPEFUL IN THE DARK,
WAITING TO CATCH ONCE MORE SOME GUIDING
      HEAVENLY SPARK.
TO DIE, TO RISE, TO HOPE IN TIME OF TRIAL,
TAKE, MASTER, THUS THY LESSONS FRCM THY DIAL !

These lines were written by the Rev. J. T. Jeffcock in 1868, and he intended to have them inscribed on the dial in the garden of the vicarage at Wolstanton, where he was then Vicar, but his-intention was not carried into execution.

50.

CADE L'OMBRA AI RAI
NEL MEZZO GIORNO,
E SINO ALL' OCCASO
IL LOR SOGGIORNO. 1853.

*The shadow falls under the rays (of the sun) at noontide, and
until sunset is their sojourn.*

Alluding to the position of the dial which faces west, and
therefore catches the sun's rays from midday to sunset. It is
on a house at La Tour, the little capital of the Vaudois
valleys of Piedmont, and is very plain in design. The motto
is in the corner, and the date below. The dial is painted on
the wall, high up betwixt the windows, which have balconies,
and look into a small square.

51.

CARPE DIEM. 1855.

Seize the (present) moment.

On a gable of one of the wings of Heslington Hall, near
York. The house is an Elizabethan mansion, and was
restored in 1855. The dial is circular in form, and painted
blue and gold. The same motto occurs on a dial in High
Street, Lewes, close to the County Hall, and is dated
MDCCXVII. It is also painted on the tower of Offchurch,
Warwickshire, where there is a full-faced sun gilt, with the
gnomon as a nose, dated 1795, "William Snow, Churchwarden;" and on a horizontal dial at Brahan Castle, Ros-
shire, engraved on the plate, with date 1794.

52.

CARPE DIEM, HORA ADEST VESPERTINA.

Seize the present moment, the hour of evening is nigh.

ASPICE, RESPICE, PROSPICE.

Look, look back, look forward.

These mottoes are upon a dial at Tornaveen, Torphius, Aberdeen; the first is engraved upon the dial plate, the latter upon the stone in which the plate is set.

53.

C'EST L'HEURE DE BIEN FAIRE.

It is the hour for well doing.

This dial motto appears at Nice; and Dean Alford found it at Porto Maurizio. It is also below a dial placed by Joseph Sidebottom, Esq., on the side of a house called "The Beeches," at Bowdon, Cheshire.

54.

CERTA RATIO.
1772.

A sure reckoning.

On a vertical dial over the porch of Deighton Church, Yorks.

55.

CETTE MONTRE PAR SON OMBRE MONTRE QUE COMME L'OMBRE PASSENT NOS JOURS.

This marker marks by its shadow, that our days pass away like a shadow.

On the wall of the church at Argentière, near Vallouse.

56.

CETTE OMBRE SOLAIRE EST À LA FOIS LA MESURE DU TEMPS, ET L'IMAGE DE LA VIE.

This solar shadow is at once the measure of time, and the symbol of life.

At Courmayeur. See No. 583.

57.

CHEMINEZ TANDIS QUE VOUS AVEZ LA LUMIÈRE. 1668.

Walk while you have the light.

UT HORA SIC VITA.

As an hour so is life.

חיום קצר והמלאכה מרבה

The day is short and the work great.

These three inscriptions are on a dial on the church wall at Hatford, near Faringdon, Berks., just below the bell turret. The Hebrew one (which is ill cut and very nearly defaced) is from the Talmud. There was formerly a Greek motto also, but it is now quite illegible.

58.

CITO PEDE PRAETERIT AETAS. 1679.

The age goes by with speedy foot.

On a dial in Over Peover churchyard, Cheshire; in a garden at Woodhouse Eaves, near Loughborough; also on the church of St. Peter, Ermington, Devon; and at Wigmore Grange, near Ludlow (see No. 702).

The words are also prefixed to the parish register at Loweswater, Westmoreland, and are taken from a passage in the poet Columella :—

Invigilate viri, tacito nam tempora gressu
Diffugiunt, nulloque sono convertitur annus:
Utendum est aetate, cito pede praeterit aetas.

F

59.

CITO PRAETERIT AETAS.

The age passes swiftly.

On Lincoln Cathedral, where there is also the common motto, *Pereunt et imputantur.* The inscriptions are on separate dials, which are fixed on the two sides of the south-east buttress of the east or lesser transept of the cathedral, and are probably about two hundred years old.

60.

COELI ENARRANT GLORIAM DEI.

The heavens declare the glory of God. Ps. xix. 1.

Roughly painted on the wall of a house near Lindau, Bavaria. It is dated 1803, and the motto is slightly defaced. The whole verse is inscribed on the dial át Moccas Court, Hereford. (See No. 635.) *Coeli enarrant gloriam Dei et operationem manuum ejus annunciat firmamentum.*

61.

COELUM REGULA.

Heaven (is our) guide.

FERT OMNIA AETAS.

Time bears all away.

IN LUCEM OMNIA VANA.

All things are vanity (when brought) into the light.

VITA FUGIT SICUT UMBRA.

Life flies like a shadow.

At Vallouse, with the date 1840, and the initials Z. G. F. and M. D. B.

62.

COME IN TIME.

On the church of Bradfield St. George, Suffolk.

63.

COME, LIGHT ! VISIT ME !

At the Knoll, Ambleside. 1846.

The history of this motto, and of the sun-dial which bears it, is given at length by Harriet Martineau in her auto-biography, vols i. and ii., pp. 80 and 265. At the age of seven she visited her grandfather, near Newcastle, and in his garden there was a large, heavy stone sun-dial. "That dial," she says, " was of immeasurable value to me. I could see its face only by raising myself on its step, and there, with my eyes on a level with the plate, did I watch and ponder, day by day, painfully forming my first clear conceptions of Time, amidst a bright confusion of notions of day and night, and of the seasons, and of the weather. I loved that dial with a sort of superstition ; and when nearly forty years after, I built a house for myself at Ambleside, my strong wish was to have this very dial for the platform below the terrace, but it was not to be had. It had been once removed already, when the railway cut through the old garden, but the stone was too heavy, and far too much fractured for a second removal. A friend in London who knew my desire for a sun-dial, and heard that I could not obtain the old one which had told me so important a story in my youth, presented me with one to stand under my terrace wall, and above the quarry which was already beginning to fill with shrubs and wild flowers. The design of the dial is

beautiful, being a copy of an ancient font, and in grey granite
to accord with the grey stone house above it. The motto
was an important affair. A neighbour had one so perfect in
its way as to eclipse a whole class. 'The night cometh.' In
asking my friends for suggestions, I told them of this, and
they agreed that we could not approach this motto in the
same direction. I preferred a motto of my own to all that
were offered in English, and Wordsworth gave it his emphatic
approbation. 'Come, Light! visit me!' stands emblazoned
on my dial, and it has been, I believe, as frequent and im-
pressive a monitor to me as ever was any dial which bore
warning of the fugacious nature of life and time."

64.

COMME UN COULANT RUISSAU DE SA SOURCE AR-
    GENTINE,
DROIT AU SEING DE THETIS PRECIPITE SON COURS
SEMBLE NE SE CHANGER ET SE CHANGE TOSIOURS
AINSV L'HOMME SANS CESSE A LA MORT SA CHEMINE
COMME L'ON ENTRE AU MONDE IL FAVLT QUE L'ON
    EN SORTE.

DANIEL IOVFROV. A Besancon, 1629.

As when a river from its silvery source
Speeds on its headlong course right to the sea,
And seeming not to change, doth change unceasingly,
So runs from birth to death man's changeful course,
So as we enter life, our exit needs must be.

On a bronze dial plate now in the possession of Charles T.
Gatty. The lines are engraved in two concentric circles,
outside the numerals, the divisions between the lines being
marked by asterisks.

65.

CONCITO GRADU.

With hurried step.

To be read a few years ago on the tower of Ruishton Church, Somersetshire, apparently the inscription of a worn-out dial. It is now quite defaced.

66.

CORRIGE PRAETERITUM.

PRAESENS REGE,

CERNE FUTURUM.

Correct the past, direct the present, discern the future.

In the Altmarkt at Dresden.

67.

CORRO A QUEL DÌ CHE DEL SIGNOR LA SPADA
UNA FARÀ L'ITALICA CONTRADA:
QUESTA FIDA CHE FA LANCE CH' IO PORTO
SEGNA L' ORA D' UN POPOLO RISORTO.

I run to that day when the sword of the Lord shall unite the Italian country. This faithful [sword] that I bear, which forms the gnomon, marks the hour of a resuscitated people.

This motto is patriotic, and a literal translation of it is most difficult. It has puzzled not only good Italian scholars, but native Italians also. The above rendering is a conjecture. There is some obscurity about the word *lance*. The dictionaries give *lancetta* as used for the gnomon on a dial; possibly, therefore, the gnomon in this case bore the form of a sword, and *questa fida* may be referred to *spada* in the first line. The inscription is placed above two dials, which stand side by side on the cathedral wall of Chieri, in Piedmont. One of them also shows the meridians of the chief cities of the world. Chieri is a few miles from Turin, on the left bank of the Po. It is an old town, but has suffered too much in the mediæval wars to retain many vestiges of antiquity. It has a round church of early Lombard architecture, which is now used as a baptistery. In its brighter days it was a free town, sending traders over half of Europe. It often changed its protectors: sometimes from choice, but more frequently from necessity; and at last gave its allegiance to the Counts of Savoy in 1347. The family of Balbo springs from Chieri; and one branch of this house, the Bertoni, refusing to accede to the treaty of 1347, emigrated to Avignon, where they assumed the name of Crillion, and were ancestors of the " Brave Crillon," *l'homme sans peur*, or *le brave des braves*, as he was called when serving under Henry IV. The other branch remained Piedmontese, to the glory and benefit of their country.

68.

COSÌ LA VITA.

Such is life.

To be read at Albizzola.

69.

CRAIGNEZ LA DERNIÈRE.

Fear the last (hour).

On the church of Notre Dame, Roscoff, in Brittany, a fishing village and sea-bathing place. It is remarkable in

history for the landing of Mary Queen of Scots when she
came from Scotland to be married to the Dauphin, afterwards
Francis II. of France. The weather being very stormy, the
young queen and her escort were glad to be put ashore at
this small village, and from thence to go forward on their
journey. The church on which this melancholy motto is
inscribed has in it the memorials of many shipwrecks, as well
as of escapes from drowning, several large votive ships being
suspended from the roof. From both these circumstances
the imperative warning of the dial gathers solemnity. The
shadow of the "last hour" stretches backward over the whole
course of Mary Stewart's life, and the fear of it has made sad
the hearts of many a fisher family on these stormy shores.
One might wish that the burden of the Tintagel bells were
re-echoed by those of Roscoff:—

> "Come to thy God in time,"
> Thus saith its pealing chime:
> Youth, manhood, old age past,
> Come to thy God at last.
>
> R. S. HAWKER.

70.

CRAS MINUS APTUS ERIT.

Tomorrow is little enough for itself.

On the Lyme Cage, Disley. See No. 700.

71.

CUM RECTE VIVAS, NE CURES VERBA MALORUM.

So thou livest aright, heed not the words of the wicked.

This dial motto is to be seen at Poirino, in Piedmont.

72.

CUM TEMPUS NON EXISTET MORIOR.

When time shall be no more,—I die.

On a dial in the garden at Cargen, near Dumfries.

73.

CUM UMBRA NIHIL,
SINE UMBRA NIHIL.

With the shadow nothing : without the shadow nothing.

Is on a dial on the Italian custom house of the Splugen Pass, near Campo Dolcino ; modern, and painted on the wall in red and yellow. The motto is also at Castasegna, a frontier village on the road to the Engadine ; and at Bececa in the Frentino, the scene of Garibaldi's battle in 1866, where the first *nihil* is written *nichil*.

74.

CUR GEIL DA'AN SCA
SHEN MYR TA'N TRA.

Observe the mark of the shadow,
In that manner is time represented.

On a dial which formerly stood in the Isle of Man (see No. 331), Mr. Jeffcott, of Castletown, has kindly translated the Manx mottoes on this dial, and he says that some of

the words are abbreviated ; if fully given, No. 73 would run
thus :—

> *Cur geill dean scaa !*
> *Shen myr tayrn traa.*

" Dean " denoting a *mark*, and " tayrn " meaning to *draw*,
delineate, or *represent*.

75.

CUR TIBI SPEM VITAE LONGOS PRODUCIS IN ANNOS?
UT MOMENTUM HORAE SIC TUA VITA FUGIT.

> *Why dost prolong the hope of life for long years to come ?*
> *As a moment of time doth thy life flit.*

On a brass dial plate in the Museum at Nuremburg.

76.

DA MATEMATICHE LINEE L'ORA VEDRAI
SI DENSA NUBE NON COPRE DEL SOLE I VAI.

1858.

> *By these mathematical lines thou shalt see the hour,*
> *If dense clouds do not cover the face of the sun.*

On a dial painted on the wall of a house at Caprile,
Venetia, bearing the face of the sun on a blue ground. It
faces south, and fronts the Monte Civita, and the weather-
beaten little column with its miniature Lion of St. Mark,
which tells of the former sway of the Venetian republic. There are two other dials in Caprile, but without
mottoes.

77.

DAMMI IL SOLE, E DEL GIORNO L' ORA È CERTA;
SOLO DEL UOMO È L' ULTIMA ORA INCERTA.

Give me the sun, and the hour of the day is certain; of man
alone is the last hour uncertain.

Inscribed on the church wall at Arola, without date, and
the dial is probably modern. Arola is a small village on a
hill-side, shaded by large chestnut trees. It is situated between
the Lago d'Orta and the Val Sesia; and the mule path from
Pella to Varallo, across the Col di Colma, runs through its
narrow roughly-paved streets.

78.

DAYS AND AGES ARE BUT AS A SHADOW OF THE
ETERNAL;
BUT THEIR USE, O MAN, DETERMINES THY FUTURE
WEAL OR WOE.

PULVIS ET UMBRA SUMUS.
We are dust and shadow.

ΕΛΕΥΣΟΝΤΑΙ ΓΑΡ ΗΜΕΡΑΙ Κ. Τ. Λ.
For the days shall come, &c.

These mottoes were formerly on the keep of Carlisle
Castle, just above the magazine, but are now obliterated.
The dial is a wreck, the gnomon gone, and only one or two
letters of the inscription can be deciphered.

79.

DEATHE JUDGMENT HEAVEN HELL UPON THIS
MOMENT DEPENS ETERNITIE. O ETERNITIE
O ETERNITIE O ETERNITIE. 1658.

The foregoing is inscribed in several lines on what is called
" Sir Francis Howard's Dial," at Corby Castle, near Carlisle.
It stands on the lawn, before the house, carved in stone, and
has four sides. Sir Francis Howard was the second son of
Lord William Howard (a son of Thomas, fourth Duke of
Norfolk), who was the " belted Will Howard " of Walter
Scott's " Lay of the Last Minstrel : "

> " Belted Will Howard is marching here,
> And hot Lord Dacre with many a spear."
>
> *Canto* iv. 6.

Sir Francis Howard was born August 29, 1588, and died in
May, 1660. He first married Margaret, daughter of John
Preston, Esq., of the Manor of Furness, Lancashire ; and
secondly, Mary, daughter of Sir Henry Widdrington, of

Widdrington Castle, Northumberland. On the so-called dial are four shields: one on each of the four sides. One side contains the family initials; another shows the emblems of the Passion in relief, namely, St. Peter's cock, the scourge, the crown of thorns, the cross and five wounds, with the hands, feet, and heart represented; the seamless garment, and below it the dice; the manacles in the form of I H S in letters of the period, and the hammer and nails. On another shield are the arms of Howard and Widdrington impaled, and on the fourth is the motto. Round the base of the pillar the following inscription has been cut, " Remounted by Henry Howard of Corby Castle, A.D. MDCCCXLII.

80.

DEFICIT SOL, NEMO RESPICIT.
When the sun sinks, of the dial none thinks.

DISEGNA LE ORE SENZA FAR ROMORE.
Tells the hours all round, without making a sound.

These two mottoes are inscribed on the wall of the Italian custom house at Fornasette, between Lugano and Luino on the Lago Maggiore. They are on a large erect south dial, which is elaborately painted with curves and flourishes. The form is that of a shield, and the letter M stands for the numeral xii., with the date below, " 15 Maggio, 1839." It is placed near the corner of the house, and beneath it are openings into a sort of corridor, where the work of the Custom House is carried on.

81.

DEL CERCHIO IL PIANO ABBRACCIA UN
 PUNTO SOLO
DEL TEMPO IM̃AGO ALL' NOM, CHE FUGGE
 A VOLO.

We cannot give a satisfactory translation of this motto, although the literal meaning of each word is quite simple. Possibly there was some emblem attached to the dial, of which we have not been told, and which would explain the text.

On the church at Tesero, Val Fiemme, Tyrol.

82.

DELLA VITA IL CAMMIN L'ASTRO MAG-
 GIORE
SEGNA VELOCE AL GIUSTO E AL PECCA-
 TORE.

To good and bad the great Star shows
How Life's rapid journey goes.

FUGIT, ET NON RECEDIT TEMPUS.

Time flies, and comes not back.

A dial motto on the outside wall, facing the road, of the Convent della Quiete, near Florence. The convent is now used as a girls' school.

83.

DELL' ORBE IN LINEE MIRO
IL DIURNO E L' ANNUO GIRO.

Lined on the dial note I here
The globe's course through each day and year.

On a church at Varazze, Riviera di Levante.

84.

DEO SOLI GLORIA.

To God alone be glory.

On a church at Sierre, in the Canton du Valais. (See No. 542.)

85.

DER MENSCH LEBT SO DAHIN UND NIMT ES NICHT
IN ACHT,
DAS JEDE STUND SEIN LEBEN KÜRZER MACHT.

Man heedless lives, nor takes to thought,
Each hour life's end hath nearer brought.

Painted on the wall of a small village inn (the sign of the "Dancing Bear") at Graf, near Landeck, Tyrol. On each side of the dial are rough frescoes, one of St. Florian, with the inscription :—

Heilige Florian beschütze dieses Haus,
Und lösch die Feuers flame aus.

Guard, St. Florian, this house about,
And put the flames of fire out.

And the other of the Blessed Virgin :—

O Mutter sey mit deinem Segen
Steh in diesem Haus zugen.

Mother, with thy blessing bide
In this house at every tide.

86.

DER SPÖTER SOL NICHTS VERACHTEN DEN ER KANS BESSER MACHEN.

HANS DVCHER, N.R.B.G.

The scorner should not aught despise
Which he can better if he tries.

On a small silvered clock, with dials on the four sides, in the British Museum; also on a cube-shaped dial, with No. 644. The spelling is old and crude.

87.

DER TOD IST GWISS, UNGWISS DER TAG,
VIELLEICHT DASS DIESE STUNDE SEIN MAG;
DARUM THU' RECHT, UND DUENKT DABEI,
DASS JEDE STUNDE LETZTE SEI.

Death certain is, its day unknown,
This very hour may be its own;
Therefore do right, and hold this fast,
That every hour may be thy last.

The sense of the second line, as it stands, is doubtful; but the probable meaning is expressed above. The dial is on Herr Weber's house at Schwyz. Some of the words are in old German, ill-spelt and imperfect. The design of the painting represents the Virgin with the Child in her lap. She is richly robed and crowned, and her head is encircled with stars.

88.

DETEGO TEGENDO.

By covering I discover.

On the south wall of a house in the Rue d'Antibes, Cannes. The plaster on which the dial is painted having been broken off, the first syllable is obliterated. It was copied in 1860.

89.

DEUS ADEST LABORANTIBUS.   1742.

God stands by those who labour.

At Hermit Hill, Wortley, near Sheffield ; also on the parish church, Leighton Buzzard.   (See No. 46.)

90.

-DEUS MIHI LUX.

God is light to me.

At Marrington Hall, Shropshire.   (See No. 605.)

91.

DEUS MONET, UMBRA DOCET :
CERNIS QVA VIVIS, QVA MORIERE LATET.

Confectum tertio calendas ivnii An. Dñi (*date lost*).

God warns, the shadow teaches.
Thou seest (the hour) in which thou livest, that wherein thou shalt die is hidden.

On a slate dial, now in the Museum at Vannes, Brittany.

Besides the above inscription it bears the signs of the Zodiac over the faces, and a crown with two blank shields. At the corners are four figures, two of which hold swords. It was the gift of M. Guizot Tomand.

92.

DI FERRO È LO STILO; D' ORO È IL TEMPO, AL PAR DI L' OMBRA PASSA E PIÙ NON TORNA.

The stile is of iron; time is golden,
It passes by like a shadow, and returns not again.

Above a dial painted in outline on the wall of a white-washed house at Ceppmorelli. The first line is also on a dial at Pie Cavallo, Val d'Oropa, near Biella. (See No. 122.)

93.

DIDST THOU NOT SEE THE LORD, HOW HE EXTENDED THY SHADOW.

Is the translation of a verse of the Koran, which is inscribed on a dial erected by the astronomer, Ali Kushaji, near the mosque of Muhammed II., by the gate of the Dyers at Constantinople.

94.

DIE AUGEN DES HERRN SIND HELLER ALS DIE SONNENSTRAHLEN.

The eyes of the Lord are brighter than sunbeams.

On a church at Hallstadt; the dial being roughly painted on the wall.

G

95.

DIE DIES TRUDITUR.

One day presses hard upon another.

John Hull. 1704.

Engraved on the brass plate of a dial, which stands upon a pedestal of red sandstone in Bispham Churchyard. In Colonel Fishwick's "History of Bispham" it is stated that the pedestal is probably the base of an ancient stone cross. The initials " R. B." are carved upon one side of the pedestal, and on the other the letters " I. H." appear, which evidently are the initals of John Hull, the probable donor of the dial. He is buried in the churchyard, and the inscription on his gravestone runs in this quaint fashion :—

" Here lye
the B
ody of Jo
hn Hvll
the son of Mathe
w Hvll of
lyttle Bisph . . . .
1709."

96.

DIJ HIJTIGE STUND UND DASS HIJTIGE GLÜCK,
SCHLICHT HIN IN EINEM AUGEN BLICK.

The hour and the fortune of to-day,
In an eye's twinkling pass away.

At Thun. Probably identical with No. 98.

97.

DIE SONNE SCHEINET ÜBERALL.

The sun shines everywhere.

On a dial in a villa garden on the banks of the Lake of Lugano.

98.

DYE JETZIGE STUND UND DAS ZYTLICHE GLUECK
SCHLEICHT HIN IN EINEM AUGENBLICK.

1792.

The present hour and this world's cheer,
Are in a moment gone from here.

The dial is on a house in the market-place at Thun, in Switzerland, placed over one of the low wide arches of the arcades, where the Bernese peasants congregate on market days. It declines S.W., and is unusually large. It is painted pink on the whitewashed wall, and is rendered somewhat indistinct by the weather. The hours are in Roman characters, and are written on a scroll. It is a venerable-looking dial, worthy of the picturesque little town.

99.

DIES AFFERT MULTA.

The day brings with it many things.

This inscription was cut on a dial, the work of an ingenious and well educated man for his time, named Daniel Rose, who placed it over the doorway of his cottage house, called

"Shutts," near Ashopton, in Derbyshire. He was the clerk of Derwent Chapel, also a schoolmaster and dial-maker—possibly, too, he wrote letters for his neighbours, and made their wills. It is said that he carved his dials in a soft slate stone during schooltime with a penknife: the dials both at Derwent Church (No. 317) and the Hall (No. 13), are specimens of his skill. Father and son were the parish clerks in succession. The father of Daniel Rose was a Welshman, and his mother is reported to have attained the age of 105. The family is not extinct in the parish of Derwent.

100.

DIES DIEM DOCET: DISCE.

One day telleth another: learn.

A block of stone with four dial faces placed over the porch of the old church at Barmston, near Bridlington, Yorkshire, is thus inscribed. The letters are much defaced. The motto was probably suggested by Ps. xix. 2 : "One day telleth another; " or, as in the Bible translation, "Day unto day uttereth speech."

101.

DIES EJUS SICUT UMBRA PRAETEREUNT.

1863.

His days pass away like a shadow.

On a church, Grand Canal, Venice.

"Le perte de la vie est imperceptible, c'est l'aiguille du cadran que nous ne voyons pas aller."—MADME. DE SEVIGNÉ.

102.

DIES MEI SICUT UMBRA DECLINAVERUNT.

My days have gone down like a shadow.

Is on the Roman Catholic church at Langen-Schwalbach; and is also traced on the marble wall of the Capella Emiliana, at San Michele in Isola, near Venice, which was built by Bergamasco in 1530. This latter dial, which has the date 1863, and the reference to Psalm cii. 11, is placed between the statues which occupy the niches of a building that has been stigmatised by Mr. Ruskin as "a beehive set on a low hexagonal tower, with dashes of stonework about its windows, like the flourishes of an idle penman." But apart from the question whether our admiration is due or not to a heavy renaissance chapel, the dial with its motto could not have been more appropriately fixed than beside the shore where the Venetians land their dead for interment in this "quiet sleeping ground in the midst of the sea." In the Church of San Michele, built on the ruins of San Cristoforo della Pace, Fra Paolo Sarpi is buried.

103.

DILIGE DOMINUM DEUM TOTO CORDE.

Love the Lord thy God with all thy heart.

At Moccas Court. See Nos. 635.

104.

DISCE BENE VIVERE ET MORI.

Learn to live and die well.

Is on a pillar dial in the churchyard at Conway, which is

further inscribed :—" Erected by the Corporation of Conway,
Robert Wynne, Jr., Esq., Alderman ; Hugh Williams and
John Nuttal, Bailiffs, 1761.   Meredith Hughes fecit.   The
difference of 20 places from Conway."

105.

DISCE DIES NUMERARE.

Learn to number the days.

On the wall of the south aisle of Arundel Church, with
the date 1744.

106.

DISCE DIES NUMERARE TUOS.

Learn to number thy days.

Is on an old school-house at Wortley, near Sheffield; and
it is also engraved on a large stone dial in the kitchen garden
at Barnes Hall, near Sheffield, the property of W. Smith,
Esq.   The date upon this dial is 1738, and without doubt it
was the handiwork of a very remarkable man, Samuel Walker,
of Masbro', the father of the Iron Trade of England.   He
was of humble origin, born in the parish of Ecclesfield, and
began life as a parish schoolmaster and dial-maker.   When
fitting this identical dial at Barnes Hall, then occupied by Sir
W. Horton, that gentleman remarked to a friend, " Sam
Walker will one day ride in his carriage."   The words were
prophetic, for in a few years Walker laid the foundation of
the largest iron-works in the country at Masbro', near Rotherham, and his descendants have since occupied, and still retain,
a good position as country gentlefolk.   See No. 117.

How soon
Our new born light
Attains to full aged noon !
And this how soon to gray hair'd night !
We spring, we bud, we blossom, and we blast
Ere we can count our days, our days they flee so fast.

They end
When scarce begun,
And ere we apprehend
That we begin to live, our life is done !
Man, count thy days, and if they fly too fast
For thy dull thoughts to count, count every day thy last.
QUARLES.

107.

DISCE MORI MUNDO.

Learn to die to the world.

A vertical dial on the church porch, Batley, Yorkshire. Recorded in " Yorkshire Post," 24 June, 1879.

108.

DISCITE JUSTITIAM, MONITI.

Learn justice, being warned.

Professor Beckmann, in his " History of Inventions and Discoveries," says: "On the side of New Palace Yard, which is opposite to Westminster Hall, and in the second pediment of the new buildings from the Thames, a dial is inserted with this remarkable motto upon it : *Discite justitiam, moniti*, which seems most clearly to relate to the fine imposed on Radulphus de Hengham being applied to the paying for a clock." The professor proceeds to state that the dial was fixed exactly where Strype describes the clock-house to have stood.

Blackstone tells the well-known story, how Chief Justice Ralph Hengham—" a very learned judge to whom we are obliged for two excellent treatises of practice "—out of mere compassion for a very poor man, altered a fine of 13*s.* 4*d.* to 6*s.* 8*d.*, and was consequently fined 800 marks by King Edward I., which were expended in building a clock-house to regulate the sittings of the Courts. This sovereign, who has been styled the Justinian of England, did so much to reform the Courts, that Sir Matthew Hale says, " that more was done in the first thirteen years of his reign to settle and establish the distributive justice of the kingdom, than in all the ages since that time put together." We may consider that the present clock tower at Westminster, from which "Big Ben" gives forth his loud utterances, is a more than sufficient substitute for that with which Judge Hengham's name is associated.

The same motto is adopted for one of the Temple dials. The quotation is from Virgil, Æn. vi. 620.

109.

DISEGNA LE ORE SENZA FAR ROMORE.

Tells the hours all round, without making a sound.

On the Italian Custom House at Fornasette, with No. 80.

110.

DO TO-DAY'S WORK TO-DAY. 1875.

On a dial at Golder's Hill, Hampstead, the residence of the eminent surgeon, Sir Spencer Wells, Bart. "Let us do, I pray, as the Hebrews express it, 'the work of the day while the day lasts,' for time slips silently away, and every succeeding hour is attended with greater disadvantages than that which went before it."—Archbishop Leighton.

111.

DOCET UMBRA.

1700.

The shadow teaches.

A large vertical dial of stone on the Dutch church in Austin Friars, London, bears this motto. It is in excellent preservation, though from its situation, closely surrounded by houses, the learners from this shadow must be few. The church was founded by Humphrey de Bohun, Earl of Hereford and Essex, for the Friars Eremites of St. Augustine, and after the dissolution of the Priory, the church (with the exception of the choir and steeple) was granted by Edward VI. to the fugitives from the Netherlands, A.D. 1550. For a few months the church was used both by the French and

Dutch congregations, but the number of refugees increased so greatly that another building was given for the use of the French. Both churches were closed during the reign of Mary, but re-opened when Elizabeth came to the throne, and Austin Friars has remained in the possession of the Dutch ever since. The motto has a singular appropriateness. The shadow teaches by its nature as well as by its progress, and it was a dark shadow, one of persecution and exile, which passed over the first congregation that worshipped in the Dutch Church. See No. 644.

112.

DONA PRAESENTIS RAPE LAETUS HORAE.

Gladly seize the gifts of the present hour.

LABITUR ET LABETUR.

It glides, and will glide away.

SCIS HORAS, NESCIS HORAM.

Thou knowest the hours, thou knowest not the hour.

TUA HORA RUIT MEA.

The hour which is mine, destroys what is thine.

ULTIMA LATET.

The last (hour) is hidden.

VOLAT SINA MORA.

It flies without delay.

All of these mottoes are recorded as being on the Franciscan Convent at Cimièz, near Nice. There are probably several dials on the building.

113.

DUBIA OMNIBUS, ULTIMA MULTIS. 1835.

Doubtful to all, the last to many.

Is painted on a house at Grasse, in the department of the Alpes Maritimes, France; also on the south wall of the village church at Cambo, Basses Pyrénées, France, where directly below it is a plain, round-arched window, with two or three cypress trees standing in the churchyard close by.

The ground behind the church slopes sharply down to the river Nive, which joins the Adour at Bayonne about fifteen miles off. Both the dials are modern.

114.

DUM FUGIT UMBRA, QUIESCO.

While the shadow fleets, I am at rest.

Inscribed by M. de Fienhet, Counsellor of State to Louis XIV., on a dial at his country house. See No. 416.

115.

DUM LICET UTERE.

While time is given, use it.

Is on a dial in the courtyard of the old Castle at Stazzano, near Serravalle Scrivia, in the province of Alessandria, North Italy. The castle is now a priests' school. The expression is used by Seneca :—

> " Quis sapiens bono
> Confidat fragili ? dum licet utere :
> Tempus te tacitum subruet, horâque
> Semper praeteritâ deterior subit."

Senec. Hippol. 775.

116.

DUM PROFICIT D(EFICI)T.

While (time) gains, it loses.

This defaced inscription may be seen in the cloisters of the cathedral at Chambery, in Savoy. The reader may amuse himself by supplying the illegible word to his own taste. A friend suggests *deficit*, which seems most probable. See No. 366.

117.

DUM SPECTAS FUGIO: SIC VITA.

Whilst thou lookest, I fly; so doth life.

In a three-sided bay-window over a shop in the High Street of Marlborough, is a handsomely illuminated glass dial of oval shape, which nearly occupies four of the twelve panes that compose the projecting centre of the window, and which is inscribed with this motto. A golden scroll on a red ground surrounds the dial face, in the centre of which is a fly so beautifully depicted, that you can hardly believe it is not a real insect incorporated in the glass, as in amber; for it is not perceptible to the touch. There is no gnomon at present; for, singularly enough, it was destroyed by lightning.

At Winchester College there is also the fly in a similar glass dial; and in Leadbetter's book many of the plates of dials have a fly figured; it is supposed that the introduction of the fly is meant for a punning suggestion of the thought, "They (the hours) fly."

The dial at Marlborough attracted the attention of Messrs. Britton and Brazley, and is mentioned by them in the "Beauties of England," vol. i. (1801), together with two similar window dials (which had also been noticed by Mr. Arthur Young in his "Six Weeks' Tour"), in the Rectory, North-hill, Beds., who gave particular praise to the execution of the fly. The dials were of green glass, on one the fly was represented with two cherries before it, and wings painted on one side of the glass, the body and legs being painted on

the other side, so as to deceive the spectator. The dials bore
the mottoes : *Dum spectas fugio* and *Sic transit gloria mundi,*
and on one of them, " John Oliver, fecit 1664." As the
rectory at North-hill had been lately rebuilt, and the paintings

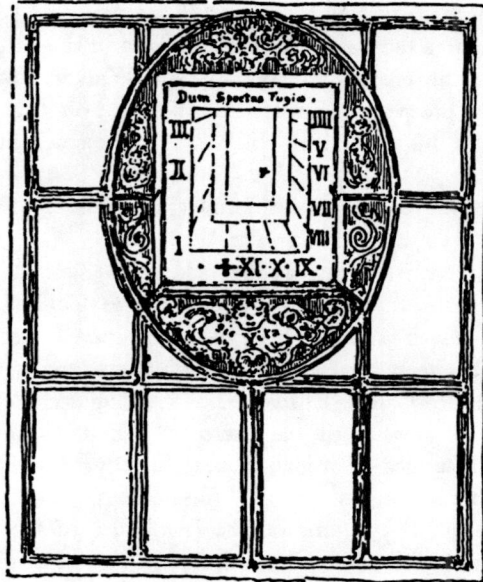

were described by M. Britton as lying useless, it is probable
that they no longer exist.

Dum spectas fugio, 1739, is (or was) also to be found on
one of four vertical dials which surmount a pillar in the
garden of " The Holmes, Rotherham." On the step below is
inscribed the name of the maker, " Sam¹ . Walker . fecit."
Walker was at this time keeping a school at Grenoside, and
had in the previous year put up the dial at Barnes Hall, in
his own parish (as mentioned in No. 106). Two years later

he and his brother started an iron foundry in an old nail smithy, and in the course of a year made eight tons of castings. In 1746, we learn from Walker's note-book, that about sixty-three tons, valued at £600, were made, and his first furnace at Rotherham was built. In 1756 he purchased from Lord Effingham a house at the Holmes, and in the garden of this residence he erected the dial. Sam. Walker died in 1784, leaving a prosperous family, and in 1796, on the retirement of one of his sons from the business, the stock in trade was valued at £213,393. The iron used in Southwark Bridge was cast at the Holmes foundry, as well as much of the cannon used in the Peninsular War.

Dum spectas fugio may be read on a dial which adorns an old gabled entrance to one of the Canons houses at Exeter. It is supported by a small carved figure, and is placed between two mullioned windows, above which is a medallion of Queen Elizabeth. Over the arched doorway is a coat of arms with the motto " Vincit Veritas." It is further inscribed on a dial, in the churchyard of Cranbrook, Kent, with the names of " John Hague, and Ellis John Troughton, 1855," and on the farmhouse of Greenbury, in the parish of Scorton, Yorkshire, with "J. Fawcitt, 1751," the " i " in *fugio* being omitted by mistake. The motto is used with others at King's Lynn (No. 316) ; Ripley, Surrey (429) ; and Thorpe Perrow (606). At Kirkby-in-Cleveland, there is a dial on the church tower dated 1815, the motto is nearly obliterated, " Dum " being the only word now legible (1887).

Dum spectas fugio is on Ingleton Church, near Settle, in Yorkshire; and in the south wall of the old tower of Willesden Church, Middlesex, there is a dial, dated 1736, which bears the same inscription, whilst immediately over it has been fixed a valuable chiming clock, the gift of a lady, to

which the words equally well apply. This reminds us of the
lines in Hood's poem of the "Workhouse Clock," which
contain the double allusion :—

> "Oh ! that the Parish Powers,
> Which regulate Labour's hours,
> The daily amount of human trial,
> Weariness, pain, and self-denial,
> Would turn from the artificial dial
> That striketh ten or eleven,
> And go, for once, by that older one
> That stands in the light of Nature's sun,
> And takes its time from Heaven ! "

118.

DUM SPECTAS FUGIT.

Whilst thou art looking, (the hour) is flying.

This inscription was probably on the dial, which, in 1869,
was still fixed to the wall of Felkirk Church, Yorkshire, a
little to the east of the porch ; the words *Dum—fugit* 1769
alone being legible. In January, 1884, the dial was seen
lying on the ground, having been blown down by a gale of
wind a few months previously. The motto is on a dial on
the south transept of the parish church, Leighton Buzzard ;
and on St. Patrick's Church, I. of Man. See Nos. 46, 372.

119.

DUM SPECTAS, FUGIT HORA.

Whilst thou art looking, the hour is flying.

On Heighington Church, near Darlington.

120.

DUM SPECTAS, FUGIT HORA: CARPE DIEM.
Whilst thou art looking, the hour is flying; seize to-day.

On a house-dial at Wolsingham, Co. Durham. The figures are gilt on a black ground.

121.

DUM TEMPUS HABEMUS, OPEREMUR BONUM.
Whilst we have time let us do good.

These words from Gal. iv. 10 (Vulgate) are on a dial on the cloister wall of the Convent of Annunziata, Florence: as also in the courtyard of a monastery at Blois (see No. 628); and in the parish of Tytherton Kellaways, Wilts. See No. 708.

122.

È DI FERRO LO STIL: MA È D'ORO IL TEMPO.
The stile is iron; but time is gold.

At Cambiano in Piedmont. See No. 92.

123.

EGO REDIBO, TU NUNQUAM.
I will return, thou never.

On the Church of St. John the Baptist, Erith.

H

124.

EHEU, FUGACES !

Alas, how fleeting !

A quotation from Horace, Carm. 2, 14, 1, " Eheu fugaces, Postume, Postume, labuntur anni."   At Sedbury Hall, near Richmond, Yorkshire, the seat of George Gilpin Brown, Esq., there is a stone pillar-shaped dial attached to the sill of the drawing-room window, with this touching motto upon it ; and it is engraved on the plate of a horizontal dial in the rectory garden, Copgrove, Yorkshire, " Goodall, Tadcaster, fecit 1816.

Also (as Dr. Doran tells us in his " Life of the Rev. Dr. Young "), the author of " Night Thoughts," set up a dial in the rectory garden of Welwyn, Hertfordshire, with the motto, " Eheu, fugaces ; " and a few nights afterwards, thieves entered the garden and proved the wisdom of the poet's choice of motto, by carrying the dial away.

On the walls of the entrance-tower at Farnham Castle, the palace of the Bishop of Winchester, there are two dials which formerly bore the inscription, " Eheu, fugaces, labuntur anni ! " Other mottoes, more appropriate to an episcopal residence, have now been substituted, as will be shown hereafter.   See No. 424.

125.

·ELECTA UT SOL BEAT ORBEM SPLENDORE.

Bright as the Sun, she blesseth the earth with brightness.

STELLT DEINS LEBENS TAG ZU DIENST MARIA EIN,
SO WIRD DEIN LETZTE STUND IN TOD DIE BESTE SEIN.

Give the day of thy life to do Mary's behest,
So will thy last hour in death be the best.

These mottoes are at Rosenheim, and are evidently lauda-
tory of the Virgin, who is represented as the crowned Queen
of Heaven, sitting richly robed on clouds, with the sun's rays
behind. A scroll above her has the Latin line, and beneath
her feet is a curling double scroll with the figures of the
hours above, and the German legend below.

126.

EN ME REGARDANT, PENSE OÙ TU VAS,
ET D'OÙ TU VIENS, CAR LA MORT TE SUIT
PAS À PAS.

1841. Z.A.F.

Remember ye that mark my face,
That Death's behind you pace by pace ;
Whence are ye come, ye do not know
Nor whither afterwards you'll go.

At Abriès in the Vallée de Queyras, a village high up amongst the Dauphiné Alps.

127.

EN REGARDANT L'HEURE QU'IL EST,
PENSE À LA MORT ET TIENS-TOI PRÊT.

As the hour here you see,
. *Think on death, and ready be.*

In the village of La Bessée.

128.

EN REGARDANT, VOUS VIELLISSEZ.

Whilst beholding, you become old.

On the church of S. Nicholas, a small village in the mountains of Haute Savoie. See Nos. 35, 482.

129.

EN SUPRA VITA FUGAX,
EN INFRA CERTA MORS:
HINC VIVERE DISCE,
ILLINC DISCE MORI.

Lo, above is fleeting life:
And below is certain death:
From the one learn to live,
From the other learn to die.

These mottoes are quoted by Mr. Leadbitter (Mechanick
Art of Dialling, 1737), as being on the two faces of the dial
on St. Mary Overy's Church (now St. Saviour's), Southwark,
which hung over the burial ground. It was probably put up
after 1647, as there is no sign of it in Hollar's etching of that
date. If not destroyed before 1822, it must then have been
cleared away when the church was altered.

130.

ERIT LAPIS ISTE
IN SIGNUM.
MDDCCIV.
PAR TA PUISSANCE.

That stone shall be for a sign.
By Thy Power.

On a small stone dial, bought at Cologne in January,
1885, by Lewis Evans, Esq. A crown, and the letters
L.P.B. in a monogram are also engraved on the face.

131.

ERRAR PUÒ IL FABBRO,
ERRAR PUÒ IL FERRO,
IO MAI NON ERRO.

The maker may err,
The iron may err,
I never err.

At Graglia in Piedmont. This claim to infallibility on the part of the dial was recently disputed, as shown by a pleasant anecdote which a correspondent has kindly supplied. A clergyman, officiating in the united parishes of Hastingleigh and Elmsted in Kent, as he was entering the church at the latter place, said to the clerk, "What's the time by the dial?" "Well, sir," was the reply, "the dial is half-past ten, but *I think it must be a little fast,* as *my watch* is only ten minutes past ten!" Both church and churchyard at Elmsted are very interesting, from their antiquity and beauty of situation. The yew trees in the churchyard are especially grand—one of them measures twenty-seven feet in circumference.

132.

'ΕΡΧΕΤΑΙ ΓΑΡ ΝΥΞ.

For the night cometh.

A sketch of this dial was made by the collector at Abbotsford in 1839, when the pedestal stood outside a small plantation near the house. But the dial-plate with its gnomon was gone: only two nails which had once served to fasten it remained. So the motto had been a prophecy; for the dial's work was over, since it could henceforth record nothing, except that the night was coming—which indeed had come as if in mockery of itself. One could not help thinking further of the night that came down upon Abbotsford, when its illustrious master was lost to the world.

The motto was also adopted by Dr. Johnson, as we learn from the following passage in Boswell: "At this time I observed upon the dial-plate of his (Dr. Johnson's) watch a

short Greek inscription, taken from the New Testament, Νὺξ γὰρ ἔρχεται, being the first words of our Saviour's solemn admonition to the improvement of that time which is allowed to us to prepare for eternity—'the night cometh when no man can work.' He some time afterwards laid aside this dial-plate, and when I asked him the reason, he said, 'It might do very well upon a clock which a man keeps in his closet ; but to have it upon his watch which he carries about with him, and which is looked at by others, might be censured as ostentatious.' " Croker adds in a note : " The inscription,

however, was made unintelligible by the mistake of writing
νμξ for νιξ." We would observe that this error is quite
sufficient to account for the learned scholar putting aside the
watch ; and we know that he did not always condescend to
fully enlighten his *shadow* "Bozzy" as to his motives.   It is
also remarkable that in both cases the word γαρ should have
been introduced, for it is not in the New Testament.
Probably, however, Sir Walter copied the passage from Johnson, without referring to the original.

There can be no doubt that Sir Walter Scott merely
adopted the inscription without critically understanding it, or
being competent in himself to refer to the original.   With
that beautiful candour which belonged to his character, and
marks the brief autobiography prefixed to Lockhart's life of
him, he confesses that when he went to the college at Edinburgh, he had no knowledge of the Greek language; and
adds, "I forgot the very letters of the Greek alphabet." His
comment on his own ignorance as a classical scholar cannot
be too often repeated : "If it should ever fall to the lot of
youth to peruse these pages, let such a reader remember that
it is with the deepest regret that I recollect in my manhood
the opportunities of learning which I neglected in my youth ;
that through every part of my literary career I have felt
pinched and hampered by my own ignorance; and that I
would at this moment give half the reputation I have had
the good fortune to acquire, if by so doing I could rest the
remaining part upon a sound foundation of learning and
science."

The same quotation, EPXETAI NUΞ, rightly rendered, is
to be found as a motto on the plate of a pillar dial in the
beautiful grounds of Dromore Castle, co. Kerry, Ireland,
inscribed by the owner, R. Mahony, Esq., in 1871, when
the dial was erected.

133.

EST DEO GRATIA.
Thanks are to God.

On pillar dial at Corpus Christi College.   See No. 134.

134.

EST REPOSITA CORONA JUSTITIAE.
There is laid up a crown of righteousness.

EST DEO GRATIA.
Thanks are to God.

POSUI DEUM ADJUTOREM MEUM.
I have placed God as my helper.

GRATIA DEI MECUM.
The grace of God with me.

HORAS OMNES COMPLECTOR.
I embrace all hours.

The first four of these mottoes are inscribed round the moulding above the square capital of the pillar dial which stands in the quadrangle of Corpus Christi College, Oxford. Above the moulding is a pyramidal block of stone, with four dial faces on its sides, and one of these is concave; the pyramid is surmounted by a globe, and the pelican, which is the crest of the College. On the four sides of the square capital below the moulding are four coats of arms carved in relief, viz., the arms of (1) Bishop Fox, the Founder of the College; (2) those of Bishop Oldham; (3) the University arms; (4) the Royal arms. In each case the scroll-work round the shield acts as a gnomon to a dial face engraved below it. The square capital stands upon a cylindrical shaft, where there is a fifth dial face, with a perpetual calendar engraved below it, and near the base the motto " Horas omnes complector " occurs. This elaborate piece of workmanship was erected in 1605 by Charles Turnbull, then a Fellow of the College; it bears the initials C. T., and the date MDCV. The pillar is said to have been regarded as " inconvenient " during the old days of threatened invasion, when the quadrangle was used as a drilling ground, but happily it was not removed from its place, and still stands as a memorial of Turnbull's mathematical skill. Four of the mottoes are adapted from the Vulgate. The dial is described in a MS. by Robert Hegge, which is preserved in the College Library, No. XL. *Codex Chartaceous 4to.*

135.

ESTEEM THY PRECIOUS TIME
WHICH PASS SO SWIFT AWAY:
PREPARE THEN FOR ETERNITY
AND DO NOT MAKE DELAY.

On Wilton Bridge, near Ross, Herefordshire, there stands a pillar surmounted by four dials, and crowned with a ball. It probably dates from the eighteenth century. The south face bears the above inscription.

136.

'ΕΤΙ ΜΙΚΡΟΝ ΧΡΟΝΟΝ ΤΟ ΦΩΣ ΜΕΘ' 'ΥΜΩΝ 'ΕΣΤΙ,
ΠΕΡΙΠΑΤΕΙΤΕ 'ΕΩΣ ΤΟ ΦΩΣ 'ΕΧΕΤΕ.

YET A LITTLE WHILE IS THE LIGHT WITH YOU,
WALK WHILE YE HAVE THE LIGHT."—*John* xii. 35.

The dial-plate on which these inscriptions appear is fixed
on an old school-house at Aynho, near Bicester, now disused.
The shape is an oblong square. The sun is represented as a
full human face, with jets of light all round. The eyes and
mouth are given, and the gnomon forms the nose. "M.C.
1671" are in the centre, being the initials of the builder and
the date of the building. "House built by one Mary
Cartwright."

> "Should not each dial strike us as we pass,
> Portentous, as the written wall which struck,
> O'er midnight bowls, the proud Assyrian pale,
> Erewhile high flush'd with insolence and wine?
> Like that the dial speaks; and points to thee,
> Lorenzo, loth to break thy banquet up!
> 'O man, thy kingdom is departing from thee;
> And while it lasts, is emptier than thy shade!'
> Its silent language such."—YOUNG's *Night Thoughts.*

137.

EUNDO HORA DIEM DEPASCIT.

As it goes, the hour consumes the day.

Inscribed on a curious sundial in the churchyard of Trelleck, Monmouthshire. (Compare No. 568.) It was erected

in 1648 by the Lady Maud Probert, widow of Sir George
Probert, and on three sides of the pedestal are represented in
relief the three marvels peculiar to the place, viz.: 1. A

tumulus, supposed to be of Roman origin, and above it the
words, " *Magna mole* " (" Great in its mound "); " *O quot
hic sepulti* " (" O, how many buried here! "). 2. Three
stone pillars, whence the name Tri-llech, the town of three
stones, with the inscription, " *Major Saxis* " (" Greater in

its stones ; " the height of the stones being also given—8 feet, 10 feet, 14 feet—as well as *" Hic fuit victor Harold"* (" Here was Harold victorious "). 3. A representation of the well of chalybeate water, and two drinking cups, *" Maxima fonte"* (" Greatest in its spring "); and below, *" Dom. Magd. Probert ostendit."*

Trelleck is supposed to have been anciently a large town and place of importance. Tradition states that the pillars were erected by Harold to commemorate a victory over the Britons, but they are known to have existed in the seventh century, and are probably of Druidical origin. Nor does the *tumulus* cover the bodies of the slain, as suggested by Lady Probert's inscription : it is simply in the neighbourhood of the battle-field. In later days it was surmounted by the keep of a castle belonging to the Earl of Clare. The motto of this dial is now (1887) nearly illegible, but a description may be found in " Archæological Journal," xi. 129.

138.

EVERY HOUR SHORTENS LIFE.

Was on the church porch at Barnard Castle, before the restoration of the building, but the dial was then removed and laid by in the church tower. The motto is also on " Turner's Hospital," at Kirkleatham, in Yorkshire, a noble charity founded at his birthplace by Sir William Turner, Lord Mayor of London in 1669. The dial is supposed to have been erected about a hundred years afterwards. A second motto is given elsewhere. (See No. 734.)

139.

EX HIS UNA TIBI.

Of these (hours) one is for thee.

This is on a church in Brittany, below a design of a radiating sun-face.

140.

EX HOC MOMENTO PENDET AETERNITAS.

On this moment hangs eternity.

On an old gable in Lincoln's Inn there was formerly a southern dial thus inscribed, which was restored in 1840, and showed the hours by its gnomon from 6 A.M. to 4 P.M., but it was taken down in 1874, and could not be replaced. A newspaper of 1812 informs us that a book was one morning found to have been suspended on the gnomon by the hand of some wag. When taken down, the volume proved to be an old edition of " Practice in Chancery." The same motto is at Sandhurst, Kent, " W. Hawney, *fecit*, 1720, and at St. Budeaux, Devon, Latitude 51,0′ 4″ ; " also on Glasgow Cathedral. (See Nos. 6 and 407.)

"O fearful moment upon which so much depends ! Admirable is the high wisdom of God which hath placed a Point in the midst betwixt Time and Eternity unto which all the time of this Life is to relate, and upon which the whole eternity of the other is to depend ! O moment which art neither Time or Eternity, which art the Horizon of both and dividest things Temporal from Eternal."—JEREMY TAYLOR.

141.

ΕΞΑΓΩΡΑΖΟΜΕΝΟΙ ΤΟΝ ΚΑΙΡΟΝ ΟΤΙ ΑΙ ΗΜΕΡΑΙ
ΠΟΝΗΡΑΙ ΕΙΣΙ.

Redeem the time because the days are evil.

In the Albert Park, Middlesbrough.   See No. 613.

142.

FAIS CE QUE DOIS, ADVIENNE QUE POURRA;
L'HEURE EST À DIEU, L'ESPERANCE À TOUS.

Do that which thou oughtest, come what may;
The hour belongs to God, hope to all.

Noted in "The Monthly Packet," Oct. 1886, but no
locality assigned.

143.

FELICIBUS BREVIS, MISERIS HORA LONGA.

The hour is short to the happy, long to the miserable.

Is painted on an oval dial on a house wall at Martigny.
The inscription is below, and the hour-glass and wings of
Time are above.   The same sentiment occurs in No. 16.
Shakespeare says, in "As You Like It," Act iii. Scene 2:
·—"Time travels in divers paces with divers persons: I'll
tell you who time ambles withal, who time trots withal,
who time gallops withal, and who he stands still withal."

144.

FERREA VIRGA EST, UMBRATILIS MOTUS.
The rod is of iron, the motion that of shadow.

The iron rod is of course the gnomon. The first letter of
the last word has been defaced, but "motus" seems to be
the most suitable term. It is painted on a large square dial
on a wall facing north, in the cloisters of the cathedral at
Chambery. See No. 366.

145.

FERT OMNIA AETAS.
Time bears all away.

On a small stone dial over the door of a farm, once the
Manor House at Lund, in the East Riding of Yorkshire;
and at Vallouse. See No. 61.

146.

FESTINA LENTE.
Hasten slowly.

Upon a square dial on a house in Deeping St. James, co.
Lincoln. This is the motto of the Onslow family, "*More
haste, less speed.*"

147.

FESTINA MOX NOX.
Hasten, the night (cometh) soon.

Noticed in the "Graphic" for August 11, 1883, as on a
sun-dial on the King's House, Thetford. This King's
House was at one time a royal mint, and was afterwards
occupied by Queen Elizabeth and by James I.

148.

FESTINAT SUPREMA.

The last (hour) hastens on.

Was copied in North Italy by Mr. Howard Hopley, and recorded by him in the " Leisure Hour."

149.

FIAT LUX, ET FACTA EST LUX, FACTUMQUE EST VESPERE ET MANE DIES UNUS.

Let there be light, and there was light : and the evening and the morning were the first day.

At Courmayeur. The motto is the Vulgate version of the passage quoted.

150.

FILI CONSERVA TEMPUS.   *Ecclus.* iv. 23.

My son, observe the opportunity.

OMNIA TEMPUS HABENT.   *Eccles.* iii. 1.

To everything there is a season.

On a dial upon the tower of the church of S. Stefano, Belluno.

In our English translation of Ecclesiasticus the first of these mottoes occurs in v. 20, and the words " My son " are omitted. The same line occurs at Palermo ; and at Carenna. It is also painted upon a modern dial on a house on the Superga, near Turin ; the dial face is square, and placed close under the roof.

I

151.

FINEM RESPICE.

Look to the end.

This motto was evidently suggested by the opening of one
of the chapters in à Kempis' " De Imitatione Christi," " *In
omnibus rebus respice finem*," Lib. I. xxiv. cap. The place
where it is inscribed is not known. See No. 232.

152.

FINIS ITINERIS SEPULCHRUM.

The grave is the end of the journey.

On the lawn at Marrington Hall, Shropshire (see No.
605). The motto recalls the more hopeful sentiment inscribed on Dean Alford's grave in St. Martin's Churchyard,
Canterbury.

DEVERSORIUM VIATORIS HIEROSOLYMAM PROFICISCENTIS.

The resting-place of a traveller on his way to Jerusalem.

153.

FLOREAT ECCLESIA. 1697. L. 54° 12'.

May the Church flourish.

Is on the church-porch at Kirkby Malzeard, Yorkshire;
and the dial is further inscribed, " This dial was given by Mr.
W. Buck, minister here in anno 1697." To be read also at
Marton cum Grafton, in the same county.

The church of Marton was pulled down (1873), and a new

one has been built. The dial was situated on the south side of the chancel of the original church. It is of stone, and is inscribed, " W. B. 1700. Floreat Ecclesia." The style was iron, and when the church was being pulled to pieces the dial fell, and the style was broken. The Rev. J. R. Lunn, then vicar, replaced it with a copper one, solid, and pierced with $\dfrac{C}{\overline{XIV,}}$ giving the golden number Sunday letter, I.R.L.

and year of rebuilding. It is now situated on the vestry chimney (1884).

The W. B. whose initials are on the dial was William Buck, who became vicar 1700, and died in 1719. He came from Kirkby Malzeard, where he had been curate, and had erected the dial recorded above. Mr. Lunn states that a much older dial of stone (without the style) was discovered at Marton, and he has had it built inside the vestry amongst other old remains. It is possibly of twelfth century date.

154.

FORTE TUA.

1760, I. C. C. fecit.

Perhaps (this hour) is thine.

At Vallouse, Départment de l'Isère ; also, with date 1831, at Les Orres, Canton d'Embrun ; and at Vars, Canton de Guillestre, dated 1827.

155.

FORTE ULTIMA,

1825.

Perhaps (this hour) is the last.

At Vallouse, Départment de l'Isère.

156.

FRONTE CAPILLATA, POST EST OCCASIO CALVA.

Opportunity has locks in front, and is bald behind.

This well-known line is inscribed on a dial on the school-house at Guilsborough, Northamptonshire, with the date 1821. It is quoted from "Distichorum de Moribus," lib. ii. D. xxv., written by Dionysius Cato, who is supposed to have lived in the time of the Antonines, in the second century. The two lines are :—

"Rem tibi quam nosces optam dimittere noli ;
Fronte capillatâ, post est occasio calva."

Lord Bacon in his xxi. Essay, "Of Delays," thus writes : "For occasion (as it is in the common verse) turneth a bald noddle after she hath presented her locks in front, and no hold taken." "Take Time by the forelock," is a proverb; and the conventional figure of Time represents an old man bald, except a tuft of hair on the crown of his head. Shake-speare recognizes the same idea in "All's Well that Ends Well," Act v. Scene 3 :—

"Let's take the instant by the forward top;
For we are old, and on our quick'st decrees
The inaudible and noiseless foot of time
Steals ere we can effect them."

157.

FUGIO, FUGE.

I fly—fly thou.

One of several mottoes on a cross-dial at Elleslie, near Chichester. See No. 48.

158.

FUGIT, DUM ASPICIS.

It flies, while thou lookest.

MANEO NEMINI.

I wait for no one.

NIL NISI CAELESTI RADIO.

Nought save by a ray from heaven.

UT UMBRA SIC VITA.

As a shadow, so is life.

In a small hamlet near Baslow, Derbyshire.

159.

FUGIT, ET NON RECEDIT TEMPUS.

Time flies, and comes not back.

Appears as a dial and a clock motto at once on the wall of a little court in the Convent della Quiete, near Florence. There is an overhanging roof, and above is suspended a tinkling bell. The convent was originally a royal villa, and received its name,—"La Quiete della Granduchessa Cristina,"—from its noble owner. It afterwards became the property of Donna Eleonora Ramirez di Montalvo, the foundress of the present existing school. See No. 82.

> " The heavens on high perpetually do move ;
> By minutes small the hour doth steal away,
> By hours the days, by days the months remove,

And then by months the years as fast decay ;
Yea, Virgil's verse, and Tully's truth do say,
That Time flieth and never claps her wings ;
But rides on clouds and forward still she springs."

GEO. GASCOIGNE.

160.

FUGIT HORA.

The hour flies.

On a square stone dial on an old house, called Moat Hall,
near Great Ouseburn, Yorkshire.

161.

FUGIT HORA, ORA.

The hour flies, pray.

On a circular dial in a square slab of stone over the porch
entrance of Catterick Church, near Richmond, Yorkshire.

The face is painted blue, the lettering is gilt, and the gnomon
springs from a golden sun which is immediately below the
motto.

The Rev. A. J. Scott, D.D., the friend and chaplain of Lord Nelson, who died in his arms at Trafalgar, was vicar of Catterick from 1816 to 1840, and was the father of the compiler of this volume.

The dial plate at Catterick, described above, was removed from the porch when the church was restored, and it was unfortunately broken ; but an exact reproduction of the original plate has been erected in its place through the kindness of William Booth, Esq., of Oran, near Catterick.

Fugit hora ora is on a dial at Gilling Church, near Catterick ; and it was formerly on the porch of Merthyr Mawr Church, co. Glamorgan, with the date 1720, but about forty years ago the church was rebuilt, and the dial taken down, and laid in the churchyard, where it still exists (1888).

Most exquisitely does Tennyson touch the three successive chroniclers of time—the hour-glass, dial, and watch, in one of the poems of his " In Memoriam."

> " O days and hours, your work is this,
>   To hold me from my proper place,
>   A little while from his embrace,
> For fuller gain of after bliss :
>
> That out of distance might ensue
>   Desire of nearness doubly sweet ;
>   And unto meeting, when we meet,
> Delight a hundredfold accrue,
>
> For every grain of sand that runs,
>   And every span of shade that steals,
>   And every kiss of toothed wheels,
> And all the courses of the suns."

162.

FUGIT HORA, ORA, LABORA.

The hour is flying, pray, work.

May be read in Southgate Street, Gloucester.

163.

FUGIT HORA SIC EST VITA.

The hour flies—so with life.

This is given as the probable reading of a dial on the church tower of Cubberley, Gloucestershire. The motto seems to be *Fugit hora suevet*, and has, says a writer in " Notes and Queries," " proved a very sphinx to enquirers." The solution is suggested by a correspondent in " Notes and Queries," 4th series, x. 254, 323.

164.

FUGIT HORA SINE MORA.

The hour flies without delay.

This may be read at North Wingfield, Derbyshire.

165.

FUGIT IRREPARABILE TEMPUS.

AD LATITUD . G . XLII.

Time passes never to be retrieved.

Sedente Gregorio XVI P.O.M. Antonius Mattevccivs Oper . Vatican . prepositus . Ioanni Antonio Teppati . hocce horarium lineari mandavit. Anno DNI MDCCCXLIII.

This sentence records that the dial was made and erected in the pontificate of Gregory XVI, A.D. 1843, by Giovanni Antonio Teppati. It is on the south corner of the balustrade on the roof of St. Peter's, Rome, the dial being engraved on a horizontal slab of white marble. It also occurs, with the date 1839, on a round dial face just below the angle of the gable and bell-cot of Vallauris Church, near Cannes; at St. Giles', Little Torrington, Devon; and at Bridgend, co. Glamorgan. Formerly on the church of St. Nectan, Welcombe, Devon; St. Nectan was the brother of St. Morwenna. See No. 269.

166.

FUGIT, SI STAS.

It flies, if thou standest still.

Not identified.

167.

FUGIT VELUT UMBRA.

It passes by like a shadow.

1881.

A mural dial upon a house near the church at Varenna, Lago di Como.

168.

FUI UT ES, ERIS UT SUM.

I was as thou art, thou wilt be as I am.

At Marrington Hall, Shropshire. See No. 605.

169.

FUMUS ET UMBRA SUMUS.

We are smoke and shadow.

Mr. Howard Hopley records this as inscribed on a dial
affixed to the broad chimney of a farm house in Italy. It
could not have been better placed.

170.

GEDENCT AM DEIN END. 1726.

Think upon thine end.

On the church at Interlachen.

171.

GEDENKE DASS DU STERBEN MUSST. 1838.

Remember that thou must die.

There is a dial thus inscribed, painted on the south wall,
close under the roof of the church at Ringenberg, near Interlachen. The gnomon is in the centre of an eight-pointed
star at the top of the dial, and the motto is on a half-circle
below. The church was built on the site and out of the
ruins of an old castle, and it stands on a hill which overlooks
the little lake of Golzwyl, or Faulensee, between the lakes of
Thun and Brienz. The tower of the former castle still
remains amongst the trees of the churchyard, and commanded
in its day a view over a large portion of the lake of Brienz.
The church was transferred to this place from Golzwyl in
1674. It has a venerable appearance, and is covered with
ivy.

172.

GIVE GOD THY HEART, THY HOPES, THY GIFTS, THY
   GOLD ;
THE DAY WEARS ON ; THE TIMES ARE WAXING OLD.

In " Tales of the Village," by the Rev. F. E. Paget, v. i.
c. i., " The Miser's Heir," contains the following passage :
" As I proceeded leisurely round Baggesden Hall, I observed
an ancient sun-dial, adorned with heraldic devices, and
grotesque emblems of mortality, carved in stone, according to
the style which prevailed at the close of the sixteenth century. On a scroll above it was inscribed ' Homfrie and
Elianor Bagges. A.D. 1598 ; ' and beneath it, in smaller but
still very legible characters, the following rhyme." We have
authority for stating that this is altogether imaginary ; but
the couplet is too pretty not to be retained.

173.

ΓΝΩΘΙ ΚΑΙΡΟΝ.
IN HORA NULLA MORA.
MISPEND NO TIME.
PEREUNT ET IMPUTANTUR.

Know the time.
In time no tarrying.
They perish and are reckoned.

These four mottoes are on a pillar dial in the rectory
garden at Micheldean, Gloucestershire. The shaft is ornamented with a Tudor rose, and a diamond in relief. On the
two sides of the plinth are the words *Rector Rectoris* (the

Rector's Director); there were apparently other words on the remaining sides, but these are nearly obliterated, and of the date only 16— remains. The pillar is rather more than four feet high, and the mottoes are engraved on the four sides of its square column; a horizontal dial plate being on the top.

174.

GO ABOUT YOUR BUSINESS.

On a buttress of St. James' Church, Bury St. Edmunds; and on Cavendish Church, Suffolk. Formerly on the church at Kilnwick on the wolds, Yorkshire, but as the motto had become entirely obliterated by the weather, another, " The time is short," was, in 1882, painted in its place.

It is said that the witty Dean Cotton, of Bangor, had a very cross old gardener, who protected his master from troublesome visitors by saying to everyone he saw near the place, "Go about your business." When the gardener died the Dean had his servant's favourite formula engraved round the sun-dial in his garden, in this wise,

Goa bou tyo urb us in ess.   1838.

The result being that the motto was usually supposed to be Welsh. After Dean Cotton's death the dial was bought by Mr. Doyle Watkins, of Glan Adda, and is now at Tanyfrou, near Bangor. (See Nos. 9 and 475.)

The same words, rather differently, but as irregularly divided, are on a sun-dial in the garden at Brook Lodge, Chester.

175.

GRATIA DEI MECUM.
The grace of God with me.

On pillar-dial at Corpus Christi College.   See No. 134.

176.

HANC QUAM TU GAUDENS IN GNOMONE CONSULIS HORAM,
FORSITAN INTERITUS CRAS ERIT HORA TUI.

This hour which now thou cheerfully readest by the pointer,
Perhaps will to-morrow be the hour of thy death.

Is on a house dial at Voltri, near Genoa.

177.

HARUM DUM SPECTAS CURSUM
RESPICE AD NOVISSIMAM HORAM.

C. C.
Walker, 1881.   I   Lat. 54° 58′.
W. R.

Watching these fleeting hours soon past
Remember that which comes at last.

On a storehouse of the Neptune Works, Newcastle-on-Tyne.   Erected by Wigham Richardson, Esq., to whom the translation is due.

178.

HASTE, TRAVELLER, THE SUN IS SINKING LOW;
HE SHALL RETURN AGAIN, BUT NEVER THOU.

At Tytherton Kellaways, Wilts.   See No. 708.

179.

Ή ΣΚΙΑ ΚΟΥΦΗ ΣΟΦΙΑΝ ΣΕ ΔΙΔΑΣΚΕΤΩ.
Let the slight shadow teach thee wisdom.

At Torrington, Devon.

180.

HERE IN CHRIST'S ACRE, WHERE THIS DIAL STANDS,
WITH PIOUS CARE AND BORNE BY REVERENT HANDS,
LONE WANDERERS GARNERED IN FROM EAST AND
    WEST,
AMONG THE HOME-LOVED LIE IN SOLEMN REST;
SEVERED IN LIFE BY LINEAGE, RACE, FAITH, CLIME,
THEY BIDE ALIKE THE LAST SOFT STROKE OF TIME;
AND WHEN GOD'S SUN WHICH SHONE UPON THEIR
    BIRTH
ENDS HIS BRIGHT COURSE AND VIGIL O'ER THE
    EARTH,—
WHEN O'ER THIS DISC THAT DAY'S LAST SHADOWS
    FLEE,
AND "DEATH NO MORE DIVIDES, AS DOTH THE SEA,"

THE DEAD WILL RISE,—RETAKE THE LIFE GOD GAVE,

CREATION'S SAVIOUR BLESS EARTH'S OPENING GRAVE !

THY WORD HATH WRIT THE BLEST—NO CONSCIENCE
    CLEAR

IN THOUGHT AND WORD, ALL MUST THY JUDGMENT
    FEAR.

ONLY OUR OWN WILD WORDS, WHICH FASHIONED
    PRAYER

WHEN LIFE WAS PARTING, STILL MOVE THE AMBIENT
    AIR,

PLEADING THAT GOD, WHO MADE, WILL GRANT
    THAT WE

MAY WITH THE PURE IN HEART THE GODHEAD SEE.

The dial, erected by Lady Burdett Coutts in St. Pancras Gardens, bears these lines. It is upwards of thirty feet in height, and in the early decorated style. It is built of Portland stone, with a marble tablet on each side, and clustered granite columns at the corners. The above lines are, with the Beatitudes, inscribed below the dial. On the other tablets are the names of the illustrious men who lie buried in the old churchyard of St. Pancras ; and also a statement that the gardens, formed out of the burying-ground of St. Giles and the churchyard of St. Pancras, are assigned for ever to the loving care of the parishioners. The dial is especially dedicated to the memory of those whose graves are now unseen, or the record of whose names may have become obliterated.

It was erected in 1879.

181.

HERE MI, NESCIS HORA
MORIERIS, SI QUAERIS, QUA.

JOHN OWEN, 1683.

My master, thou knowest not, if thou askest, the hour in which thou shalt die.

A motto in bad Latin on a spirally-carved stone dial in the garden of the Hon. W. O. Stanley, at Penrhos, Holyhead. Let no one imagine that this motto is either misspelt or mis-transcribed. Mrs. Vaughan, from whom the collector received it, with a drawing of the dial, vouches for its accuracy on the authority of the Master of the Temple, who compared it with the original inscription, and found it correctly copied, however incorrect in itself. It afterwards brought a smile to the lips of the Laureate, who, when translating it broke out into exclamations, "But you've no notion what bad Latin it is ! But you can't imagine how vile the Latin is ! " *Oh ! my master, if thou shouldest seek to know the hour of thy death, thou shalt be ignorant of it.*

182.

HEU, PATIMUR UMBRAM.

Alas ! we endure the shadow.

On a dial at Sleningford Hall, near Ripon, the seat of the Dalton family. It may be feared it is no longer there. A friend of the collector had a search made for it a few years ago, in order to let her know whether it was on the house, or in what part of the grounds. The result was unfortunate ; it could not be found at all.

183.

HEU, QUAERIMUS UMBRAM.
Alas! we pursue a shadow.

Recorded by Mr. Howard Hopley.

184.

HIC LICET INDULGERE GENIO.
Here you may indulge your taste.

"Indulgere genio" is from Persius, v. 151. Dean Alford
says, " I observed between Mentone and Bordighera, a brand
new villa conspicuously inscribed," as above. "On inquiry
I found that it belonged to an eccentric lady."

185.

HINC —— DISCE ——

In Malvern churchyard stands a graceful shaft, nineteen
feet high, of a cross of the fifteenth century, crowned with a
cube and ball. The dial on the sides of the cube present four
faces to the points of the compass. On the north face there
is an illegible inscription which apparently consisted of two
lines, one above and one below the gnomon, and the initials
W. K. From the position of the only two words which can
be made out, it seems as if the motto had been that which
was formerly on St. Mary Overy, Southwark, " *Hinc vivere
disce, Illinc disce mori.* (See No. 129.) Half way up the

K

shaft is a pretty niche, in which no doubt was a figure of the
Virgin.

Hinc disce is also engraved, with three other mottoes, on
the dial upon the West Pier, Brighton.   (See No. 206.)

186.

HINC VIVERE DISCAS.

Hence learn to live.

On a pedestal dial at Mount Melville, St. Andrews. The plate is a metal one, and is inscribed: "J. Dougall fecit. Kirkaldy 1778"; it also tells the latitude and longitude of the spot, and states that the time at Constantinople is 2 hrs. 10 min., and at Bergen 57 minutes earlier than at Craigtown (as St. Andrews is called, by its old name), whilst at Kingston it is 5 hrs. 5 min. later. There is a second pillar dial at Mount Melville of a much more elaborate description, but it bears no motto, so will be found in the Notes on Remarkable Dials at the end of the book.

187.

Ὁ ΚΑΙΡΟΣ ΟΞΥΣ.

Time is swift.

ΑΜΕΡΑΙ ΕΠΙΛΟΙΠΟΙ ΜΑΡΤΥΡΕΣ ΣΟΦΩΤΑΤΟΙ.

The days that remain are the surest witnesses.

Is on a dial on Alleyne's Grammar School, at Uttoxeter. It was originally on the school-house that was built in 1568, and was removed to the new one erected in 1859.

188.

HOC AGE DUM LUMEN ADEST.

Be diligent, while the light abides.

On a vertical dial which is fastened to the lower stone of a gable of the parish church at Chirnside, Berwickshire. The building has been recently restored, but part of it is Norman. The dial is dated 1816. Mr. Thomas Ross, who copied the motto in 1888, had difficulty in deciphering the word which we have rendered *lumen;* but there is every reason to believe that the above reading is correct.

189.

HO LA VITA NELLA LUCE, LA MORTE NELLE TENEBRE.

I have life in light, death in darkness.

At Cessila, near Biella.

190.

HOMO QUASI UMBRA.

Man is as a shadow.

On a vertical wooden dial on the south wall of Cumwhitton Church, Cumberland. It has a table of the equation of time, and is of modern make.

191.

HONI SOIT QUI MAL Y PENSE.

Evil be to him who evil thinks.

On a dial which Charles II. caused to be erected at Windsor, on the east terrace, close to what are still known as " The Star Buildings." The plate is a circular horizontal one, and in the centre the star of the Garter is engraved, with the motto upon it ; the gnomon rises from this, and is perforated, with the king's monogram and crown entwined therein. The pedestal is marble, and decorated with carving in high relief, which is said to have been the work of Grinling Gibbons. " Henricus Wynne, Londinii fecit" is also engraved upon the plate.

192.

Honor DoMIno pro paCe popVLo sVo parta.

Honour be to the Lord for the peace procured for His people.

Mentioned in Mr. Hilton's work on " Chronograms," as a motto on the upper border of a sun-dial formerly at the west end of Nantwich Church. It was removed in 1800. The date 1661 points to the year after the Restoration of Charles II.

193.

HORA BIBENDI.

The hour of drinking.

Is a dial motto which is aptly used as the sign of a public-house, near Grenoble. That it is not an uncommon one is shown by a writer in the " Bulletin de la Société Astronomique de France," vii. 1860, who, speaking of the country about Abriès (near the Monte Viso), says, " toutes les eglises que nous avons vues dans notre excursion portaient sur leur clocher un cadeau solaire, orné d'une devise latine, quelque-fois assez singulièrement choisie—*Nunc hora bibendi*, par exemple."

194.
HORA, DIES, ET VITA FUGIT, MANET UNICA VIRTUS.

The hour, day and life, all fly away: virtue alone remains.

Is noted in Cyrus Redding's " Fifty Years' Recollections, Literary and Personal," vol. iii. p. 86.

195.
HORA EST BENEFACIENDI.

It is the time for well-doing.

At Hyères.

196.
HORA FLUIT, CULPAE CRESCUNT, MORS IMMINET:
HEU, VITAE CORRIGE FACTA TUAE.

The hour flows on, faults increase, death impends: alas, amend the deeds of thy life.

This dial motto is on the church of St. Pierre, in Switzerland, and the words are illegibly traced. There is no date; but age or the tempests of those high regions have defaced the inscription. St. Pierre is on the road to the pass of the great St. Bernard, 5,302 (Swiss) feet above the level of the sea. It is a wild and dreary looking village. Dark rough châlets, raised a foot or two from the ground, are scattered about the neighbouring fields. The river roars and foams in the deep defile below; and pine trees, the remains of the forest through which Napoleon's army struggled with so much difficulty in 1800, cover in patches the mountain sides.

The dial is painted on the church wall protected by a buttress, and facing the snowy Mont Velan. The church dates from 1018, and a Latin inscription, placed by its founder, Bishop Hugo of Geneva, commemorates a Saracen invasion. A Roman military column, dedicated to the younger Constantine, and said to have replaced a statue of Jupiter on the summit of the Pass, but destroyed by Constantine about 339 A.D., attests the great antiquity of the place.

197.

HORA FUGIT: MEMENTO MORI.

Time passes : remember death.

On a dial which, until the recent restoration, stood on the porch of the parish Church of Rotherham. This motto replaced an older one, *Pereunt et imputantur.*

Remember Death! for now my tongue
　To sing of death shall tuned be:
Remember Death! which else ere long,
　Will to thy pain remember thee.
　　Remember Death! whose voice doth say,
　　This night a man, to-morrow clay.

Remember, Death no truce hath made,
　A year, a month, or week to stay ;
Remember how thy flesh doth fade,
　And how thy time does steal away.
　　Remember, death will neither spare
　　Wit, wealth, nor those that lovely are.

Remember, death forgoes the dooms,
  Which due to thy deservings be;
Remember this before it comes,
  And that despair oppress not thee.
    Remember Death! remember Him
  Who doth from death and hell redeem.
                    G. WITHER.

198.

HORA FUGIT, MORS VENIT.

Time passes, death advances.

SOL NON OCCIDAT SUPER IRACUNDIAM VESTRAM.

Let not the sun go down upon your wrath.

On a dial which is painted upon the wall of the old Court House at La Fiera di Primiero. It is dated 1703, and there is a skull, crowned by an hour glass, in the corner of the dial-face. The motto is now (1888) somewhat defaced.

199.

HORA HORIS CEDIT, PEREVNT SIC TEMPORA NOBIS:
VT TIBI FINALIS SIT BONA, VIVE BENE.

An hour yields to hours, so our time perishes:
That thy last hour may be good, live well.

Many years ago the collector's old and kind friend, the late Lord Chief Justice Tindal, brought over for her from Karlsbad a mysterious inscription, which he had carefully copied in scholarly handwriting. The dial was formed on two sides of the angle of the upper storey of a substantial house in the market-place. The Chief Justice wrote, " The letters which are written in capitals were so in the original inscription, and were coloured red: probably the anagram of some one's name is concealed under them." By consulting that useful oracle, " Notes and Queries," we had the difficulty solved. We suggested that it might be a chronogram, but for the introduction of the letter E. A correspondent replied that probably CEdIt ought to be written CeDIt, when the following numerals could be extracted: MDCCVVVVIIIIIIIIII : MDCCXXX : 1730, which we may suppose to be the date of the building.

It is amusing to record further, that some friends who were staying more recently at Karlsbad, kindly looked after this dial, which they found, but in a dilapidated state. They made out the motto, however, with the help of the Burgomaster of the place, who owned that he had lived opposite to it all his life, but had never noticed it. Nevertheless, he became much interested, and said he would give orders that it should be cleaned and repainted. The Doctor, too, confessed that he had never seen it before, but should henceforth point it out to his patients for their contemplation and improvement.

200.

HORA PARS VITAE.

An hour is a portion of life.

Fixed to what appears to have been the shaft of a cross in Brading Churchyard, Isle of Wight, is a metal dial-plate dated 1815, with the foregoing motto. " J. James, G. Hearn, Churchwardens. J. Wood, *fecit.*" The stone column is about four feet high, rising from three circular steps, which are much worn, and, like the shaft, appear to be of considerable age. As the date 1715 also appears, this probably refers to a previous dial, from which the motto may have been borrowed.

The same inscription is on a dial fixed on the eaves of Stokesley Church, Yorkshire, dated 1822 ; and on the church of St. Eustachius, Tavistock, dated 1814 ; also on Thursley Church, Surrey ; on Kirk Whelpington Church, Northumberland, dated 1764 ; and at Charlton, Somerset.

201.

HORA PARS VITAE, HORA PARS UMBRAE.

The hour is a portion of life, the hour is a portion of shadow.

Is on the plate of a horizontal dial in the old churchyard of Castleton, in Derbyshire.

202.

HORA RUIT.

The hour hurries away.

At Val-de-la-Haye, on the Seine, near Rouen.

Grotius, it is said, " used to take for his motto *Hora ruit,* to put himself in continual remembrance that he should usefully employ that time which was flying away with extreme rapidity."—SEWARD's *Anecdotes.*

203.

HORAE PEREUNT ET IMPUTANTUR.

The hours perish and are reckoned.

This is found on the Riviera. The phrase comes from Martial's " Epigrams," v. 20, 23, only that he has *soles*, not *horae*.

204.

HORAM SOLE NOLENTE NEGO.

The hour I tell not, when the sun will not.

May be read at Poirino, in Piedmont.

205.

HORAS IMPLE, UMBRAM RESPICE, OCCASUM TIME.
UMBRAE TRANSITUS EST TEMPUS NOSTRUM.
UTERE PRAESENTI MEMOR ULTIMAE.
PEREUNT ET IMPUTANTUR.

Fulfil the hours, consider the shadow, fear the sunset.
Our time is the passing away of a shadow.
Use the present (hour), mindful of the last.
They perish, and are reckoned.

On the four sides of the campanile of the church of S. Crocifisso, Pieve di Cadore.

206.

HORAS NON NUMERO NISI SERENAS.
I count the bright hours only.

This motto is known to be on dials at the following places :—Sackville College, East Grinstead; the Moot Hall (or assembly house), at Aldeburgh, in Suffolk, which was built circa A.D. 1500: at Highclere, Newbury; at Leam, near Leamington; in the garden of Beard Sheppard, Esq., at Frome, having been removed from the Rectory garden of Compton Basset, Wilts; in front of a farmhouse near Farnworth, Lancashire; at Cawder, near Glasgow (see No. 710); at Arley Hall, Cheshire; Ember Court, Surrey (see No. 535); Stoke Edith Park, Worcestershire; and on a walk behind the chapel at Harrow, the dial being erected to the memory of George Frederick Harris, formerly assistant master and lower master of Harrow; on a house in a village near Como; at Campo Dolcino; according to Hazlitt, near Venice. On the four faces of the dial on Brighton West Pier, there are mottoes of which this is the chief. The other three are *Umbra docet, Hinc disce, Sine umbra nihil* (*The shadow teaches, Hence learn, Without a shadow —nothing*). In truth, the saying is too good to be uncommon. It is thus alluded to by Sir Arthur Helps, in his " Friends in Council " (1st series, vol. i. bk. ii.): "Milverton had put up a sun-dial in the centre of his lawn, with the motto, *Horas non numero nisi serenas*, which gave occasion to Ellesmere to say, that for men the dial was either totally useless or utterly false."

In 1875 this motto was chosen from " Friends in Council," and inscribed upon an old dial in Weaverham Churchyard, by the direction of the vicar, Rev. T. H. Gillam.

We cannot resist giving the well-known testimony of Shakespeare in favour of the shepherd's life for serenity and peace. Henry VI. thus soliloquizes on the battle-field at Towton :—

" O God ! methinks, it were a happy life,
To be no better than a homely swain ;
To sit upon a hill, as I do now,
To carve out dials quaintly, point by point,
Thereby to see the minutes how they run :
How many make the hour full complete,
How many hours bring about the day,
How many days will finish up the year,
How many years a mortal man may live.
When this is known, then to divide the times :
So many hours must I tend my flock ;
So many hours must I take my rest ;
So many hours must I contemplate ;
So many hours must I sport myself ;
So many days my ewes have been with young ;
So many weeks ere the poor fools will yean ;
So many years ere I shall shear the fleece :
So minutes, hours, days, weeks, months, and years,
Pass'd over to the end they were created,
Would bring white hairs unto a quiet grave."

207.

HORAS OMNES COMPLECTOR.

I embrace all hours.

On pillar dial at Corpus Christi College. See No. 134.

208.

HORTUS UTRAMQUE TULIT, NOS ET MEDITEMUR IN HORTO.

The garden bore both, let us also meditate in the garden.

This motto is on a dial in the Nuns' Garden at Polesworth, near Tamworth. It must be imperfect; and it has been suggested that a previous line may have referred to the two trees of Life and Knowledge in the Garden of Eden. If so, the meaning is clear.

Peculiar interest attaches to the foundation of the Benedictine nunnery at Polesworth. Dugdale gives the following account: "Egbert, king of the West Saxons, built this monastery of nuns, and made his daughter Edith the first abbess, having caused her to be instructed in the Rule of St. Benedict by Modwen, an Irish lady, whom he had sent for out of that country, because she had there cured his son, Arnulf, by her prayers, of a leprosy. King William the Conqueror gave to Sir Robert Marmyon the castle of Tamworth, with all the lands about it, in which was the nunnery of Polesworth. This knight turned out the nuns; but a year after, being terrified by a vision, he restored them, they having retired during that time to a cell they had at Oldbury or Aldbury, given to their monastery by Walter de Hastings. However, the aforesaid Marmyon was afterwards reckoned the founder of Polesworth."

This spot appears to have been the site of the first religious house that was planted in the centre of England, and one of the first that found a local habitation in the kingdom. The name of the foundress is still preserved in the neighbourhood. The parish church of Burton-upon-Trent is dedicated to the joint names of St. Mary and St. Modwenna. The site of her chapel is still called " St. Modwen's Orchard," and " St. Modwen's Well" was celebrated, two hundred years ago, for the sanatory properties of its water. The nunnery became the place of education to which the young ladies of the highest families were sent before they entered the society of the world.

The nunnery was dissolved in 1539, when Sir Francis Nethersole became possessed of the conventual lands, and built the hall out of the ruins of the nunnery. It is supposed that the dial was then created in the centre of a square garden on the site of the cloisters. It is now placed on the corner of an old wall, as if to get it out of the way. The garden has disappeared, but the spot is still an orchard with a pretty green sloping to the river side. As to the construction of the dial: there is a projecting base surmounted by several courses of wall stone on which is the principal object. This consists of a curved pediment of stone, supporting a square block, on the east side of which is represented a tomb: below is the motto, and on a scroll above are the words, " Non est hic: resurrexit "—*He is not here: he has risen.* The top is finished off so as to correspond with the pediment, and contains the Nethersole coat of arms. Among the devices are the Death's head and cross bones: also an apple, which seems to identify the reference in the motto with—

" The fruit
Of that forbidden tree, whose mortal taste,
Brought death into the world, and all our woe.

209.

HORULA DUM QUOTA SIT QUAERITUR, HORA FUGIT. 1678.

While one asks how long the little hour is, the hour flies by.

On a dial which formerly stood upon a pedestal in the churchyard of Kirk-Arbory, Isle of Man, " Thomas Kirk-dale de Bolton fecit," and a coat of arms being also engraved upon the bronze plate.   The dial has been missing for some years, but the plate was found in 1887 on a shelf in a cottage in the parish, where it had lain for so long that the tenant had no recollection of how it came into his possession ! He willingly gave it up, however, and it is hoped that it will soon be replaced in the churchyard.   The same motto used to be upon a dial in Rushen churchyard, but it has been replaced by one without a motto, dated 1829.

210.

I ALSO AM UNDER AUTHORITY.

As this motto has been published in the pages of " Aunt Judy's Magazine," it may claim to take its place with those culled from the writings of Wordsworth and Mr. Paget ; and all of them may be regarded as suggestions for new dial inscriptions.

211.

I AM A SHADE, A SHADOW TOO ART THOU;
I MARK THE TIME, SAY GOSSIP, DOST THOU SOE?

At the Manor House, Chew Magna, Somerset. The lines also are to be found in "Vignettes in Rhyme," by Austin Dobson.

212.

I AM A SHADOW, SO ART THOU:
I MARK TIME, DOST THOU?

Inscribed on a dial in the Grey Friars' churchyard, Stirling; and in 1884 placed on West Lodge, Carthorpe, Yorkshire. See No. 218.

213.

I MARK NONE BUT SUNNY HOURS.

At Bournstream House, Wotton-under-edge; now (1887) belonging to Miss Austin. The date of the house is 1614.

214.

I MARK NOT THE HOURS UNLESS THEY BE BRIGHT,
I MARK NOT THE HOURS OF DARKNESS AND NIGHT,
MY PROMISE IS SOLELY TO FOLLOW THE SUN,
AND POINT OUT THE COURSE HIS CHARIOT DOTH
RUN.

NON NUMERO HORAS NISI SERENAS.

I count no hours that are not bright.

These mottoes are engraved upon the pedestal of a dial in the garden of Downham Hall, Brandon, together with the following inscription :—

" Taken from a gun battery on Kelbouroun Spit, at the entrance of the Dnieper, captured by the English and French on Oct. 17th, 1855, being the first fort and portion of territory of Russia proper, taken by the allied forces in the war of 1854-55."

The dial face is made of slate, it was presented to the Duchess of Cleveland, who at one time owned Downham Hall, and was erected on a stone pedestal and inscribed by her orders.

215.

I MARK THE MOMENTS TROD FOR GOOD OR ILL.

On a vertical dial at the Priory, Warwick, with the initials T. H. and the date, 1556.

216.

I NUMBER NONE BUT SUNNY HOURS.

At Galtfaenen, Wales, the seat of Townsend Mainwaring, Esq.

217.

I ONLY MARK BRIGHT HOURS.

There is a square stone pedestal, panelled on the four sides, and surmounted by a dial which bears this motto ; and it was so inscribed by the late Countess of Tyrconnel, in whose garden at Kiplin Hall, near Catterick, Yorkshire, it was erected.

> " For as in sunshine only we can read
> The march of minutes on the dial's face,
> So in the shadows of this lonely place
> There is no love, and Time is dead indeed."
> *Sonnet,* by HOOD.

218.

I SPEAK NOT, YET ALL UNDERSTAND ME WELL,
I MAKE NO SOUND AND YET THE HOUR I TELL.
I AM A SHADOW, SO ART THOU:
I MARK TIME, DOST THOU?

These mottoes have been placed on a dial at West Lodge farm, near Carthorpe, Yorkshire, by G. J. Serjeantson, Esq. The two first lines are Dean Alford's paraphrase of No. 486.

219.

I STAND AMID Y^E SUMMERE FLOWERS
TO TELL Y^E PASSAGE OF Y^E HOURES.
WHEN WINTER STEALS Y^E FLOWERS AWAYE
I TELL Y^E PASSINGE OF THEIR DAYE.
O MAN WHOSE FLESH IS BUT AS GRASSE
LIKE SUMMERE FLOWERS THY LIFE SHALL PASSE.
WHILES TYME IS THINE LAYE UP IN STORE
AND THOU SHALT LIVE FOR EVER MORE.

Sent to the collector by her friend, the Rev. Greville J. Chester, as being inscribed on the four sides of a dial in a flower-garden at S. Windleham. It was an ingenious practical joke, as the lines were invented for the occasion; but they are so pretty and quaint, that she is loath to let them pass away unrecorded.

220.

ICH DIEN.

I serve.

SHADOWS WE ARE, AND LIKE SHADOWS DEPART.

UT HORA SIC VITA.

As the hour, so is life.

On a dial in the garden of B. B. Kent, Esq., Menwith Hill, Darley, Ripley, Yorkshire.

221.

IF O'ER THE DIAL GLIDES A SHADE, REDEEM
THE TIME; FOR, LO, IT PASSES LIKE A DREAM.
BUT IF 'TIS ALL A BLANK, THEN MARK THE LOSS
OF HOURS UNBLEST BY SHADOWS FROM THE CROSS.

These lines are on a dial made in the form of a cross, and
placed in a slanting position on a pillar in Shenstone churchyard, near Lichfield. The hours are marked on the sides,

and the shadow is thus thrown by the cross upon the cross.
It was put up by the Rev. R. W. Essington, who, on taking
possession of the living of Shenstone, found the pillar of the
dial standing, while the metal plate and gnomon had disappeared. Having seen a cross-dial at High End near Calne,
Wilts, he caused a copy of it to be placed upon the pillar,

and composed the motto for it, A.D. 1848. The motto was afterwards inscribed in a slightly altered form upon another cross-dial, placed, about A.D. 1857, in the churchyard at Collaton, Devon. It is a pretty cross of white marble on a pedestal of red sandstone. Another cross-dial was afterwards erected by Mr. Essington in the Rectory garden (No. 545). A dial of similar construction was placed by the Rev. Canon Eden in the garden of Aberford Vicarage, Yorkshire, but he gave it no motto. For a further example with a motto see No. 599.

In the "Dundee Advertiser" (16th August, 1888) an article was published called "The Castles and Mansions of Fife and Kinross," by A. H. Millar, in which he described and figured a cross-dial at Scotscraig, near Tayport, N.B. The dial was stated to have belonged to James Sharp, Archbishop of St. Andrew's, who was assassinated by a party of Covenanters on Magus Muir in 1679. The present owner of Scotscraig is Admiral Maitland Dougall, and he says that the dial is not formed of *marble*, as Mr. Millar described, but of a close-grained brown stone, probably some form of sandstone. Archbishop Sharp lived at Scotscraig, and his family were in possession of the estate for nearly one hundred years. Two years before his death an entrance gate to the Court was built, which still bears his arms and initials.

222.

IL EST PLUS TARD QUE VOUS CROYEZ.
1851, L. G. F.

It is later than you believe.

At Abriès, Dauphinée.

223.

IL PASSATO FUGGI, FUGGE IL PRESENTE
VERRA FUGGENDO L'ARVENIR REPENTE.

1854 Gmo. Bdi feece.

The present flies, the past is fled and gone,
Swiftly the fleeing future will come on.

On a plain dial traced upon the church wall at Campitello,
Val Fassa, in the Italian Tyrol.

224.

IL TEMPO AVARO OGNI COSA FRACASSO,
IL TEMPO ANNULLA OGNI GRACE FAMA IN TERRA,
OGNI COSA MORTAL COL TEMPO PASSA.

Envious Time destroys all things ;
It obliterates all earthly fame ;
Whatsoever is mortal passes away with Time.

Dean Burgon, writing to the "Guardian," Feb. 26th,
1874, an account of the ancient inscriptions of Ravenna,
concludes his letter with the above lines, copied from a sun-
dial in front of the church of St. Apollinari in Classe, and
which, after wandering over the scenes of vanished greatness
and around the old city, struck him as possessing peculiar
pathos. "After traversing," he says, "for miles the level
plain outside Ravenna, and noting with interest the heaps of
flat, rounded pebbles, alternating with heaps of detritus from
the Bosco—which record the nature of the change which
has passed over the entire aspect of the country, the humble
words inscribed on this sun-dial struck me very forcibly."

225.

IL TEMPO PASSA, E L'ETERNITÁ S'AVVICINA.

Time passes away, eternity draws near.

On a dial at Riva, Val Sesia.   See No. 332.

226.

ILLE EGO SUM, LONGUM QUI METIOR ANNUM, OMNIA QUI VIDEO, PER QUEM VIDET OMNIA TELLUS, MUNDI OCULUS.

I am he that measures the length of the years, that seeth all things;—through whom the earth seeth all things; the eye of the universe.

On a white freestone dial, inserted in the gable of an early English porch at Wootton Church, Oxon, with the initials and date as follows : " R. H., 1623, J. R. Ch. Wa." The motto is taken and altered from Ovid's " Metamorphoses : "—

> " Ille ego sum, dixit, qui longum metior annum,
> Omnia qui video, per quem, videt omnia tellus,
> Mundi oculus."   (Book iv., line 226.)

227.

IMPROVE THE TIME.   1765.

On an oval dial on the Unicorn Inn at Uppingham ; and on Market Harborough Church, dated 1850.

228.

IMPROVE THE PRESENT HOUR, FOR ALL
    BESIDE
IS A MERE FEATHER ON A TORRENT'S
    TIDE.

May be read at Fredericton, in New Brunswick, Canada,
as the motto of a dial, which is placed on a wooden shaft
shaped like a ninepin, standing in the garden of the late
Mrs. Shore. [The dial has now, 1888, disappeared, a railway
line having been taken through the garden where it stood.]

229.

IN COELO QUIES.

1793.

In heaven is rest.

On a vertical dial affixed to the walls of the church at
Glaisdale, North Riding of Yorkshire. ("Yorkshire Post,"
June 24th, 1879.)

    " Death's but the dawning of that happy day,
    Where, without setting, shines the eternal sun ;
    Wherein who walk, can never, never stray,
    Nor fear they night who to the dayward run.

    " There's rest eternal for thy labours rife,
    There's for thy bondage boundless liberty ;
    There where death endeth, she begins thy life
    And where there's no more time, there's eternity."
        Jos. Sylvester, " Memorials of Mortalitie."

230.

IN HORA NULLA MORA.

In hours of day
Is no delay.

In the Rectory garden at Micheldean.   See No. 173.

231.

IN LUCEM OMNIA VANA.

All things are vanity (when brought) into the light.

On a hydropathic bath-house at Biella-alta in Piedmont; and on a house at Vallouse.   See No. 61.

232.

IN OMNIBUS REBUS RESPICE FINEM.

In all things look to the end.

This line from Thomas à Kempis has been inscribed on a pedestal sun-dial which stands in the garden of Crowder House, in the parish of Ecclesfield, Yorkshire. The old house and farm attached to it are now the property of Bernard Wake, Esq., who inscribed the dial. They previously belonged to a yeoman family named Wilkinson, that seems to have held the farm for more than four hundred years; as there is the copy of a deed in existence, relating to Julyan Wilkinson of Crowder House, bearing date 1402. See No. 151.

233.

IN REASON'S EYE THY SEDENTARY SHADOW TRAVELS HARD.
1819.

On a dial which is now at Ardkeen, Inverness, but which previously stood at Port Elphinstone, Aberdeenshire.

234.

IN SUCH AN HOUR AS YE LOOK NOT FOR, THE SON OF MAN COMETH. 1793.

Is on a plain oval dial erected on the south porch of Bakewell Church, Derbyshire, nearly under the roof. [The motto is now (1885) nearly obliterated.]

235.

IN THE HOURE OF   HE THAT WILL THRIVE   FOR AS TYME

DEATHE   MUSTE RISE AT FIVE;   DOTH HASTE

GOD BE MERCIFUL   HE THAT HATH THRIVEN   SO LIFE DOTH

UNTO ME.   MAY LIE TILL SEVEN;   WASTE.

HE THAT WILL NEVER THRIVE

MAY LIE TILL ELEVEN.

In front of Stanwardine Hall, near Baschurch, Shropshire, a fine old Elizabethan mansion, now converted into a farmhouse, stands a pillar-dial, having a silver plate, on which these homely maxims are engraved. The face of the dial is circular, but drawn in a square; and the four vacant corners of the square are occupied above by the two couplets we have given; and below, on one side, by an elephant with a castle on his back, and in the opposite corner is a squirrel

sitting up and eating. The advice for early rising is in the centre of the face; beneath is a bird on a shield, and lower down "anno 1560." Stanwardine Hall belonged to the Corbet family, from which it passed to the Wynnes; and it is now in other hands. The elephant and squirrel are the Corbet crests.

236.

IN UMBRA DESINO.

In shadow I cease.

Seen on the picture of a dial in a scrap-book, in a shop window at Florence.

237.

INCESSANT DOWN THE STREAM OF TIME,
AND HOURS, AND YEARS, AND AGES ROLL.

On the plate of a pillar-dial in the kitchen-garden at Lansdowne Lodge, Kenmare, County Kerry.

" Time is a river or violent torrent of things coming into being ; each one, as soon as it has appeared, is swept off, and disappears, and is succeeded by another which is swept away in its turn."—*Meditations of Marcus Aurelius Antoninus.*

238.

InDeX Vt VMbras sIC tVos IesV regIs. 1635.
NesCItIs In qVa hora DoMInVs Vester VentVrVs.
1635.

As the gnomon rules the shadows, so dost Thou, O Jesu, rule Thine own.

Ye know not at what hour your Lord will come.

These lines are given in Hunter's " South Yorkshire " as having been "formerly on a piece of marble fixed over a gate," near Darfield Church, Yorkshire. They can hardly have belonged to anything but a sun-dial. The capitals are chronograms, and can be transposed so as to form the date 1635 in each line.

239.

INDUCE ANIMUM SAPIENTEM. 1775.
Take to thyself a wise mind.

May be seen on the south porch of the church in the pretty retired village of Eyam, in Derbyshire ; noted for a fearful visitation of the plague, which nearly depopulated the place in 1666. The dial is very elaborate, and has the tropics of Cancer and Capricorn, &c., marked upon it; also the names of places, showing their difference from English time. The names of " Wm. Lee, Tho. Froggatt, Churchwardens," are recorded.

240.

INSTAR GLOBI STAT MACHINA MUNDI.

Like a ball stands the framework of the world.

At Moccas Court.   See No. 635.

241.

IO VADO E VENGO OGNI GIORNO
MA TU ANDRAI SENZA RITORNO.

I go and come every day,
But thou shalt go without returning.

This sentiment is on the wall of a modern house in the Rue de France, Nice.   At the side of the inscription is the dial, a large semi-oval in shape.   It is sketched in brown on the white-washed wall.   The late Dean Alford translated the motto as follows :—

" I come and go, and go and come, each day ;
But thou without return shalt pass away."

In 1880 the dial was repainted, and the last two lines of the motto altered thus :—

MA TU SE VAI
PIU NON RITORNI.

This new rendering is now (1888) becoming illegible owing to the effects of weather upon the thin coating of plaster on which the words are painted, and the original motto can be discerned below. The dial was erected in 1830.

The same motto may also be seen at Arma di Taggia, on the Riviera; and at Pisa. It is also inscribed on a pillar dial which stands in the Italian garden of the Manor House, Monkton Farleigh, Wilts. The dial was erected by Mr. Wade Browne, a tenant of the manor (1842-57), in memory of his younger brother, who was killed in the Caffre war.

242.

IRREVOCABILE.

(Time) that cannot be recalled.

On Little Milton Vicarage, Oxon.

243.

IRREVOCABILIS HORA. 1842.

The hour that cannot be recalled.

The Bridge over the Siagne, not very far from Cannes, is crossed by the high road from Toulon to Nice; and on the eastern side of the river there is a small house for the toll-keeper, facing south, with an almost round dial painted white on its yellow wall, and super-inscribed as above. Below is the garden widow of the *garde du pont*, with its green shutters to keep out the strong sunshine. Beyond the corner of the house are olive-covered plains, from which the hills rise suddenly, and the glowing range of the Alpes Provençaux forms the background. The same motto was found in the neighbourhood, badly written and mis-spelt, dated 1850, over a south dial on the door of a shed in the valley of Gourdalou, two miles from Cannes. The shed was a roughly plastered building, standing in the midst of heath, which in some places rose to six feet in height, and sheltered by pine trees that had happily escaped the axe which laid bare the surrounding hills.

244.

ISTA VELUT TACITO CURSU DIŁABITUR
UMBRA, TRANSIT IN AETERNOS
SIC TUA VITA DIES.

As that shadow glides away with silent passage,
So thy life passes into the days of eternity.

This was read somewhere in Tuscany.

245.

ITALICUM SIGNAT TEMPORA SACRA DEO.
AD LATITUD. GRADUM XLII.

SEDENTE . GREGORIO XVI . PONT . MAX . PONTIFICATUS . SUI .
ANNO XIII . ANTONIVS MATTEVCCIVS . CURATOR . OPER .
TEMPLI . VATICANI . ADSCITA . OPERA . IOANNIS . ANTONII .
TEPPATI . HOC . HORARIUM . INDICE . COMODUM . ORNA-
TUMQ . AUXIT.

An Italian (dial) shows times sacred to God.

The inscription states that in the thirteenth year of the pontificate of Gregory XVI., Giovanni Antonio Teppati restored and embellished this dial, by the order of Antonio Matteucci, clerk of the works of the church of the Vatican.

On a large horizontal dial of white marble placed on the balustrade which surrounds the roof of the nave of St. Peter's at Rome. It tells the hours from x to xxii, following the old Italian method by which the twenty-four hours are counted from the ringing of Ave Maria, half an hour after sunset. This dial, and its companion No. 165, placed on the corresponding corner of the balustrade, are remarkable from their position, standing as they do at more than a hundred and fifty feet above the ground. Probably no other dials in the world have been raised so high. Their use is, however, undeniable. The roof of St. Peter's is a village in itself. "There are," says Mr. Wey, "workshops, huts, sheds for domestic beasts, a forge and carpenter's stores, washhouses, ovens. For several families it is a native land. The workmen of St. Peter's, called San Pietrini, succeed one another from father to son, and form a tribe. The natives of the terrace have laws and customs of their own," and as it appears, their timekeepers also. See No. 308.

The hours are marked in Roman numerals. The motto, probably, refers to the Italian hours, which are shown on this dial as the ordinary ones are on its fellow. It recalls a saying suggested by the sight of a clock on a northern cathedral :

"I was thinking," said I, "why it was that men placed clocks in the towers of churches."

"That is easily answered, man ; to teach you that Time is a sacred thing." ("Old Church Clock").

M

246.

J'AVANCE.

I go forward.

This dial motto is in the garden at Hall Place, near
Maidenhead, Berkshire. It is the family motto of Sir
Gilbert East, Bart., whose crest is a horse, passant sable.

247.

JAM PROPERA, NEC TE VENTURAS DIFFER
IN HORAS, QUI NON EST HODIE, CRAS:
MINUS APTUS ERIT.

Haste now, nor until coming hours delay,
Less fit tomorrow he, unfit today.

On a house near Newton House Woods, near Whitby.
The first line is above, the second below the dial face.
They are from Ovid, Rem. Amor. 93-4. See Nos. 444 and
700.

248.

JE LUIS POUR TOUT LE MONDE,
MON OMBRE PASSE AVEC VITESSE,
ET TA FIN APPROCHE AVEC RAPIDITÉ, O MORTEL

I shine for the whole world,
My Shadow passes on swiftly,
And thy end rapidly approaches, O Mortal.

The sun's full face, surrounded by rays, forms the dial, the
gnomon projecting from the centre. Below the solar por-

trait is the first line: the other two being written under the
dial plane.   The initials of the maker, and date, F. M. 1833,
are on the face.   It is placed over the door of a village inn
at Rougemont, in the Canton de Vaud, Switzerland, one of
the picturesque wooded châlets of the country, and there is

an elaborate cornice supporting the deep over-hanging roof.
The windows, fitted with little square panes of glass, are
small, and flanked by solid shutters ; and probably only one
pane in the whole house can be opened to admit the outer
air, which is so unwelcome to the Swiss domestic hearth.
Below is a second cornice over a round arched porch, with
thick heavy doors ; where may be seen the hostess on a seat
knitting, in her black silk cap and lace lappets, with her bee-

hive hat hanging on the wall beside. Such are the last remains of the old costume of the Canton, which, though dying out on the shores of the Lake of Geneva, still linger in the high valleys, where fields creep up to the foot of the precipices, and rocks uprear their sharp peaks against the sky—where too, as Mr. Ruskin boldly says, "the pine forests cover the mountains like the shadow of God, and the great rivers move like His eternity."

249.

JE MARQUE LE TEMPS VRAI, L'HORLOGE MARQUE LE TEMPS MOYEN.

I show the true time—
The clock shows mean time.

This is inscribed above a dial on a house at Pau, opposite the Halle. Beneath it are the words : "Les horloges et les Cadrans indiquent à quelques secondes près la même heure le 25 x^{bre}, le 15 Avril, le 25 juin, et le 1^{ière} 7^{bie}.

250.

JE VIS DE TA PRESENCE, ET MON UTILITÉ FINIT EN TON ABSENCE.

I live by thy presence, and my usefulness ends in thy absence.

This is the last half of a motto, near Courmayeur. As some words at the beginning have been defaced, it is impossible to give the meaning of the whole inscription ; but it was probably an address to the sun.

251.

JUBILATE DEO.
June 21. 1887.
Rejoice in God.

On a dial in the garden at Elm Hall, Wanstead, Essex.

252.

ΚΑΙΡΟΝ ΓΝΩΘΙ.
Know the season.

Is over a dial placed on the wall of the south transept of Ely Cathedral. The face of the sun seems to emit the lines to the surrounding figures, as well as the gnomon ; and between the lines are the signs of the zodiac. There is no date, but the dial is probably older than the clock, which was placed in the tower about the middle of the eighteenth century, and later than the Dissolution, as the chapter house, which formerly projected from the south face of the transept is believed to have been destroyed at that time.

253.

L'AMOUR ET LA JEUNESSE
C'EST UN SIMPLE PASSAGE
COMME LE SOLEIL ET SON OMBRAGE.
The transit of love and youth
Is as direct as that of the sun and its shadow.

In a village near Courmayeur.

254.

LA VIE DE L'HOMME PASSE COMME L'OMBRE.

The life of man passes as a shadow.

At La Saxe, near Courmayeur.

255.

LA VIE EST COMME L'OMBRE,
INSENSIBLE À SON COURS,
ON LA CROIT IMMOBILE,
ELLE AVANCE TOUJOURS.

SIC VITA DUM FUGIT STARE VIDETUR.

> *Our life is like the shade,*
> *Unseen upon its way ;*
> *At rest we deem it laid,*
> *It moveth on for aye.*

So life while it flies seems to stand still.

Both these mottoes are on a house dial at Bourges. There is a similar sentiment to the second motto in Ovid, Eleg. i. :

> *Labitur occulte, fallitque volubilis aetas,*
> *Et celer admissis labitur annus equis.*

256.

LABITUR ET LABETUR.

It glides, and will glide away.

On a dial over the church porch at Leake, Yorks ; and at at the Convent of Cimiez, Nice. See No. 112. The words are from Horace, Epist. ii. 43. The simile is that of the countryman who when he comes to the river waits stolidly for the water to flow away so that he may be able to cross to the other side.

> " Qui recte vivendi prorogat horam,
> Rusticus expectat dum defluat amnis ; at ille
> Labitur et labetur in omne volubilis aevum.

Ovid has a similar passage :

> " Runt anni more fluentis aquae.
> Nec quae praeteriit cursu revocabitur unda,
> Nec quae praeteriit hora redire potest."
> *De Arte Amandi.*, iii. 62. -

Dr. Young has adopted a like metaphor in his " Night Thoughts."

> Life glides away, Lorenzo, like a brook ;
> For ever changing, unperceived the change.
> In the same brook none ever bathed him twice ;
> To the same life none ever twice awoke,
> We call the brook the same ; the same we think
> Our life, though still more rapid in its flow ;
> Nor mark the much, irrevocably lapsed
> And mingled with the sea.
> (*Night fifth*).

257.

LABUNTUR ANNI.

The years glide away.

On Burnham church, Somerset. See No. 329.

258.

LAS KEINE STUND FURUBER GHAN
DU HABST DEN ETWAS GUT GETHAN.

Of the hours let there none
Pass when thou no good hast done.

QUAELIBET EST INDEX FUNERIS HORA TUI.

Any hour is signal for thy death.

On an ivory portarium in the National Museum at
Munich.

259.

LATET ULTIMA.

The last (hour) is hidden.

At Bispham Hall, Lancashire, on a dial in the garden;
and at Alagna.   See No. 639.

260.

L'HEURE QUE TU CHERCHES TE CONDUIT
À LA MORT.

The hour that thou lookest for leads thee to death.

Les Orres, Canton d'Embrun, Dauphiné.

261.

L'HOMME EST SEMBLABLE À LA VANITÉ; SES JOURS
SONT COMME UN OMBRE QUI PASSE.

*Man is like a thing of naught; his time passeth away like a
shadow.*

On a dial above the porch of St. Brelade's church, Jersey.

262.

LE TEMPS PASSE, L'AMITIE RESTE.
C'EST L'HEURE DE BIEN FAIRE.

Time goes, friendship stays,
This is the hour for doing good.

It is intended by Lord Ilchester to erect a sun-dial on the
south-west front of Melbury Castle, Dorset, bearing the
above mottoes, when the alterations are completed, which
are now (1887) being made in the house. The oldest part
of the building is about 1450 in date.

263.

LE TEMPS PASSE, L'ETERNITÉ S'AVANCE.

Time passes, eternity approaches.

At Entrèves, near Courmayeur; where there is a second
line, so much defaced that no sense can be made of it.

264.

LET NOT THE SUN GO DOWN UPON YOUR WRATH.

Is St. Paul's monition (Ep. iv. 26) and was admirably used by Bishop Coplestone for a dial motto in a village near which he resided. See No. 535.

265.

LET OTHERS TELL OF STORMS AND SHOWERS,
I'LL ONLY COUNT YOUR SUNNY HOURS.

This motto, belonging to the numerous family of *Horas non numero nisi serenas,* is inscribed on the dial plate of a pillar in the grounds of Lansdowne Lodge, Kenmare, Co. Kerry, and was placed there about A.D., 1870.

266.

LEX DEI, LUX DIEI.
The law of God is the light of day.

On the church of St. Thomas à Becket, Dodbrooke, Devon ; and over the south entrance of Mickleton Church, co. Gloucester. It was formerly on the church of Great Smeaton, Yorkshire (see No. 437); and is recorded as existing at Rugby, but the exact locality is not known.

267.

LIFE'S BUT A SHADOW,
MAN'S BUT DUST.
THIS DYALL SAYES,
DY ALL WE MUST.

On the church of All Saints, Winkleigh, Devon.

268.

LIFE'S BUT A WALKING SHADOW. 1769.

From *Macbeth*, Act v., Scene 5, is on a dial facing to the
south of an old house in Salisbury Close, formerly inhabited
by James Harris, the author of " Hermes," a Salisbury
man; who, as he died in 1780, may have erected and
inscribed the dial.

269.

LIFE IS LIKE A SHADOW.

On the porch of the fine old church of St. John the
Baptist, Morwenstow, or Moorwinstow, Cornwall, which
dates its foundation from the ninth or tenth century. The
entrance door to the nave is of very good Norman work, and
the font is one of the oldest Saxon ones in England. The
dial appears to be modern. Morwenstow, according to the
late Vicar, the Rev. R. S. Hawker, means the " stow " or
" place " of St. Morwenna.

My Saxon shrine ! the only ground
Wherein this wearied heart hath rest !
What years the birds of God have found
Among thy walls their sacred nest :
The storm—the blast—the tempest shock,
Have beat upon those walls in vain,
She stands—a daughter of the rock—
The changeless God's eternal fane.

Firm was their faith, the ancient bands
The wise of heart in wood and stone ;
Who reared with stern and trembling hands
These dark grey towers of days unknown ;

*　　　*　　　*　　　*

They pitched no tent for change or death,
No home to last man's shadowy day !
There ! there ! the everlasting breath
Would breathe whole centuries away.

R. S. HAWKER.

270.

LIFE IS SHORT, TIME IS SWIFT,
MUCH IS TO BE DONE. J. S. 1833. Lat. 54, 30.

The dial-plate is circular and made of slate, and is erected
on a barn near Bassenthwaite, Cumberland.

271.

LIFE STEALS AWAY, O MAN THIS HOUR IS
LENT THEE,
PATIENTLY WORK THE WORK OF HIM WHO
SENT THEE.

At Tytherton Kellaways, Wilts. See No. 708.

272.

L'OMBRA CHE VEDI O PASSAGIER DA VELOCISSIME
ORE
E DA UN MOMENTO
T'ATTESTA
UN ORA PAŠA, UN ORA MEN TI RESTA
L'ETERNO GIOIR
PENDE OPUR TORMENTO.
1852.

The shadow's hours, traveller, swiftly speed,
One moment grants it, bidding thee take heed;
One hour hath gone, one hour the less remains,
Ere joys eternal, or eternal pains.

On a house in a village near the Lago di Garda. The

words *Soli. Soli. Soli* are written between the numerals. See No. 543.

273.

L'OMBRA È FIGURA DELLA TUA LABIL
    VITA
SEGNANDO L'ORE A MEDITAR T'INVITA.
                1868.

The shadow is a symbol of thy fleeting life,
By telling the time it calls thee to reflection.

On a house, Grand Canal, Venice.
" Men desire thousands of days and wish to live long here ; let them rather despise thousands of days, and desire that one which hath neither dawn nor darkening, to which no yesterday give place, which yields to no to-morrow."— *S. Augustine, quoted by Archbishop Leighton.*

274.

L'ORA CHE L'OMBRA MIA FEDEL TI ADDITA,
PENSA CHE FU SOTTRATTA DALLA TUA
    VITA. 1862.

The hour my shadow marks with faithfulness,
Hath made thy life, remember, so much less.

AMICIS QUAELIBET HORA.

To friends—any hour they please.

On a house at Murano, near Venice.   See No. 19.

275.

L'OROLOGIO PUÒ ERRAR SEGNANDO LE ORE,
MA LA SFERA DEL SOLE GIAMMAI TRAS-CORRE.

The clock may mistake in the hours of the day,
But the orb of the sun never goeth astray.

On a mill near Riva, Lago di Garda.

276.

LO SOL SEN' VA, SOGGIUNSE, E VIEN LA SERA :
NON V'ARRESTATE, MA STUDIATE IL PASSO
MENTRE CHE L'OCCIDENTE NON S'ANNERA.

" The sun," it added, " sinks, and eve is nigh :
Linger not here, but swift pursue your way,
Ere night arriving shrouds the western sky."

WRIGHT'S *Trans.*

On a dial erected by the late Lord Iddesleigh on the terrace at Pynes, Devon, and inscribed, " Sir Thomas Dyke Acland, Bart. In memory of a friendship of three generations, 1787-1876."

The lines are from the " Divina Commedia " of Dante. Purgatorio, c. xxvii.

277.

17 LOOSE NO TIME 13

A (The Royal Crown) R.

WILLIAM MUNDEN.

May ye 5.

On the south side of High Street, Kensington, nearly midway between Young Street and the entrance to Jenning's Buildings (pulled down by Baron Grant), the old Red Lion Inn was entered by a yard which still remained in 1874. About forty feet from the ground on the south wall of the old house, a large stone slab let into the wall formed the plate of a sun-dial, the gnomon of which was propped by an S-like bar of iron. The above inscription was found to be engraved on the dial. Mr. W. Munden was a barber chirurgeon, (surgery was not constituted a distinct service till 1745.) He held property in various parts of Kensington, and was churchwarden of the parish church, 1698. (*Notes and Queries*, 5th S., 1874).

278.

LOQUOR, SED NON CAECIS.

I speak, but not to the blind.

In Mrs. Schimmelpenninck's account of her visit to the ruins of Port Royal, she states that in the burying-ground attached to the chapel, dedicated to the Blessed Virgin, there was a sun-dial which bore this motto: and she adds,

" above the portal entrance to the burying-ground were the following inscriptions :—without,

> ' Time is yet before thee ; '

within,

> ' Time is for ever behind thee.'

A quaint verse in old French was also often repeated :—

> ' Tous ces morts ont vécu, toi qui vis, tu mourras :
> Ce jour terrible approche, et tu n'y penses pas.'

which might be thus rendered :

> ' These dead once lived, and thou who liv'st shalt die :
> Thou heed'st it not, yet that dread day draws nigh.' "

279.

LORD REMEMBER ME
WHEN TIME NO MORE SHIL BE.
WE SHALL DIE ALL.

These mottoes with the initials M. M. R. and the date 1658, are inscribed on a dial plate now in the Museum of the Peterborough Natural History and Archæological Society. It was " taken out of the wall of an old public house when it was pulled down."

280.

LORD THROUGH THIS HOUR
BE THOU MY GUIDE,
SO BY THY POWER
NO FOOT SHALL SLIDE.

Copied from an almanack, and there called "a sundial motto : " no further particulars were given.

N

281.

LORSQUE TU SONNERAS, JE CHANTE.
When thou shalt strike, I crow.

On a house in the Rue d'Antibes, at Cannes, is a circular dial, surmounted by a gaily-feathered cock. Right and left of the bird spreads a scroll, which is thus inscribed. It is of course the cock's challenge to the dial. The dial faces south, and is green in colour. No date appears, but the once brilliant plumage of the cock, and the condition of the dial face, testify that they have long passed their prime.

282.

LOSE NO TIME.

On a very large dial, which is fastened outside the chancel wall of Middleton Church, Lancashire. The church is an old one, and contains several interesting monuments, in addition to some armour, which was worn at Flodden by the lord of the manor of Middleton.

283.

LUX EST UMBRA DEI.
Light is the shadow of God.

On a dial at Finchley.

284.

LUMEN ET UMBRA DEI. 1672.

Light and shadow of God.

" At Tredegar Park, Monmouthshire, in a room panelled with cedar, one pane of the window is marked with the lines and hours for a sun-dial radiating from an ancestral projecting gnomon, and beneath it is the above motto burnt in the glass." (*Notes and Queries*, 4th S. iv. 143).

> " Think, the shadow on the dial
> Is the Nature most undone,
> Marks the passing of the trial,
> Proves the presence of the sun."
>
> E. B. BROWNING.

285.

LUMEN ME REGIT, VOS UMBRA.

The light guides me, the shadow you.

At Barlow Hall, Lancashire, on a dial supposed to have been erected about the year 1574 by Alexander Barlow.

286.

LUX POST UMBRAM.

Light after shadow.

May be read as a dial motto in the north of Italy.

287.

LUX TUA VITA MEA.

Thy light (is) my life.

On Mapledurham House near Reading, the motto is that of the Blount family, to whom the place belongs.

288.

LUX UMBRA DEI.

Light the shadow of God.

Seen in the north of Italy; also on Dymock Church, Gloucester; and at Ripley, Surrey, see No. 429. It was formerly on the church of Great Smeaton, Yorkshire. See No. 437.

289.

1740 YEARS OF
ממשיר
A STONE OF STUMBLING.
SEE ISAIAH VIII. 14, 15.
PS. CXIX. 165. EZEK. III. 20.
A STUMBLING BLOCK.
BEWARE OF HIM.
MAL. I. 11.
BEZALEEL BENEVENT.
SCULPTOR ISRAELITE. ISAIAH, XLIV. 5.
MAKER. I AM 58 YEARS OLD.

This extraordinary inscription is carved in stone on the two sides of a dial plate which is inserted in the slab, and fixed against a house in the village of Wentworth, on Earl Fitzwilliam's Yorkshire estate. It has puzzled many passers by; but the Rev. Dr. Moses Margoliouth has offered a solution of the mysterious motto in "Notes and Queries," 1st Ser., vol. iv., p. 378. He assumes it to have been the work of a Jewish mason, probably employed in the erection of Wentworth Woodhouse, who had become a convert to Christianity, and who sought to allure his Hebrew brethren to a like change of faith. The Hebrew characters form no word that can be found in the language, but they are the initial letters of the following words :—

סלך משיח שילה יהוה רעי

which express, "The King Messiah, the Shiloh, the Lord my Shepherd." Dr. Margoliouth regards the motto as a veiled admission on the part of the Israelite of his conversion to Christianity, given after a national mode of Eastern communication. It will be observed that the Scriptural references are confined to the books of the Old Testament, so as not to alarm the inquiring reader. Dr. Margoliouth concludes his criticism thus : "One may well imagine an Israelite or two observing from the road the Hebrew characters, ממשיר, for they are very large, and are seen afar off— and after puzzling over their intent and purport for some time, proceed to ask for an explanation from the major-domo. The master, delighted that the bait caught, vouchsafes, in his peculiarly eccentric style, to lecture on his own device, and thus reads to his brethren a sermon in stone." By referring to the passages cited in the inscription, the reader will better understand the learned Hebraist's interpretation.

290.

MACHINA, BIS SEXTAS QUAE JUSTE DIVIDIT
    HORAS,
JUSTITIAM SERVARE MONET, LEGESQUE
    TUERI.

This engine marking right the hours of day
Bids you guard justice, and the laws obey.

This appears in Paris, on a turret of the Palais de Justice,
where formerly was a sun-dial.

291.

MAESTIS LENTAE, CELERES GAUDENTIBUS
    HORAE.

Slow to the sorrowing,
Swift to the joying,
(Pass) the hours.

At Stra, near Padua. Also on a house by the roadside,
between Ventimiglia and Bordighera, where the first word is
missing :—

    " How lazily time creeps about
    To one that mourns ! "

                Bp. H. KING.

292.

MAN BEST ERWÄHLT
DER NUR HEITERE STUNDEN ZÄHLT.

He hath made his choice aright,
Who counteth but the hours of light.

At Nuremburg, quoted from memory by a writer in " The Monthly Packet," Oct., 1886, p. 396.

293.

MAN FLEETH AS A SHADOW.

A square dial, once painted red with a green border, is on a gable over the porch of the picturesque old church at

Wycliffe on the Tees, and bears the above motto from Job xiv. 2. The dial is now quite defaced and useless. Wycliffe is the reputed birthplace of the Great Reformer, and is very beautifully situated. The same motto formerly was on the church porch at Staindrop, county Durham ; and it still exists on a square dial upon the south wall of the aisle of Maxey Church, Northamptonshire.

294.

MAN IS A SHADOW. 1808.

Is on a dial over the south-west porch of Stowmarket Church, Suffolk.

295.

MANE PIGER STERTIS, FUGIT HORA.

In the morning thou snorest sluggishly — the hour flies.

Recorded as a dial motto, but no locality assigned. The first three words are from Persius 5. 132.

296.

MANEO NEMINI.

I wait for no one.

There is a dial which bears this inscription, surrounded by creeper foliage, on Middleton Tyas Hall, near Richmond, Yorkshire. The same motto occurs in a small hamlet near Baslow, Derbyshire. See No. 158.

297.

MARK WELL MY SHADE, AND SERIOUSLY ATTEND
THE COMMON LESSON OF A SILENT FRIEND,
FOR TIME AND LIFE SPEED RAPIDLY AWAY,
NEITHER CAN YOU RECALL THE FORMER DAY.
YOU ARE NOT ABLE TO RECALL THE PAST,
BUT LIVE THOU THIS DAY AS IF THE LAST.

On the sun-dial of Thornby Church, Northamptonshire.

298.

MAY THE DREAD BOOK AT OUR LAST TRIAL,
WHEN OPEN SPREAD, BE LIKE THIS DIAL;
MAY HEAVEN FORBEAR TO MARK THEREIN
THE HOURS MADE DARK BY DEEDS OF SIN;
THOSE ONLY IN THAT RECORD WRITE
WHICH VIRTUE, LIKE THE SUN, MAKES BRIGHT.

On a dial which projects from the sill of the library window
at Arley Hall, Cheshire, the seat of R. Egerton-Warburton,
Esq. It has also *Horas non numero nisi serenas.* (See No. 599.)

299.

MAY THOSE BE BLEST WITH LENGTH OF
    DAYS
WHO STILL PROCLAIM KING WILLIAM'S
    PRAISE.

This pious tribute to the " glorious and immortal memory "
is recorded in " Notes and Queries," 4th Ser. x., Nov. 1872,

as an Orange inscription in the Green county of Roscommon.

300.

ME LUMEN VOS UMBRA REGIT.

The light rules me, the shadow you.

At Lesneven, in Brittany ; also on the south wall of the Town Hall, Saltash, with " Edward Stephens, fecit 1727."

301.

ME ORTUM VIDES FORSAN NON OCCASUM.

Risen thou seest me (the sun) perhaps not set.

On the south dial face of a pillar at Borranshill House, near Carlisle ; on the opposite side is *Tempus fugit.* The dials were erected by a member of the Heysham family ; they stand on a pedestal, and are surmounted by a vase ornamented with doves, and crowned by a lion passant regardant—the Heysham crest. The whole erection is about seven feet high. The property now belongs to Colonel Wybergh.

302.

MEAM NON TUAM NOSCIS.

Thou knowest my hour, not thine own.

At Poirino, Piedmont.

303.

MEDIUM NON DESERIT UNQUAM.

It never leaves the middle.

On a dial upon the tower of the parish church, Capolago.
The motto, perhaps, refers to the gnomon.

304.

MEMENTO FINIS.

Remember the end.

On a dial at Le Villard, Dauphiné (see No. 151). The
words are from the Vulgate of *Ecclus.* xxxvi. 10.

305.

MEMENTO HORAE NOVISSIMAE. 1798.

Remember thy last hour.

This is inscribed on a semi-circular dial on a low cottage
or shed beside the road, on the eastern side of Bordighera,
near Ospedaletti. It is placed almost immediately under the
roof, the motto and date being below. On the right-hand
side a lamp projects from the wall, and hangs in front of a
niche, where there is an image of the Madonna.

306.

MEMENTO MORI.

Remember death.

Is on a circular dial, fixed in a sort of hatchment frame, on
the wall of Croft Church, in Yorkshire, and half concealing

a window.   The motto is above, the date 1816 on the sides, and the numerals and lettering are gilt.   The same motto, dated 1804, is at Monthey, Canton Vallais, in Switzerland.

Also on the church porch at Skipton, Yorkshire.   The porch was built in 1866, and replaced an old structure on which there was a stone sun-dial.   The present dial is of brass.   The words also occur in the parish register, with a note of the burial, in 1665, of Robert Sutton, M.A., who for " fforty & three years was Vicar of the sayde place.   His funeral sermon was preached by his son and onely son, Thomas Sutton, on this text (2 Kings xi. 12), 'Memento mori.   One generation goeth and another cometh!'" An older dial, without a motto, is traced on the church tower, which was destroyed during the siege of Skipton Castle in the Civil Wars, 1642-5, and was rebuilt by Anne, Countess of Pembroke in 1655.

The motto is also on the church at Amsoldingen, Canton, Berne ; and at Wetherall, Cumberland (see No. 28) ; and was formerly at Rotherham, Yorks (see No. 187).

The same words were chosen by Thackeray for the dial at Castlewood, which figures in one of his beautiful descriptions : " There was in the court a peculiar silence somehow ; and the scene remained long in Esmond's memory.   The sky bright overhead ; the buttresses of the building and the sundial casting shadow over the gilt 'Memento mori' inscribed underneath ; the two dogs—a black greyhound and a spaniel nearly white, the one with his face up to the sun, and the other snuffing amongst the grass and stones ; and my lord leaning over the fountain, which was plashing audibly.   'Tis strange how that scene, and the sound of that fountain, remain fixed on the memory of a man who has beheld a hundred sights of splendour 'and danger too, of which he has kept no account " (" Esmond," chap. xiv.).

A correspondent reminds us that a certain well-known Fellow of Worcester College, Oxford, suggested as the motto for a snuff-box made out of an old mulberry tree, " Memento mori "—*remember the mulberry tree.*

307.

MEMOR ESTO BREVIS AEVI. 1764.

Bear in mind how short life is.

There is a circular dial placed over the porch entrance at Bittadon Church, North Devon, which contains this inscription. The whole porch is enveloped in ivy, from which the dial face peers out. The same motto, without date, also occurs at Checkley, Staffordshire.

So Hotspur :—

> O gentlemen, the time of life is short,
> To spend that shortness basely were too long
> If life did ride upon a dial's point
> Still ending at the arrival of an hour.
> SHAKESPEARE, Hen. IV.

308.

MEMOR ULTIMAE UTERE PRAESENTI.

Declinat. G. R. xxxvi. An. Dom. mdcccxxxiv. Joh. Antonivs Teppati, Tavrini, delineavit.

Mindful of the last [hour], employ the present.

On a large dial painted on the wall of a court in the Hospital della Consolazione, or Santa Maria in Portico, Rome.

309.

MENTIRI NON EST ME(I).

It is not possible for me to lie.

Formerly on Ebberston Church, near Scarborough, with
No. 407.

310.

MI FECE D' ARCHIMEDE L' ALTA SCUOLA,
IL SOL MI DÀ LA VITA E LA PAROLA.

The high teaching of Archimedes made me,
The sun gives me life and speech.

The dial plate is oval in shape, but wider than it is long.
The motto is on the top, the points of the compass are
marked in the centre, and the date, 1859, is below, with the
name of the maker, *Carolus Sachi, Trigon, Desine, Pinxit.*
It is erected on the wall of one of the courts of the immense
chateau of the Counts Arconati, at Rho, near Milan. The
last descendant of this ancient Milanese family, which
dated from the fourteenth century, was buried at Milan in
1870.

311.

A. D. S.

MIA VITA È IL SOL: DELL' UOM LA VITA
È DIO;
SENZA ESSO È L' UOM, QUAL SENZA SOL
SON' IO.

My life is the Sun : God is the life of man ;
Man without Him, is as I am without the sun.

On the wall of a monastery, now suppressed, in the neighbourhood of Florence.

312.

MIhI DeVs LVX et saLVs.

God is my light and salvation.

At Hadleigh, Suffolk (see No. 604). A chronogram,
A.D. 1627.

313.

MIND YOUR BUSINESS.

On a house at Falsgrave, Scarborough.

314.

MISPEND NO TIME.

At Micheldean (see No. 173).

315.

MONEO, DUM MOVEO.

I warn whilst I move.

Formerly on a summer-house at Danby Hall, near Leyburn, Yorkshire; but the dial has now been moved, and
placed above the principal door of the stables.

316.

MONEO, DUM MOVEO:
DUM SPECTAS FUGIO:
SAPIENTIS EST NUMERARE:
SIC PRAETERIT AETAS.

*I warn whilst I move: While thou lookest I fly: It is for the
wise man to number (his days): So time passes.*

In the private diary of a gentleman, dated 1790, has been
found an entry of an interesting group of four mottoes, no
longer existing, at King's Lynn, Norfolk. "The market-
place at Lynn very fine and spacious; a very fine Market
Cross, as it is called—a very elegant building, standing on
pillars, adorned with statues and four dials, on which are the
four mottoes"—as written above. This building was put
up in 1710, and having become dilapidated was replaced by a
market house.

317.

MORS DE DIE ACCELERAT. 1796.

Death hastens on day by day.

This inscription was on a dial over an archway in the stable-yard at Kiplin Hall, near Catterick.

When the collector last saw it, in 1864, the motto had been painted over. The dial was made by a villager named Bonner, who died about 1818; and in 1838 the collector sketched his widow at her cottage in Kiplin, and received the information from her.

The same motto is in the churchyard at Derwent, in Derbyshire. This dial is made of a soft grey stone or slate, in shape like an heraldic shield, and is mounted on an oak beam, which was probably taken out of the old chapel of the fourteenth century. (See Nos. 13 and 99.)

318.

MORTAL, WHILE THE SUNNY BEAM
TELLS THEE HERE HOW TIME IS FLYING,
HASTE THE MOMENTS TO REDEEM,
FOR ETERNITY PROVIDING.

WINTERS PASS AND SPRINGS RENEW
TO MATURITY ADVANCING,
YOUTH TO PLEASURE SIGHS ADIEU
IN THE FIELDS OF CHILDHOOD DANCING.

o

MANHOOD SINKS TO HOARY AGE
AND A NIGHT THAT HAS NO MORNING;
O LET WISDOM NOW ENGAGE,
HEAR HER DICTATES AND TAKE WARNING.

WISELY STILL THE MOMENTS USE
MAN IS EVERY MOMENT DYING;
WHILST THIS TABLET YOU PERUSE,
O REMEMBER TIME IS FLYING.

W. LAMB.

The "Gentleman's Magazine" for 1829, ii. p. 34, states that the above stanzas are written on a sun-dial on Gainford Church porch. They are no longer there.

319.

MOX NOX.

Soon (cometh) night.

Is a dial motto on the south porch of Elsworth Church, near Cambridge; and on a house in Double Street, Spalding, with the date 1773. It also occurs on a flint-built church, near Dennington, Suffolk, where the dial is fixed on the battlement, and beneath, on a scroll, is—

Mox Nox.
THE MOMENT PAST,
LAID MANY FAST.

Many of these flint-built churches are very handsome. Round the base of this one the flints are arranged in patterns, to represent the emblems of the Passion, &c., &c.

320.

, MOYLL Y LAA MIE FASTYR
BAASE JIU AGH BIOYS MARAGH.

Praise the good day in the evening,
Death may be greedy of life on the morrow.

On a dial which formerly stood in the Isle of Man. See
No. 331.

321.

MULIER, AMICTA SOLE,
ORA PRO NOBIS, SANCTA DEI GENITOR.

Lady, clothed with the sun, pray for us, holy Mother of God.

These lines are to be read on the house of the Roman
Catholic Priest at Hallstadt, near Salzburg. Evidently new,
and roughly painted on the wall, is the figure of the Virgin
holding the gnomon of a dial, which casts its shadow on a
scroll beneath, on which the hours are figured.

322.

MY CHANGE IS SURE, IT MAY BE SOON,
EACH HASTENING MINUTE LEADS ME ON:
THE AWFUL SUMMONS DRAWETH NIGH,
AND EVERY DAY I LIVE TO DIE. 1697.

These lines are beneath a sun-dial attached to the south
wall of Blackley Chapel.

323.

MY DAYS ARE LIKE A SHADOW THAT DECLINETH.

From Psalm cii. 11, is inscribed over the south door of St. Vigean's Church, Arbroath, N.B.; and on the plate of a pillar dial, formed by a cluster of three slight columns at Haley Hill Cemetery, near Halifax. There is no date, but the dial was probably erected in 1856, when the cemetery was opened. The spire of the fine church, built by Mr. Akroyd, and the chimney of his mills, rise in the background, above the trees which surround the enclosure. See No. 609.

"Every day is a little life, in the account whereof we may reckon a birth from the womb of the morning, our growing time from thence to noon (when we are as the sun in his strength); after which, like a shadow that declineth, we hasten to the evening of our age, till at last we close our eyes in sleep, the image of death; and our whole life is but a tale of a day told over and over."—Sir William Waller.

324.

MY TIME IS IN THY HAND.
R. A. G.: F. E. G. 1875.

On the base of a stone pillar bearing a horizontal dial, and erected and inscribed by the Rev. R. A. Gatty. It stands in the centre of a grass plot in front of Bradfield Rectory, near Sheffield. The flower beds which surround it are cut after the pattern of astronomical figures, a crescent moon, Saturn and his ring, Jupiter and his satellites, &c. The

motto is taken from Psalm xxxi. 15, Prayer Book Version.
It has also been placed, by Bernard Wake, Esq., on a vertical
dial, at Abbeyfield, Sheffield.   See No. 493.

325.

NASCE, MUORE.

It is born, it dies.

At Dolce Acqua, near Bordighera.   See No. 327.

326.

NATUS HOMO EX UTERO, BREVIORI TEMPORE VIVENS, UT FLOS EGREDITUR, SED VELUT UMBRA FUGIT.

Job. xiv. 1, 2.

Man born of woman, living for a very short time,
Cometh forth like a flower, but fleeth as a shadow.

This is on a square-shaped dial, which is traced on the
wall of a church, near Menaggio, that stands high above the
Lake of Como on the western shore.   The dial is probably
not old, and is placed close to the corner of the church wall,
at an angle with the west, or rather south-west front, where
there is a large porch supported on light pillars, and shaded
by cypress trees.

327.

NATUS MORTUUS.

Born dead.

On a dial at Bellentre, near Bourg S. Maurice.   It is very
difficult to understand this motto.   Dr. Littledale thinks it

perhaps means that time is gone immediately on coming, so that its birth and death are at once. But then the words ought to be feminine to agree with *hora*, or neuter to agree with *tempus*, not masculine.

328.

NE COMPTE PAS SUR LA PREMIÈRE,
CAR TOUT DÉPEND DE LA DERNIÈRE.
Z. G. F.   1869.

Reckon not upon the beginning,
For all hangs upon the end.

At Le Villard; and also on the church of Mélézes, Dauphiné, dated 1853.

329.

NE QUID PEREAT.
Let nothing be lost.

LABUNTUR ANNI.
The years glide by.

On a square dial face, upon the south porch of Burnham Church, Somerset.

330.

NEC ULTIMA SI PRIOR
DENOTAL FALLACES ANNOS.

This somewhat mysterious inscription occurs on two faces of a dial which is painted upon the wall of the courtyard of an old Hôtel, No. 47, Rue Vieille du Temple, Paris. There are four faces, on blue grounds, and possibly the painter may have made a mistake in rendering the inscription. It has been suggested that the words should run thus :—

> " Nec ultimos si priores,
> Fallaces denotat annos."

Nor does it mark the last years as deceiving, though it may the first.

If the lines are quoted from a poem, the context might throw light on their meaning; but we have failed to discover whether this is the case. Some difficulty has arisen in copying the motto, as the present inmate of the Hôtel evidently objects to its being transcribed, and on two occasions has come out and driven away people who were attempting to make a copy of the lines.

331.
NEMO SINE CRIMINE VIVIT.

No one lives without reproach.

QUID CELERIUS UMBRA?

What swifter than a shadow ?

CUR GEIL DA'AN SCA,
SHEN MYR TA'N TRA.

Observe the mark of the shadow,
In that manner is time represented.

UT UMBRA SIC VITA.

As a shadow so is life.

WHILST PHŒBUS ON ME SHINES,
THEN VIEW MY SHADES AND LINES.

TEMPUS ABIT, MORS VENIT.
Time goes, death comes.

MOYLL Y LAA MIE FASTYR,
BAASE JIU AGH BIOYS MARAGH.
Praise the good day in the evening,
Death may be greedy of life on the morrow.

John Kewley, Ballafreer.   Fecit 1774.

On a pillar-dial, which formerly stood in the Isle of Man.
The pillar is made of Pooilvaish marble, about two feet in
height, and pointed at the top.   It is supposed to have originally belonged to Sir George Moore, of Ballamoore, Patrick,
but in 1879 it was found on a rubbish heap at Peel, and sold
to Mr. Meyer, the well known collector of antiquities.   It
was purchased after his death by Mr. Lewis Evans, of
Hemel Hempstead, and is now (1888) in his possession.
The dial shows the time at Boston, Port Royal, and other
places.   Kewley, the maker, is said to have lived at the farm,
Ballafreer, and he erected another dial there.   See Nos. 22
and 635.

332.

NESCIES QUA HORA VENIAM.
Thou wilt not know at what hour I will come.

IL TEMPO PASSA, L'ETERNITÁ S'AVVICINNA.
Time passes away, eternity draws near.

On a dial at Riva, Val Sesia.

A fine old watch in the York Museum, dated " H. K.
1640 ", has the inscription, *Nescies quâ horâ, vigila.*

333.

NESCIT OCCASUM LUMEN ECCLESIAE.

The light of the Church knows no setting.

At Standish Vicarage, Gloucestershire. There is a hidden meaning in this motto, due to its having been chosen by Bishop Frampton, who was deprived of the See of Gloucester as a non-juror, but was permitted to hold the vicarage of Standish, and died there in 1708. He erected the dial, and in addition to the allusion to his career, which he put into the motto, he had the gnomon shaped like the sword of the See, reversed, and pointing upwards, as an emblem of martyrdom. He is buried within the sanctuary of Standish Church, and his gravestone bears the quaint inscription, " Robertus Frampton Episcopus Gloucestrensis, caetera quis nescit ? "

334.

NIHIL VOLENTIBUS ARDUUM.

Nothing is difficult to the willing.

Is on a dial at Fyning House, in Sussex, which was erected in the reign of George II.

335.

NIL NI SIT SOL MI.

Less than none without the sun.

At Alzo, on the Lake of Orta, in North Italy.

336.

NIL NISI CAELESTI RADIO.

Nought save by a ray from heaven.

Applicable alike to the dial, the church and the services, this motto is over the south door of the church of St. Mary the Virgin, at Lower Heyford, in Oxfordshire, where there has been a church from before the Conquest. It is also found near Baslow. See No. 158.

337.

NIL SINE NOBIS.

A. B. F. 1674.

Nothing (exists) without us.

A dial on the wall of a courtyard on the south side of the Hôtel Cluny, Paris, has this inscription. The word *nobis* refers to the rays of the sun which are represented on its face. The Hôtel Cluny is a very beautiful specimen of rather elaborate fourteenth century Gothic architecture. In 1625 it was bought for the abbess and nuns of Port Royal, and was known as Port Royal de Paris. It was re-established by Louis XIV. in 1665, on a fresh basis, and was looked upon as schismatic by the community of Port Royal des Champs. This dial must have been erected in the time of the first abbess of the new foundation, Sœur Dorothée Perdreau, who held the office till 1684.

338.

No light unthinking fondness, such as oft
Enshrines in pomp th' unworthiest of their line,
Prompted the tender thought which here found
    words
To tell of him we valued; one whose form
Under this turf is mingled with the dust,
No more to *live;* but whose recorded name,
Endear'd to all, reminds us how to *love.*

Near to this time-recording pillar's base
Entomb'd, and, as became his merits, mourn'd—
Poor Neppy lies! the generous and the fond—
The brave and vigilant—in whose nature shone,
United, all the virtues of his race:
Nor grudged be this memorial, if its truth
Enforce the charge, " Be faithful unto death."
    Obiit Sep. 9, 1839, anno aetatis decimo.

In the garden of the Vicarage House at Borden, near Sittingbourne, Kent, there is a pedestal, surmounted by a sun-dial, which bears on its eastern and western sides two tablets inscribed with these acrostic epitaphs to the memory of a favourite Newfoundland watchdog, called " Neptune," by his sorrowing owner. These lines recall Lord Byron's " Inscription on the Monument of a Newfoundland dog," dated " Newstead Abbey, Oct. 30, 1808."

339.

NO MARBLE POMP, NO MONUMENTAL PRAISE;
MY TOMB THIS DIAL, EPITAPH THESE LAYS.

PRIDE AND LOW MOULDERING CLAY BUT ILL AGREE,
DEATH LEVELS ME TO BEGGAR, KINGS TO ME.
ALIVE, INSTRUCTION WAS MY WORK EACH DAY,
DEAD, I PERISH, INSTRUCTION TO CONVEY.
HERE, READER, MARK (PERHAPS NOW IN THY PRIME)
THE STEALING STEPS OF NEVER-STANDING TIME;
THOU'LT BE WHAT I AM, CATCH THE PRESENT HOUR,
EMPLOY THAT WELL, FOR THAT'S WITHIN THY POWER.

Quoted in the "Gent. Mag.," vol. xiv, p. 332, A.D. 1744, from Faulkner's "Dublin Journal," as "Inscription on a dial to be erected by his desire on the grave of Edward Bond, of Bondvil, in the county of Armagh, Esq."

340.

NOISELESS FALLS THE FOOT OF TIME
WHICH ONLY TREADS ON FLOWERS.

This quotation from a song by W. H. Spencer (see No. 16) is inscribed on the base of a stone pillar with a horizontal dial, in the garden of Jordangate, Macclesfield, erected by Samuel Pearson, Esq., and Jane his wife. The name "Quiz," and date 1876, are also carved on the stone, in memory of a favourite terrier who was buried close by. On the dial plate is the motto "Post tenebras spero lucem."

341.

NOLI CONFIDERE NOCTI.
Trust not to the night.

On the Manor House, Mickleton, co. Gloucester.

342.

NON DEDERUNT TIBI DI QUAM PRAESENTEM SUPERI
HORAM
AD FINEM ASPICIAS, HORA FUTURA LATET.

The gods above have given thee but the present hour.
Look on to the end, the future hour lies hid.

At Carville Hall, an old mansion on the Roman wall near
Wallsend, is a fine old sun-dial with faces so that the pointer
is parallel to the face. The motto given above is perhaps of
more recent date than the dial itself. (*A Correspondent in*
"*The Guardian.*")

343.

NON NISI CAELESTI RADIO.

Not save by a ray from heaven (do I tell the time).

On the church porch at Haydon Bridge, Northumberland.
The dial is square, and the motto is above: the words being

divided by a full-faced sun, which emits rays all round. They bear an obvious moral signification. There is no date on this dial, but the church was built out of the nave of an older church, and opened for service July, 1796. The features of the Sun God are too decidedly Hanoverian to suppose a much earlier date.

344.

NON NUMERO HORAS NISI SERENAS.

I count no hours that are not bright.

On a dial at Downham Hall, Brandon, with No. 214.

345.

NON NUMERO NISI SERENAS HORAS.

I count only bright hours.

On an old mural sun-dial in the garden of the Château of Passy, and said to have been erected by an ancestor of Arago.

346.

NON REDIBO.

I shall not return.

CHARLES GREENWOOD, FECIT, 1790.

On a house in Westgate, Grantham.

> " Be watchful thou ; Time posts away amain,
> Nor can the hour that's past return again."
> THOS. ELWOOD, " *To such as stand idle in*
> *the market place.*"

347.

NON REGO NISI REGAR.

I rule not if I be not ruled.

On the Crown Inn at Uppingham. The dial is square—
black and gilt—and the motto acknowledges submission to
the sun. It also illustrates the profound truth that—as à
Kempis expresses it—" No man ruleth safely, but he that is
willing to be ruled."

348.

NON SINE LUMINE.

Not without light.

On the south wall of the church of St. Catherine Cree,
Leadenhall Street, London. The dial is cut in the stones of
the building between two of the windows facing the street,
but is now (1884) so covered with dirt as to be nearly illegible. A little care and pains would soon make it as useful
and ornamental as its neighbour in Austin Friars, though
owing to the height of the opposite houses there must be
many hours of the day in which " sine Lumine " would be
only too appropriate a motto. St. Catherine Cree is one of
the few churches built in the seventeenth century. It was
consecrated by Archbishop Laud in 1631. The dial is shown
in an engraving of 1736, as bearing the date MDCCVI.
There was a dial on the tower also at the same period.

349.

NON TARDUM OPPERIOR.

I tarry not for the slow.

There is a stone figure of Time, bearded and with wings, on the terrace at Duncombe Park, Yorkshire, the seat of the Earl of Feversham, which is represented as about to carry away a vase-shaped pedestal, on the top of which is a dial thus inscribed. The figure, which is boldly sculptured, was the work of a local artist, the Helmsley stonemason, about the year 1750, when the terrace was made. Dr. Drake, in his "Lines on Duncombe Park" (Gent. Mag. 1823), describes the place :—

> Where Saturn's statue bids the iron shade
> Point the swift minutes as they rise and fade.

350.

NONE BUT A VILLAIN WILL DEFACE ME.

Is to be seen at Kidderminster.

351.

NORMA DEL TEMPO INFALLIBILE IO SONO.

I am the infallible measure of the time.

On the church at Pieve, near Cento, in the Romagna.

352.

NOS EXIGUUM TEMPUS HABEMUS, SED MULTUM PERDIMUS.

We have little time, but we waste much.

At Hatherley, in Gloucestershire. Sir W. Scott says likewise :—

" Redeem mine hours—the space is brief—
While in my glass the sand-grains shiver ;
And measureless thy joy or grief,
When time and thou shalt part for ever."

353.

NOS JOURS PASSENT COMME L'OMBRE.

Our days pass by like the shadow.

On a house in a street of Antibes, in the department of the Alpes Maritimes, is a dial painted on the wall, with the above motto. It is so close under the roof that the tiles overshadow it.

354.

NOSCE TEIPSUM, 1740, T. S.

Know thyself.

This is on Whitley Hall, an Elizabethan house, in the parish of Ecclesfield, which belonged to Thomas Shirecliffe in 1740 : also on a house which stands in High Street, Lewes ; and on the cross-dial at Elleslie, near Chichester. See No. 48.

P

" For how may we to other things attain,
When none of us his own soul understands ?
For which the devil mocks our curious brain,
When—Know thyself, his oracle commands.

For why should we the busy soul believe,
When boldly she concludes of that and this ;
When of herself she can no judgment give,
Nor how, nor where, nor whence, nor what she is.

If aught can teach us aught, afflictions looks
Making us pry into ourselves so near,
Teach us to know ourselves beyond our books
Or all the learned schools that ever were."

SIR JOHN DAVIES' Nosce Teipsum.

355.

NOUS AVONS BESOIN DE PEU, ET POUR PEU DE TEMPS.

We need but little, and for a little time.

This sentiment is versified by Goldsmith in " The Hermit " :—

" Man wants but little here below,
Nor wants that little long."

The motto is on a house near Aigle, in Canton de Vaud, Switzerland.

356.

NOW IS THE ACCEPTED TIME.

From Rom. xiii., was engraven over a stone dial, which rested on the top of a low wall, against an overshadowing

tree, with water below, near Danby Mill, in the parish of Leyburn, Yorkshire, but has been removed or destroyed. It could not be found in 1884.

357.

NOW IS YESTERDAY'S TO-MORROW.

This quaint motto is on the porch of East Leake Church, in Nottinghamshire. The dial is of slate, and of no great age.

"To-morrow, and to-morrow, and to-morrow,
Creeps in this petty pace from day to day,
To the last syllable of recorded time ;
And all our yesterdays have lighted fools
The way to dusty death."

Macbeth, Act v. Scene 5.

358.
NOW OR NEVER. 1614.

Is rudely engraven on a vertical dial fixed on the top of a buttress of Monk Fryston Church, Yorkshire, but is now (1884) nearly obliterated.   The inscription runs thus :—

"N O V O R N E V E R
Ivne + 1614"

It has also been deciphered on a square-faced dial, with four gnomons, and surmounted by a ball, which rests on a tall elegant stone shaft in Bolton Percy Churchyard, Yorkshire.   It is on the south face, and on the north side there is a faint trace of a former inscription, now wholly illegible from time and weather.   The rector says a tradition exists that the effaced words were "rationibus suis computandis," which may be supposed to be an exhortation to sum up your accounts.   On Bolton Percy Rectory is an uninscribed dial, bearing the date 1698.

359.
NOW OR WHEN.

On a plain black and white dial, which is erected on the south-west tower of Beverley Minster.

360.

NOX VENIT.

Night cometh.

REDIME.

Redeem (the time).

LUX ES.

Thou art Light.

These inscriptions are respectively on the west, south, and east faces of a square dial which stands upon a horizontal

tombstone in Greystoke Churchyard. On the north side of the block is engraved, "Graystock . Lat . 54″ 46 J. G. MDCC . x .". There are gnomons on three of the faces.

361.

NULLA DIES SINE LINEA.

No day without its mark.

On the cross-dial at Elleslie, near Chichester (see No. 48). Also on a pocket universal dial and calendar, made of brass, bearing the date 1716, and the maker's name, Schindler. This specimen is in the collection of Lewis Evans, Esq.

362.

NULLA É PIÙ PREZIOSA DEL TEMPO.
1859.

Nothing is more precious than time.

At Pieve di Rendana.

363.

NULLA EST AUSTRALIS UMBRA.

There is no shadow in the south.

On a house at Campo Rosso, near Bordighera.

364.

NULLA FUIT CUJUS NON MEMINISSE VOLO.

There has been no hour which I do not wish to remember.

This is on a dial which is painted on the wall of a house at Fréjus, in the south of France.

365.

NULLA FLUAT CUJUS NON MEMINISSE JUVET.

May no hour pass which it is not a delight to remember.

At Bruges.

366.

NULLA HORA SINE LINEA.
No hour without its mark.

DUM PROFICIT D(EFICI)T.
While (time) gains, it loses.

SI SOL DEFICIT, NEMO ME RESPICIT.
If the sun fails, no one regards me.

FERREA VIRGA EST, UMBRATILIS MOTUS.
The rod is of iron, the motion that of shadow.

There are four dials in the cloisters of the cathedral at Chambery, all of large size, one on each side of the quad-

rangle. They are traced on the plaster, but two of them are much broken and defaced. From their ancient appearance they have evidently borne many years of Alpine storms. The first motto here quoted belongs to the dial on the south-east cloister. No date is on any of the dials; but old as they are, they must be considerably more modern than the adjoining cathedral, which was finished in 1430, in the reign of Amadeus III. (afterwards the Anti-Pope Felix V.), four years before his abdication and retirement to Ripaille, on the Lake of Geneva.

In " De Symbolis Heroicis," Lib. vi. 250 (Antwerp, 1634), the first motto is given with the design above. Under it is inscribed, " Laurentij Prioli, Ducis Venetæ Reipublicæ, symbolum fuit solare horologium cum eâ epigraphe. Nulla hora sine linea. Nullam in Principatu horam transigere sine linea, et benefactio ars est et laus multò praestantior, quàm cùm Apelles non fuit dies sine lineâ."

367.

NULLI OPTABILIS

DABITUR MORA;

IRREVOCABILIS

LABITUR HORA:

NE SIT INUTILIS

SEMPER LABORA,

NEVE SIS FUTILIS.

VIGILA, ORA.

None from Time's hurrying wain
Winneth delay;
Ne'er to come back again
Speedeth each day:
While its few hours remain
Labour alway.
Lest thou should'st live in vain,
Watch thou and pray.

These lines, and the free English rendering of them, were written by the Rev. S. E. Bartleet, and put by him upon a dial which stood on the lawn of the vicarage garden at Crompton (or, as it is more commonly called, Shaw), near Oldham, Lancashire. The dial-plate has since been moved into the churchyard and placed upon the shaft of the old mortuary cross, from which a previous plate had been stolen. The Latin lines were inserted in the "Guardian," and they have been inscribed, but in slightly different order, upon a dial erected by Henry H. Gibbs, Esq., at Aldenham House, Elstree.

368.

NULLA VESTIGIA RETRORSUM.
INDICE UTERE.

There are no footsteps backward.
Mark the pointer.

On a horizontal dial with a stone pedestal, at Lake House, Wilts, an interesting building, of Elizabethan date, now the property of the Rev. E. Drake. See No. 679.

369.

NUMQUAM AURI,
SED OCULO
SAEPE GRATA. 1742.

Never acceptable to the ear, but often to the eye.

This motto may be read on a south-west declining dial, which is on the wall of the courtyard of the Mairie at Perpignan. It stands betwixt windows, some distance below the overhanging Spanish roof, whose border of greenish glazed tiles rests here and there on carved wooden owl-like figures, which project like gurgoyles from the wall. There are two or three dials in this court over the low marble arcades, but only one bears an inscription. The building itself forms a part of the old Loge—from the Spanish " Lonja," or " Exchange of the Merchants." The façade, with its pointed arches, " exhibiting flamboyant ornaments, foliage, and tracery," dates from the fifteenth century. The carving is a good deal injured; the arches are now filled with glass, and that portion of the building is used as a café. It is one of the most remarkable structures in the old capital of Roussillon. The dial, however, is not of Spanish construction, as Perpignan came into the posssssion of the French in 1650.

370.

NUNC EX PRAETERITO DISCAS.

Now mayst thou learn from the past.

Is on Warrington School.

371.

O BEATA SOLITUDO, O SOLA BEATITUDO;

MIHI OPPIDUM CARCER EST,

ET SOLITUDO

PARADISUS.

W ✠ H

DEUS NOBISCUM,

ET CORONA MANUUM OPUS NOSTRUM.

1663.

VIVAT CAROLUS SECUNDUS.

O blessed solitariness—O solitary blessedness: The town to me is a prison, and solitude my Paradise. O God, be with us, and crown the work of our hands. Long live Charles II.

The dial which is thus inscribed is circular, but has square ends below. The hours are marked round the lower half of the circle, and the lines of motto are above, and bend with the shape of the dial; the word " Paradisus " in the centre being straight, and from it the gnomon springs. It is formed

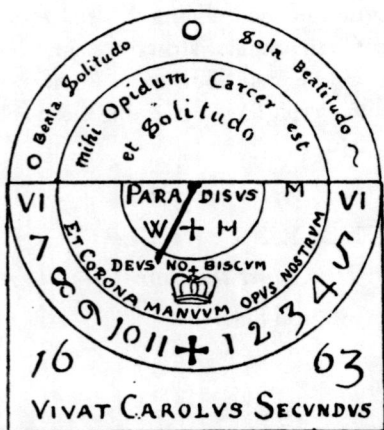

of a single stone let into a plastered gable of a house fronting a garden in Priestgate, Peterborough, and belonging to Mr. G. Wyman. It was once held by a family named Hake, which may account for the initials W. H. There is a crown on the lower part of the dial face, which was gilt, but is now so much worn that only the general outline can be traced.

372.

O COONIEE CRE CHA GIARE AS TA MY HRAA.

Oh remember how short my time is.

" THE SMALL AND GREAT ARE THERE ; AND THE SER-
VANT IS FREE FROM HIS MASTER."—*Job* iii. 19.

UT HORA SIC VITA ; DUM SPECTAS FUGIT.

As the hour, so is life ; while thou lookest it flies.

These mottoes, the first of which is in Manx (Ps. lxxxix,
v. 46), are on a sun-dial which stands at the gateway of St.
Patrick's Church, in the village of Patrick, near Holm Peel,
Isle of Man. The dial is of Pooilvaish marble from the
quarries near Castletown.

373.

O JUNGFRAU DIE DER SCHLANGE FEIND,
BLEIB IM̃ER ELEPHANTENS FREŨND :
MIT DEINEM SCHŨTZ BEDECKE DIESES HAUS,
TREIB KRANKHEIT NOTH UND JEDES UNHEIL AUS.

*O maiden, enemy of the serpent, remain ever the elephant's
friend, with thy protection cover this house, drive sickness, want,
and every evil out.*

This motto, on the wall of the Gasthof zùm Elephanten,
Brixen, Tyrol, can only be explained by a description of the
dial. It represents the Blessed Virgin crushing the serpent
which has wound itself round the globe on which she stands.
One foot is on the serpent's body, the other rests on the
crescent moon, from beneath which the reptile strives to lift

its head. The Virgin's eyes are raised to heaven, and she holds in her hand the lily and the cross. The hours are marked on a scroll across the globe, and the inscription is on another scroll below. The hotel takes its name from the Elephant which is painted in fresco on the other side of the house, where also is an inscription in old German explaining the picture, as follows :—

Als mà sagt 1551 Jar dĕ 2 tag Juni furwar
Was dises thier Elephãdt in teutschlãd unerkãt
Al hier durch gfuere worde unsĕre dĕ gros nan f^{tu} un Hern
Maximilian In Behan Kugreich Erhz^{gn} sũ Ost^{reich} de
Andre Bosch der liesz maln Lenhart Mair daz vefahn
Gott Will das haùs in seiner verhuetung haben
Des Inhaber leib Ehr und guet allizen bewaren
Au 1645 hat Lenhart Muller dis wider beerneurn lasen.

(As they say, 1551 year 2nd day of June in truth was this animal the Elephant unknown in Germany, brought here by our high and mighty Prince our Lord Maximilian in Bohemia kingdom, Archduke of Austria. Andre Bosch who experienced this made Lenhart Mais paint it. God will have the house in His protection the inhabitants' body, honour, and property, to keep from harm. In 1645 Lenhart Muller had this renewed again.)

There are also the following inscriptions :—

Wen da baut an der strassen muss Jederman au davon ròden lassen. 1713.

In Jahre 1870 hat Hanns Heiss diese Bilder wieder erneuern lassen v. mal. AR.

He who builds in the street must expect everyone to talk about it. 1713.

In the year 1870 Hanns Heiss caused these pictures to be renovated by the painter (?) A. R.

The sun-dial was probably painted at the same time.

374.

O SOLEIL, TU PARAIS, TU SOURIS, TU CONSOLES LA TERRE.

1852.

O sun, thou appearest, thou smilest, thou comfortest the earth.

On a house in the first hamlet on the road from Briançon to the Mont Genèvre. The dial is simply outlined, and has a peacock painted at the top.

375.

'Ω Θεὸς ὁ Θεὸς μοῦ πρὸς Σὲ ὀρθρίζω.

O GOD, Thou art my GOD, early will I seek Thee.

Ps. lxiii. 1, from the LXX. This verse is on a dial over the south porch of the church at Walkern, Herts. "The inscription is nearly obliterated," said Archdeacon Grant of St. Albans, in 1878, "but ought certainly to be preserved."

The following passage from Geikie's "Life of Christ" (vol. i., pp. 219, 222), helps to reveal the full meaning of this and similar verses in the Psalms. "The morning sacrifice could not be slain before the first appearance of the morning light. A watcher, therefore, standing on the roof of the Temple looked out for the first glimpse of Hebron, far off, on the hills, as the sign of morning having come. When it

was visible the summons was given—" Priests, to your
ministry! Levites, to your places! Israelites, take your
stations!" The priests then once more washed their feet and
hands and the service finally began. " With the first sight
of the rising sun every one bowed his head in prayer, wherever at the moment he may be. Yonder a Pharisee, who has
purposely let the hour overtake him in the street, suddenly
stops, and ties his Tephillin broader and larger than common on his forehead and arm. The olive gatherer, with his
basket, prays when he is in the tree. Pilgrims and citizens
are alike bent in prayer."

376.

O TV CHE IN ME GVARDI
VICIN MI TROVERAI QVÃDO
IO TIRO I COLPI SE BEN NON VEDI
CHE PIV CHE TV SCHIVAR IO BEN SO FARLI.

O thou who gazest on me here,
Time will be thou shalt find me near,
When I deal blows thou canst not see,
Ay, more of them than thou canst flee,
So deft in striking them I be.

On the church of Madonna di Campagna, near Pallanza.
The dial lines are traced in red on a plastered wall; a
skeleton, half-length, is resting his right hand on the gnomon,
and in his left holds a torch or scythe. The gnomon is gone,
and the dial much defaced. Trees now intercept the light.

377.

O TU, QUI BINAM UNO GNOMONE CONSPICIS HORAM,
HEU! MISER, IGNORAS QUA MORITURUS ERIS. 1822.

On one dial hours twain thou canst descry,
But not, alas! the hour when thou shalt die.

The "hours twain" referred to in this motto indicate the
arrangement of the figures on the dial, which, besides telling
the hour of the day in the usual manner, do also show the
time by the Italian mode of reckoning : that is, as the hours
are counted from sunset to sunset, going through the whole
course of the twenty-four numbers. The lines of these additional hours, from xii to xxiv, which are traced upon the
dial plane, declare the time by the shadow of a point in the
stile, as it falls upon them. The dial itself is a large and
wide one, the figures being represented in rolling clouds ;
and it is painted on a house wall that faces the sea at an
opening of the main street of Cogoletto, a fishing village
about eighteen miles west of Genoa, and a reputed birthplace
of Christopher Columbus. The room in which, it is said,
he was born, is still shown, and there are many inscriptions
on the outside of the house testifying to the tradition, which
were placed there by a member of the family in 1650. The
tradition is firmly held by the inhabitants ; and Washington
Irving, who disputes the claims of all other places, save
Genoa, nevertheless admits that there is some evidence in
favour of Cogoletto. Admiral Colombo, with whom the
great discoverer first sailed, was a native of this place ; and
the portrait of Colombus has been preserved here by his descendants. Tennyson seems to yield to this local claim :

"How young Columbus seem'd to rove,
Yet present in his native grove,
  Now watching high on mountain cornice,
And steering, now from a purple cove,
Now pacing mute by ocean's rim ;
Till in a narrow street and dim,
  I stay'd the wheels at Cogoletto,
And drank, and loyally drank to him."

378.

O VIATOR, HORAM BIBENDI ASPICE.

O wayfarer, behold the hour of drinking.

On the wall of a house at Champs, on the Col de Sestrières, near Fenestrellis, dated 1870. (See No. 193.)

379.

O WRETCHED MAN

REMEMBER THOU

MUST

DIE.

SENCE ALL THINGS

PASSE AND NOTHINGE

CERTAINE

BE.

This is one of the mottoes engraved on two sides of the square top to the solid pillar dial at Brougham Hall. On one of these sides is UT HORA SIC VITA with a skull carved below ; and on the other side is TEMPUS UT UMBRA PRAETERIT, with an hourglass beneath. The two remaining

Q

sides are occupied with the date 1660 : the initials $_{TE}^{B}$ (Thomas and Elizabeth Brougham) on one face, and on the

other an armorial shield, which bears a fret, the coat of either Fleming or Huddlestone.

380.

OBREPIT NON INTELLECTA SENECTUS.
1714.

Old age creeps on unawares.

On St. Bridget's Church, Bridestowe; and on St. Andrews', South Tawton, Devon.

The motto is from Ansonii Epigramm. 13.

> Senescimus, effugit aetas,
> Obrepit non intellecta senectus,
> Nec revocare potes, qui periere, dies.

381.

OBSERVE HOW FAST, TIME HURRIES PAST,
THEN USE EACH HOUR, WHILE IN YOUR POWER.
FOR COMES THE SUN, BUT TIME FLIES ON,
PROCEEDING EVER, RETURNING NEVER.

R. B.   1810.

On a fine pillar dial at Newhall, near Penicuik, N.B., which stands in the garden, upon four steps. Round the base of the pillar there are eight panels, arranged round the four sides, one above another. The motto is engraved on one of these panels, in another there is the following inscription : "Here Alexander Penicuik of Newhall M.D. is said to have given Allan Ramsay the plot of his celebrated Pastoral Comedy of the Gentle Shepherd." This explains the contents of the six remaining panels. (1) Contains a design consisting of shepherd's crook, and other pastoral implements. (2) Habbie's How, and Mause's Cottage, (Habbie's How is a romantic spot in the neighbourhood of Newhall, and Mause is one of the characters in the comedy). (3) The Washing Green, and Symon's house. (4) The Craigg Bield and Gland's On-stead, (Gland and Symon are also characters in the poem). (5) A ship enclosed in an oval margin. (6) "Here Allan Ramsay recited to his distinguished and literary patrons, as he proceeded with them, the scenes of his unequalled Pastoral Comedy, amid the objects and characters introduced into it."

382.

O'ER EVERY HOUR THAT'S BRIGHTEST
    A SHADOW CREEPS;
AND HE WHOSE LAUGH IS LIGHTEST
    FULL OFTEN WEEPS.
O LOOK WE FOR THE MORROW
    WHICH HATH NO NIGHT,
WHERE LOST IS EVERY SORROW
    IN GOD'S OWN LIGHT.

Suggested as a motto by the Rev. S. E. Bartleet.

383.

OF SHADE AND SUNSHINE FOR EACH HOUR
SEE HERE A MEASURE MADE:
THEN WONDER NOT IF LIFE CONSIST
OF SUNSHINE AND OF SHADE.

On a pleasant villa house at Wadsley, near Sheffield, called
" Dial House," is a stone dial let into the wall, which bears
the foregoing inscription.

384.

OGN' ORA UN ALTRA AL VIVER TUO SCHEMA
NON AL USARNE MAL PENSATI E TEMA.

Each hour is another in thy scheme of life,
Lest thou should use it ill—think and fear.

On a house, Piazza San Michele, Ventimiglia.

385.

ΟΥΡΑΝΟΝ . ʹΑ . ΧΩΡΥΣΑ . ΣΟΦΑ . ΛΙΘΟΣ .
ʹΑ . ΔΙΑ . ΤΥΤΘΟΥ . ΓΝΩΜΟΝΟΣ .
ΑΕΛΥΩ . ΠΑΝΤΙ . ΜΕΡΙΣΔΟΜΕΝΑ .

Exaequat caelum sapiens Lapis indice parvo,
Mensus quod solis flamma diurnat iter.

" *Behold, epitomised in this small space*
The swift revolving earth's diurnal wheel."

A writer in the "Gentleman's Magazine," Feb., 1792,
p. 121, said: "I found yesterday, in the 'Anthologia,' a
curious philosophical bagatelle, an inscription for a dial containing twelve words, and, as it seems, intentionally limited
to that number. It is well known to your Grecian readers
that λιθος, in the feminine, denotes a gem. This was probably therefore a very small dial."

The Latin and English versions of the inscription were
also given in the "Gentleman's Magazine." Both they and
the Greek lines have been exactly copied. We are not
responsible for the spelling. Probably ΑΕΛΥΩ should be
ΑΕΛΙΟΥ.

386.

OH, EARLY PASSENGER, LOOK UP, BE WISE,
AND THINK HOW, NIGHT AND DAY, TIME EVER FLIES.

At Tytherton Kellaways, Wilts. See No. 708.

387.

OH QE LE TEMP PASSE VITE!

Oh, how quickly time passes.

This quaintly spelt motto appears over the door of a small house which stands in a garden a little off the road between Cannes and Grasse. The dial is round, facing south, with a green background. It represents the sun's full face, broad and smiling, with his hair dressed after the fashion of a king in a pack of cards. He holds the gnomon like a pipe in the corner of his mouth, and seems to be regretting the swift passage of a jolly life.

388.

OMNES SECANT, ULTIMA NECAT.

All wound, the last kills.

At Vispthal.

389.

OMNES TIME PROPTER UNAM.

Fear every hour because of one (the last).

At Visp, in Switzerland.

390.

OMNIA CVM TEMPORE PRAETEREVNT.

All things pass away with time.

On a small brass sun-dial in the British Museum. It is

round in shape and beautifully engraved, showing the face of the sun and other ornaments. On one side is the dial, and on the other a perpetual calendar.

391.
OMNIA SOMNIA. A.D. 1680.
All things are dreams.

On the convent of St. Ursula, Valetta.

392.
OMNIA SUNT HOMINUM PENDENTIA FILO.
A.D. 1764.
All things that are of men are hanging on a thread.

On the Lodge, Wentworth Woodhouse, Yorkshire. See No. 701.

393.
OMNIA TEMPUS HABENT.
Eccl. iii. 1.
To everything there is a season.

On the church of St. Stefano, Belluno, see No. 150.

394.
OMNIBUS LUCET.
(The sun) shines for all.

On the tower of Long Sutton Church, Lincolnshire.

395.
OMNIS SPIRITUS LAUDET DOMINUM.
Let everything that hath breath praise the Lord.

Formerly at Great Smeaton.   See No. 437.

396.
ON THIS MOMENT HANGS ETERNITY.

On the church tower of Alfrick, Worcestershire, is a dial which until the last repainting bore this motto.   It is now no longer visible.

397.
ONCE AT A POTENT LEADER'S VOICE I STAY'D,
ONCE I WENT BACK WHEN A GOOD MONARCH
      PRAY'D ;
MORTALS : HOWE'ER WE GRIEVE, HOWE'ER DEPLORE,
THE FLYING SHADOW WILL RETURN NO MORE.

Taken from Cyrus Redding's "Fifty Years' Personal Recollections."

398.
OPPOSTO DI ME,
PENSI DI TE.
Think of thyself instead of me.

At the chateau of the Count Pinsuti, in Piedmont.

"Opposto" is in Piedmontese, "Au" (or "Al) posto." As is often the case in this dialect, a French word has been used, but here it has been misspelt.

399.

ORA ET LABORA.

Pray and work.

On the church at Northallerton, Yorkshire. The dial is quite plain in form.

400.

ORA, NE TE RAPIAT HORA.

Pray, that thou fallest not a prey to the hour.

This is inscribed high up on the tower of a large modern church in a small village of the Val Sesia, near Varallo, North Italy. The village has narrow shady streets, steep-roofed houses, and garden walls with vines straggling over them.

401.

ORDINATIONE TUA, REGE ET PROTEGE.

By thy ordainment, rule and protect.

On Visp church in the Rhone Valley, Switzerland. The motto is on the dial face, which also has the sun and a church painted on it.

402.

ORIENS EX ALTO VISITAVIT NOS:
MEMOR ESTO OCCASUS TUI.

The day-star from on high hath visited us :
Be thou mindful of thine own setting.

The first line is on the east face, the second on the west
face, of a dial at Round House Farm, Haverfield,
Gloucestershire.

403.

ORIMUR, MORIMUR.

We rise up, we die.

SEPTEM SINE HORIS.

Seven without the hours.

On a gable at Packwood Hall, Warwickshire. We are
told that when this motto was last painted, the artist unfor-
nately put *mortimur* for " morimur." We cannot doubt that
this is a true account of the position, for a sketch of the
square-shaped dial, immediately under a small window in the
angle of the gable, is before us, with the legend below. An
obliging communication, however, from Bishop Hobhouse,
informs us that the same words are also on a clock-face at
Packwood ; the word "orimur" being over an increasing
series of figures, and the word "morimur" over a de-
creasing series.

404.

OUR DAYS ON EARTH ARE AS A SHADOW
AND THERE IS NONE ABIDING.
1 *Chron.* xx. 15. 1860.

On a house at Lyme, Dorsetshire; and on a church at Charlton Kings, Somerset. Also on a dial placed on a buttress of Tutbury Church, Staffordshire.

The first part of the verse, " Our days upon earth are as a shadow," is on the church at Thornton, near Poulton-le-Fylde, Lancashire. This church was built in 1835.

405.

OUR DAYS ON EARTH ARE AS A SHADOW:
SO SOON PASSETH IT AWAY, AND WE ARE GONE.

In the gardens fronting the house at Gale Syke, Wastwater, is a horizontal dial thus inscribed. It was erected about 1852-3, and presented to the then owner of the place, Stansfield Rawson, Esq., by one of his daughters. It was said to have been designed by Mr. Rawson's son-in-law, the Rev. Dr. Worsley, late Master of Downing College, Cambridge.

406.

OUR DAYS PASS LIKE A SHADOW.

Is on the old church at Whitby, Yorkshire, cut in the stone, and dated 1757.

407.

OUR LIFE'S A FLYING SHADOW, GOD'S THE POLE:
THE INDEX POINTING AT HIM IS OUR SOUL;
DEATH'S THE HORIZON WHEN OUR SUN IS SET,
WHICH WILL, THROUGH CHRIST, A RESURRECTION
　　　GET.

This motto, together with *Mentiri non est me* (No. 309)
F. Thorpe, delineavit, 1843, might be read on the dial
on Ebberston Church, near Scarborough, until the recent
restoration. It was placed on the porch, but is now laid
aside. The same motto was on Glasgow Cathedral, together
with *Ex hoc momento pendet aeternitas,* and *Umbra labitur, et
nos umbrae,* but the dial was removed before the year 1852.
The stanza was placed alone on a dial on Milton Church,
Berks, in 1859.

408.

ΠΑΝΤΑ ΣΚΙΑ.

EDMOND BURTON.

נֵצֶל יְחֵינוּ עֲלֵי אָרֶץ.

MAUD BURTON, 1607.

HORA FUGIT

SIC TV.

All things are but shadow,

Our days on earth (are) as a shadow.

Time passes, so dost thou.

On the copper plate of a dial which has stood in the

Rectory Garden at Sutton Montis, Somerset, ever since it was put up in 1607. Edmond Burton was rector at the time of its erection.

409.

PAR LE SOLEIL JE DONNE L'HEURE,
ET EN DIEU TU TROUVES TON ESPOIR.

> *The sun reveals the hour by me,*
> *And God it is gives hope to thee.*

At Abriès, Dauphiné.

410.

PARTE L'OMBRA COL SOL, COL SOL RITORNA:
MA L'UOM QUAL OMBRA FUGGE, E PIÙ NON TORNA.

> *The shadow departs with the sun, with the sun returns:*
> *But man as the shadow flees, and returns no more.*

At Sordevole, in Piedmont.

411.

PENSA, UN DIO, UN ANIMA, UN ETERNITÀ.
RIPENSA, UN ORA IL TUTTO DECIDERA.

> *Think,—One God, one soul, one eternity.*
> *Think again—one hour will decide all.*

At Saure, near Tione, in the Trentino.

412.

PER I FELICI ED I TRISTI SEGNO UGUALMENTE LE ORE.

I mark the hours alike for the happy and the sad.

On a farmhouse in the neighbourhood of Lari, Tuscany, recorded by a writer in " Macmillan's Magazine."

413.

PEREUNT ET IMPUTANTUR. ᴛ.ᴊ.ᴬ. 1861.

They perish and are reckoned.

This is one of the Temple dial mottoes. The dial which bears it in Temple Lane has lately been restored, and placed in a slightly different place from that which it formerly occupied. The same motto was also on the south porch of Gloucester Cathedral, but at the recent restoration the dial was removed, and the older canopy work restored. At one time this inscription might have been read on Rotherham Church; St. Bunyan, Cornwall (dated 1757); and Bamburgh, Northumberland ; but the restoration of these churches has been fatal to the dials. There is a possibility of the Bamburgh one being put up in another place. St. Margaret's Church, Ipswich, once had a vertical dial over the porch with this same motto, but in 1867 it was removed, and after remaining for some time in a stonemason's yard, was sold by auction ; it is now in a meat salesman's yard at Ipswich, and has been regilt and painted. The elaborate dial placed by Sir Christopher Wren on the college of which he was a fellow, All Souls, Oxford, bears this motto. It may further be read on Lincoln Cathedral (see No. 59);

Kildwick Church, in Craven; on the cross dial at Elleslie (see No. 48); in the rectory garden at Micheldean (see No. 173); on the Municipio, Palermo; the Moot Hall, Aldeburgh, with No. 206; in the churchyard at Garstang, with the date 1757; at Brympton, near Yeovil, with 647; on the church of S. Crocifisso, Pieve di Cadore (see No. 205); and on the curious clock in Exeter Cathedral. The words are from an epigram by Martial, 5. 20. 11, the four last lines of which are as follows :—

> " Nunc vivit sibi neuter, heu ! bonosque
> Soles effugere atque abire sentit,
> Qui nobis *pereunt et imputantur ;*
> Quisquam vivere cum sciat, moratur ? "

Cowley translates these :—

> " Now to himself, alas ! does neither live,
> But sees good suns of which we are to give
> A strict account, set and doth march away :
> Knows a man how to live, and does he stay ? "

The sentiment is remarkable from a heathen writer, and somewhat more Christian, though often not more true, than that given to a lady who was being lionized at Oxford, and asked the meaning of the words—" They perish," said her waggish companion, " and are not thought of."

Pereunt et imputantur is also in the gardens of Bremhill Rectory, Wilts, on a dial which stands on a twisted column in the midst of flower-beds. It was put up by the Rev. W. L. Bowles, who also inscribed the following lines upon a hermitage, now destroyed, which stood near it :—

> To mark life's few but fleeting hours,
> I placed the dial 'midst the flowers

Which one by one came forth and died,
Still withering by its ancient side.
Mortal, let the sight impart
Its pensive moral to thy heart!

414.

PERGE SECURUS MONSTRO VIAM.

Proceed trustfully, I show the way.

On the outside of an ivory portarium, now in the possession of Charles T. Gatty. The motto evidently refers to the compass which is included in the portarium, rather than to the sun-dial. The name of Hans Troschel is given on the face of the dial. The portarium was bought at Nuremburg, and is apparently of the seventeenth century.

415.

PETITO QUOD JUSTUM.

Seek what is just.

In Jamaica there is an old Spanish sun-dial placed on the parapet of the platform, before the main entrance to Great Pond House, parish of St. Anne, just in front of a pomegranate tree, which springs from the rock opposite the dial. The dial is inscribed as above.

416.

PLURES LABORI, DULCIBUS QUIDAM OTIIS.

Most to work, some to pleasant ease.

M. de Fienhet, Counsellor of State to Louis XIV., set up

many dials, and the one which he erected on his house in
Paris bore the above motto. It was supported by figures of
Labour and Rest. For the motto on his country house, see
No. 114.

417.

PORTATRICE A VOI DI BENE,

L'ORE SIAM DE' DI SERENI,

SI ANNOTTA, O TUONA, O PIOVE

NOI FUGGIAM IN GREMBO A GIOVE.

Bearers of wealth to you, the sons of men,
Are we, the sunlight hours of days serene;
If night, or rain, or thunder blur the sky,
Into our Father's bosom back we fly.

So the late Dean Alford translated the motto which he
found at Vignale, in Piedmont.

418.

POST EST OCCASIO CALVA.

Opportunity is bald behind.

"Take Time by the forelock," says the adage. The
whole line is: "Fronte capillatâ, post est occasio calva," as
already stated (see No. 156). The above motto is on the
church tower at Yaxley, Huntingdonshire. The dial bears
the date of its renewal in 1818, but the motto is now almost
obliterated. It is also on Horton Church, Dorset.

"The moment that is past returns no more ;
The hour mis-spent can never be recalled !
Old Chronos has but one poor lock before,
His head, behind, is altogether bald.
Take that from me.

THOS. ELWOOD.

R

419.

POST TENEBRAS LUX.

After darkness light.

A modern dial, near the corner of a house with a high
garden wall, at Varenna, on the Lake of Como, bears this
inscription.   The Rev. Samuel Clark, writing in 1656
(" Mirror for Saints and Sinners "), observes that these words
were written upon " a marble table in the town house of
Geneva.   Before Master Calvin opened their eyes by his
ministry, their motto was *Post tenebras spero lucem.*   Since
they altered it to *Post tenebras lux."*

420.

POST TENEBRAS SPERO LUCEM.

After darkness I hope for light.

At Jordan gate, Macclesfield.   (See No. 340.)

421.

POSUI DEUM ADJUTOREM MEUM.

I have placed God as my helper.

On pillar dial at Corpus Christi Coll.   (See No. 134.)

422.

PRAESTANT AETERNA CADUCIS.

The things eternal excel the transient.

Noted in North Italy.

423.

PRAETERIT AETAS NEC REMORANTI
LAPSA RECEDUNT SAECULA CURSU,
UT FUGIT AETAS UTQUE CITATUS
TURBINIS INSTAR VOLVITUR ANNUS,
SIC QUOQUE NOSTRA PRAECIPITANTER
VITA RECIDIT OCIOR UNDIS.

*Time passes, and with no lingering passage the ages vanish.
As time flies, and as the year rolls on, hurried as the whirlwind,
so suddenly doth our life fail, swifter than the waves.*

On the back of a curious old sun-dial formerly at Park
Hill, near Oswestry. On the sides were the following
mottoes :

TEMPUS OMNIUM PARENS.

Time the father of all things.

TEMPUS EDAX RERUM.

Time the devourer of all.

At the base :

TEMPORI PARE.

Obey time.

1578.

The " Archæological Journal " (xiii. 417), gives a figure
of the dial, and says, " It measures about four feet in height,
exclusive of the two footing courses. There has evidently
been another inscription which is now defaced. There are
seven dials on this curious example. At the time when the
dial was erected the family of Ap Howell or Powell owned

Park Hill, and it remained in their hands till 1717." This
was written in 1856. Unfortunately the dial no longer
exists. An attempt was made to move it, and it fell to
pieces.

424.

PRAETEREUNT. IMPUTANTUR.

They pass by.   They are reckoned.

There are two sun-dials at Farnham Castle, on the walls
of the entrance tower.   They had formerly the inscription
" Eheu, fugaces labuntur anni ;" but have now the more
befitting words " Praetereunt," on the one, and " Imputantur " on the other.

425.

PRAETERITUM NIHIL,
PRAESENS INSTABILE,
FUTURUM INCERTUM.

*The past is nothing, the present unstable, the future
uncertain.*

Once in the pleasure ground of Knole Park, Sevenoaks,
stood a white marble pillar dial, the gnomon of which is supported by an earl's coronet.   It has been removed to the
garden of a neighbouring farm-house, and bears the foregoing motto.   Knole was the property of the Duke of
Dorset, whose co-heiresses were his two sisters, the elder of
whom married the Earl of Plymouth, and inherited the estate.
She afterwards became the Countess Amherst.   In default
of issue, the estate passed to the younger sister, the wife of
Earl Delawarr, who was created Baroness Buckhurst in her
own right, with remainder to her second son, who is now in
possession of Knole.

426.

PRAETERITUM NIHIL,
PRAESENS INSTABILE,
FUTURUM IGNOTUM.

The past is nothing, the present unstable, the future unknown.

On a silver dial in the Museum at Copenhagen, which was made by Thomas Tuttell.

427.

PRAY, FOR THE HOUR PASSETH AWAY.

Recorded in the "Leeds Monthly" as being inscribed on a dial which hangs upon the front of a house at Monk Fryston, near Selby.

428.

PREPARE TO MEET THY GOD.
LAT. 53 DEG. 26 MIN.
TEMPUS FUGIT UT UMBRA.
Time flies as a shadow.

GLORIA DEI.
The glory of God.

These mottoes are on the porch dial of Bradfield Church, in the parish of Ecclesfield, Yorkshire. The church is a fine one of fifteenth century date, and is nobly placed, over-looking the moors and the valley, through which the flood, caused by the bursting of the Dale Dyke Reservoir, poured down into Sheffield in the night of March 11, 1864, when 250 persons were drowned. The church was well restored during the years 1871-1888, whilst the Rev. Reginald A. Gatty was rector.

429.

PROPERAT HORA MORTIS:
ULTIMA CUIVIS EXPECTANDA DIES.
LUX UMBRA DEI.
DUM SPECTAS FUGIO.
TENERE NON POTES, POTES NON PERDERE DIEM.
JOHANNES WATKINS, 1695.

The hour of death hastens on: the last day is to be looked for by each one. Light is the shadow of God. Whilst thou lookest I fly. Thou canst not hold, thou canst not destroy a day.

These mottoes were on a dial which formerly stood in a garden at East Harptree, belonging to Lieut. Wm. Hooper, R.N. It is not known whether he found the dial there in 1831 when he bought the place, or whether he erected it. The dial stood on a pedestal. In 1861, Mr. Hooper died, and his widow removed the dial to Bath, where it remained unused till 1870, when Mrs. Hooper went to live with her son, Rev. H. Hooper, at Ripley, Surrey, and the dial was re-erected in his garden. In 1879 his house was made the Vicarage of Ripley.

430.

PUDOR SIT UT DILVCVLVM.

A.D. MDCCCIL. ÆQVI NOCTIALIS.

Let shame be [*rosy*] *as the dawn.*

The dial which bears this inscription is on a horizontal

slab of white marble in the cloisters of the Certosa, Val
d'Ema, near Florence. It tells the hours from two to six, p.m.
to the few remaining inmates of

> " . . . . The huge battlemented convent block
> Over the little forky flashing Greve
> That takes the quick turn at the foot o' the hill
> Just as one first sees Florence."
> *The Ring and the Book.*

431.

PULVIS ET UMBRA SUMUS.

We are dust and shadow.

In Leyland churchyard, Lancashire; also in Grappenhall
churchyard, Cheshire, dated 1714; and formerly on the
keep of Carlisle Castle, see No. 78. The line is from
Horace, Book iv., Ode 7. Hogarth inscribed it under a
mural sun-dial in his picture of "Chairing the Member;"
a skull and cross-bones ornament the gate posts below.

432.

PUÒ FALLARE LA CAMPANA IL FERRO,
MA RISPLENDE (IL) SOLE IO NON ERRO.

The iron bell may wrongly tell,
I err not, if the sun shine well.

At Comano, in the Trentino.

433.

QUA HORA NON PUTATIS FILIUS HOMINIS VENIET.

Luc. 12. v. 40.

The Son of Man cometh at an hour when ye think not.

On a brass portable universal dial in Trêves Museum.

434.

QUA REDIT NESCITIS HORAM.

You know not the hour in which He returns.

A western dial thus inscribed stood formerly on an old gable in Lincoln's Inn. It was renewed in 1794, when the great William Pitt was treasurer, and bears this date and the initials W. P. When the old buildings were taken down the dial was removed to the Stone Buildings, and placed near the windows of Mr. Pitt's chambers. The same motto, is at the Chantry, Newark (See No. 505); and on Threckingham Church, Lincolnshire.

435.

QUAE LENTA ACCEDIT QUAM VELOX PRAETERIT HORA.

Simpson. A.D. 1820.

The hour that comes slowly, how swiftly doth it pass.

On a dial at Wigton Hall, Cumberland.

436.

QUAELIBET EST INDEX FUNERIS HORA TUI.

Any hour is the signal for thy death.

On an ivory portarium in the National Museum at Munich, see No. 258.

437.

QUALIS VITA FINIS ITA. 1809. W. DEACON.

As the life, so the end.

OMNIS SPIRITUS LAUDET DOMINUM.

Let everything that hath breath praise the Lord.

LEX DEI, LUX DIEI.

The law of God is the light of day.

LUX UMBRA DEI.

Light is the shadow of GOD.

Formerly on the church of Great Smeaton, Yorkshire, but the dial was removed in 1872, when the church was restored. The first motto is at Ballafreer Farm, Isle of Man. See No. 22.

438.

QUAM CITO JUCUNDI PRAETERIERE DIES.

How quickly the pleasant days have passed away.

On a cruciform dial erected by the Rev. W. L. Bowles in the grounds of his canonical residence in the Close, Salisbury, 1829.

439.

QUANDO DI NUBI AL SOL SGOMBRA É LA VIA,
ALLO STANCO VISITANTE ADOTT' É L' ORA
CHE LO CHIAMA AL RISTORO E ALL' ALLEGRIA.

When the path of the sun is free from clouds,
To the weary traveller is brought round the hour
Which calls him to refreshment and mirth.

Beyond Varenna the road to Colico winds along the shores
of the Lake of Como, and passes a little roadside *osteria*, over
the door of which is a rough sun-dial with the above motto.
It serves as a sign to the inn, as well as to indicate the
time.

440.

QUASI PHOENIX EXICINERE MEO
RESURGAM.

Like the Phœnix I shall arise from mine ashes.

AMICIS QUAELIBET HORA.

To friends—any hour they please.

At Chatillon, Val d'Aosta. Recorded in " Notes and
Queries," 4th Series, ix. Sep. 73.

441.

QUE TOUTES LES HEURES DU JOUR VOUS TROUVENT
TRAVAILLENT POUR L'ÉTERNITÉ.

1849.   Z. G. F.

Let every hour of the day find you working for eternity.

At Abriès, Dauphiné.

442.

QUELLE HEURE EST-IL?
PEUT-ETRE LA MIENNE.
1853. Andeyer.

What is the hour?
Perchance my (last).

At Les Orres, Canton d'Embrun, Dauphiné. "Andeyer" is the name of a former Maire.

443.

QUI LUCEM DE TENEBRIS LUCET IN CORDE.

He who sends light from darkness shines in our heart.

"God who commanded the light to shine out of darkness hath shined in our hearts," 2 Cor. iv. 6, will have suggested this motto, which is on the old Grammar School at Wellingborough, near the church ; and there is the further inscription :—

ΉΜΕΡΑΙ ὡσεὶ ΣΚΙΑ.

Our days are as a shadow.

A sun with rays occupies the upper part, and the Latin line is written round it. The school was rebuilt in 1620.

444.

QUI NON EST HODIE.

Which is not to-day (lit.).

Above a window dial in The Hall at Nun Appleton, Yorkshire. It is difficult to suppose that the rest of the line from whence these words are taken (Ovid, Rem. Amor., 94), did not at one time occupy the corresponding place below

the dial, but it is not there now. See Nos. 76 and 247. At the four corners of the dial are figures representing the four seasons, with the following lines from Ovid (Rem. Amor. 187-88):—

POMA DAT AUTUMNUS, FORMOSA EST MESSIBUS AESTAS,
VER PRAEBET FLORES, IGNE LEVATUR HIEMS.

> *Autumn gives fruits, Summer fair with corn appears,*
> *Spring bestows flowers, Winter fire cheers.*

In the centre pane a Cupid holds contemplatively a smaller dial.

The window probably dates from the beginning of the eighteenth century, when the greater part of the house was rebuilt by Sir William Milner, whose arms are displayed in a

corresponding pane of glass. The hall itself may possibly
belong to the older house built by the great Lord Fairfax,
and written of by Andrew Marvel, who fondly predicts
that :—

> " The after age
> Shall hither come on pilgrimage,
> These sacred places to adore,
> By Vere and Fairfax trod before."

445.

QUID CELERIUS TEMPORE ?

What is swifter than time ?

One of the mottoes on the cross-dial at Elleslie, near
Chichester, see No. 48.

446.

QUID CELERIUS UMBRA ?

What swifter than shadow?

On a dial which formerly stood in the Isle of Man. See
No. 331.

447.

QUOD FUIT, EST, ET ERIT, PERIT ARTICULO BREVIS
ORAE (*sic*)
ERGO QUID PRODEST ESSE, FUISSE, FORE?
ESSE, FUISSE, FORE, HEU! TRIA FLORIDA SUNT SINE
FLORE,
NAM SIMUL OMNE PERIT QUOD FUIT, EST, ET ERIT.

> What is, has been, shall come,
> Fades in a moment brief :

Three flowers that never bloom,
  Nought do they bring but grief,
What is, has been, shall come,
  Dies like the fallen leaf.

Inscribed beneath a sun-dial at Monza.   See " Notes and
Queries," 7th Series, vol. i., p. 187 (March, 1886).

448.

QUOD PETIS UMBRA EST.
What thou seekest is a shadow.

At Hebden Bridge, near Halifax, Yorkshire.

449.

QUOTA SIT HORA PETIS, DUM PETIS IPSA FUGIT, NEC QUAE PRAETERIT, HORA REDIRE POTEST.

You ask the hour : meanwhile you see it fly,
Nor can the hour return that passes by.

At the Villa Modena, Varese.

450.

QUOTIDIE MORIOR.
I die daily.

On a dial over the porch of St. Ive's Church, near Liskeard.
The plate is ornamented with a coiled serpent at the top,
and a Tudor rose at the bottom.   It is dated 1695.

451.

REDEEM Y(ᴱ) TIME.
V.R.I. Reg. Annº Domⁱ 1849.

Over the porch of Shelton Church, Long Stratton, Norfolk.
Possibly this dial has been restored, or it may have been put
up to replace the older one which is figured in Ladbroke's
" Churches of Norfolk," 1820-30, as being on the porch. The
same motto is on St. John's Church, Cookbury, Devon ;
and at Brackley, Northamptonshire ; and it is probably a
mutilated version of the same inscription which remains as
" Rede the time" on one of the chimneys of Weston Mill
farmhouse, in the parish of St. Budeaux. This dial plate is
of Delabole slate, and is dated 1670 ; the letters of the
inscription are cut in bold Roman characters. Mr. Harry
Hems, in the " Western Morning News," said that the
dial was erected in the same year as the one which is over
the church porch, and the charge for this is entered in the
churchwarden's accounts thus :—

" For the Diall	.	.	. £1	17	6
— time a fetching the Diall	.			1	6
— beere for the workman when					
hee set up the Diall	.			0	6."

Richard Knighton and John Marten were churchwardens at
this time, and the former was owner of Weston Mill farm.
For more than two hundred years the Knightons were connected with St. Budeaux' parish. Mrs. Janet Knighton was
chosen churchwarden in 1690, and her name appears at
different times in the parish accounts. In 1684 she charged
for two repairs to parish property, " 6ᵈ for mending the
Dyell," and 9ᵈ for repairing the stocks.

452.

REDEEMING THE TIME.

1725. T.T.

These words from Eph. v. 16 are on the Dial House at Twickenham, the property of Richard Twining, Esq.

The dial was put up by Mr. Thomas Twining, who died in 1741, and was the founder of the well-known tea warehouse in the Strand. It is thought that from continually observing the

dial on St. Clement Danes as he went to and from his business, he desired to have one of his own, and so added this to the house which he built at Twickenham. Some years ago it was taken down, and repainted, and under it was found a fresco painting of a figure of Time, with an hour-glass in his hand, and a cock at his feet.

453.

REDIBO, TU NUNQUAM.

I shall return, thou never.

At Erith, in Kent. Also at Tytherton Kellaways, Wilts. See No. 708.

454.
REMEMBER. 1803.

At West Ham.

455.
REMEMBER NOW THY CREATOR IN THE DAYS OF THY YOUTH.

On the Lyme Cage, Disley.   See No. 700.

456.
REMEMBER THY LATTER END.
A.D. 1810.

On the tower of Haworth Church, Yorkshire.

457.
REMOVE NOT THE ANCIENT LANDMARK WHICH THY FATHERS HAVE SET UP.
RICHARD HART, *Vestry Clerk*, 1802.

The above verse from Prov. xxii. 28, is inscribed round the shaft of a dial which stands upon four old steps in the parish churchyard at Folkestone, and marks the spot where by the ancient charters of the Corporation, the Mayor of Folkestone was annually elected.   It was restored in 1863. On the dial plate the names of Thomas Baker, and John Bolder, Churchwardens, are engraved, with the date, 1783.

s

458.

RES SACRAS CLERI, THEMIDIS, MARTISQUE LABORES,
ET PATRIOS COETUS, LUMEN ET UMBRA REGIT.

The sacred work of the church, the toils of Themis and of Mars,
the councils of the nation too, light and shadow rule.

The Cathedral of Fréjus in the Department du Var,
France, is a Romanesque building of the eleventh and twelfth
centuries. Over one of the doors, with ivy growing up the
side, is a wooden dial, painted blue with gilt lettering, and
thus inscribed.

459.

RESPICITE, NON MIHI SOLI LABORAVI, 1593.

Mark ye, not for myself alone have I toiled.

On the triangular Lodge at Rushton, Northamptonshire,
which was built by Sir Thomas Tresham, and is an architectural curiosity. The building is in fine preservation, and
has on each side three gables, which severally terminate in a
pinnacle, and on the centre gable of each side there is a sun-
dial with an inscription. On one is the word " Respicite ; "
on another, " Non mihi ; " and " Soli laboravi " on the third.
The plan of the building is symbolic of the Trinity, which is
also expressed in the trefoil that forms part of the family
crest.

Sir Thomas Tresham, who founded this lodge on his
estate, was knighted by Queen Elizabeth at Kenilworth
Castle ; but being a firm adherent of the Roman Church,
like his ancestors before him, he suffered a long imprison-
ment in the Castle of Wisbech for recusancy. Indeed, for
this offence he was three times in custody ; his last commit-

ment being on the 31st December, 1596, from which he was
discharged by warrant on the 8th December, 1597. He was
a skilful architect, and built the market-house at Rothwell.
" Having many daughters," says Fuller, " and being a great
housekeeper, he matched most of them into honourable, the rest
of them into worshipful and wealthy families." They were six
in number. The following extract from a letter, written by
Sir Thomas Tresham, about 1584, is curious :—" If it be demanded why I labour so much in the Trinity and Passion of
Christ, to depaint in this chamber, this is the principal instance thereof; That at my last being hither committed, and
I usually having my servants here allowed me, to read nightly
an hour to me after supper, it fortuned that Fulcis, my then
servant, reading in the ' Christian Resolution,' in the treatise
of ' Proof that there is a God, &c.' there was upon a wains-
coat table at that instant three loud knocks (as if it had been
with an iron hammer) given, to the great amazing of me and
my two servants, Fulcis and Nilkton." This story remains
to show that there is nothing new under the sun—not even
" table-rapping." The triangular Lodge is rich in pious
emblems and inscriptions — a noble monument of Sir
Thomas's zeal for Trinitarian doctrine. His family was
ancient and influential by wealth and character.

460.

RETAIN YOUR LOYALTY, PRESERVE YOUR RIGHTS.

This motto is engraved upon the base of a tall pillar dial
at Appleby, which was erected and inscribed by Anne
Clifford, Countess of Pembroke, Dorset, and Montgomery.
The dial pillar stands in a prominent position at the top of the

principal street, opposite to the parish church, in which there is a monument with a life-sized recumbent figure of the countess. She lived 1590 to 1675, and was a lady of very strong character and determined will. She fought successfully for her own "rights" on several occasions against strong enemies. James I. tried to prevent her from succeeding as her father's sole heiress to the office of hereditary high sheriff of Westmoreland, but she eventually obtained the post, and held it to the end of her life. She defended her castles against Cromwell, and had disputes with the court of Charles II., so it may fairly be concluded that the precept which she chose for her dial was one which she had practised herself under considerable difficulties. For a description of another dial erected by her near Brougham, see " Further Notes on Remarkable Dials."

461.

RITORNA IL SOL DALL' OMBRA SPARITA :
MA NON RITORNA, NO, L'ETÀ FINITA.

The sun returns which has been made to disappear by the shadow :
but there is no return, none, of Time gone by.

This was on a house, 22, Via Gregoriana, in Rome. Also on the wall of the Douane at Isella is the same motto, somewhat varied :—

TORNA TORNANDO IL SOL DALL' OMBRA SPARITA,
MA NON RITORNA PIÙ L'ETÀ FUGITA.

Turning returns the sun in shadow thrown,
But never Time returns which once hath flown.

The writing, which is very much defaced, may be just

read between arches that run along the front of the building. This stands close upon the great Simplon road, and is the first or last halting-place on the Italian frontier. [The motto has now, 1888, entirely disappeared.]

462.

SACRA THEMIS MORES UT PENDULA DIRIGIT HORAS.

Sacred Justice guides manners, as the dial does the hours.

At the Palais de Justice, Paris.

463.

SANS DIEU L'ON NE PEUT RIEN. SOL EST REGULA.

Without God one can do nothing.
The sun is the rule.

On a house at Briançon.   The dial is merely outlined.

464.

SANS LA CLARTÉ NI LA CHALEUR N'AURIONS NI HEURE NI FLEUR. 1844. Z. G. F.

'Tis the light that marks the hour,
'Tis the heat that makes the flower.

At Argentière, near Vallouse.

465.

SANS LE SOLEIL JE NE SUIS RIEN, ET TOI,
SANS DIEU TU NE PEUT RIEN.   1843.

*Without the sun I can do nothing, and thou, without God thou
canst do nothing.*

On an out-lined dial seen at the top of the Mont Genèvre
Pass.

466.

SAPIENS DOMINABITUR ORBI.

The wise man shall rule the world.

On a small brass dial-plate seen in a shop in Nuremburg.

467.

SAPIENTES NUMERANT HORAS.

The wise count the hours.

Upon a dial on the front of Langston House, South
Devon, which is the property of the Courtenay Bulteels, but
the inscription is the punning motto of the Wise family.

468.

SAPIENTIS EST NUMERARE.

It is the wise who counts.

Formerly at King's Lynn.   See No. 316.

469.

SCIS HORAS, NESCIS HORAM.

Thou knowest the hours, thou knowest not the hour.

On the convent of Cimièż, near Nice.   See No. 112.

470.

SE IL MOTO TALOR NON SEGNO L' ORE,
DELLA NATURA SOLO È COLPA IL GIOCO;
SE SI SPIEGA LA CENSURA IL SUO FURORE,
INVIDIA E NON RAGION VI PUÒ DAR LOCO.

L' ETERNO FACITOR CON GIUSTO PESO
L' OPRE SUE COMPARSE CON MISURA;
SE IN CIÒ CREDE TALUN D' ESSERNE LESO,
STOLTO! L' OPRE DIVINE ALLOR CENSURA.

SE IL SOL RESPLENDE IN PIENO GIORNO,
SE IL MONTE OPPOSTO NON TOGLIE I RAGGI,
VERGATE ORE AVRAI A TE D' INTORNO,
QUETI E MUTI FARÒ I MENO SAGGI.

If the shade sometimes fail the hour to name,
The freak of Nature is alone to blame;
And if to wrath the critic be inclined,
Anger, not reason, governeth his mind.

The Eternal Maker all His works hath made
With justest measure, in right balance weighed;
If man there be who thinks they do him wrong,
Fool! what he blames to works divine belong.

If the sun shineth forth in fullest day,
And if the mount in front hide not his ray,
The hours thou shalt then have all marked around,
And the least wise must still and dumb be found.

These inscriptions are the mottoes on three separate dials, which are placed on the sides of the tower of the Campanile at Trafiume, near Canobbio, on the Lago Maggiore. Near the top of the tower is the date thus given :—" Anno Domini MDCCCVIII Ristaurato nel 1808. Capo Maestro Andrea de Bernardi." Each verse is written below its respective dial. We may assume there were dials before the year named.

471.

SE IL SOL BENIGNO MI CONCEDE IL RAGGIO,
L'ORA TI MOSTRA, E IL CIEL TI DIA BUON VIAGGIO.

If the sun granteth me his kindly ray,
It shows the hour, Heaven guide thee on thy way.

Was read somewhere on the route between Florence and Bologna.

472.

SE ME MIRAS, ME MIRAN.

If thou lookest at me, they look at me.

In Spain. The sun speaks to the dial, of men. See No. 33.

473.

SECULA SIC FUGIENT, SIC LUX, SIC UMBRA THEATRUM
DONEC (S)TELLIGERUM CLAUSERIT UNA DIES.
SIC PETIT OCEANUM PHOEBUS, SIC VITA SEPULCRUM.
(D) UM (SENSIM) TACITA VOLVITUR HORA ROTA.

> *So fly the ages, light and shade shall fly,*
> *Till one day close the starry scene on high.*
> *So Phœbus seeks the ocean, life the urn,*
> *While on still wheels the hours softly turn.*

Inscribed round the circle of hours, on a slate dial face, at
Balla Killey, near Rushen, in the Isle of Man. On referring to No. 499 it will be seen that the lines are identical
with an " Inscription on a sun-dial in a circle," which was
published in the " Gentleman's Magazine," September, 1802.
There, however, the first two lines are those which in the
Balla Killey motto are placed last. It seems probable that the
maker of the Manx dial in 1830, copied the inscription from
the " Gentleman's Magazine," and was a better mathematician than scholar, since he treated the Latin and Greek
mottoes in a very reckless fashion. The word *sensim* was
omitted, thereby preventing the fourth line from scanning,
and *clauserit* written as two words—*claus erit*. There is a
motto at each corner of the plate—

(1) Ζωὴ ατμὴ σκιὴ,

rendered below *Life is the Spectator* (query *Spectre?*) *of a
shadow,* instead of *Life* (*is*) *smoke, shadow,* which is the
literal interpretation. In the word ατμη the smooth breath-
ing ought to be over the letter α instead of τ. The usual
form of the word is ἀτμὸς.

(2) VENI, VIDE, VALE (*Come, see, farewell*).

(3) LEARN TO VALUE YOUR TIME.

(4) EVERY DAY BRINGS LIFE NEARER.

On the dial is further written :—

RICH^D. WATTERSON'S
DIAL,

Kentraighmill, in the Isle of Man.

Lat. 54°, 20 N. ; Long. 4°, 30′ W.

MDCCCXXX.

474.

SED FUGIT INTEREA, FUGIT IRREPARABILE TEMPUS,
SINGULA DUM CAPTI CIRCUMVECTAMUR AMORE.

JOHN DEVASTON fecit. 1789.

But meanwhile time flies, flies irretrievably,
While we, love stricken, dwell on each thing.

These lines from Virgil, Georg. III., 284-5, were placed by Mr. Devaston on a house dial at West Felton, Salop.

475.

SEE, AND BEGONE ABOUT YOUR BUSINESS.

On a dial over the south porch of Chesterton Church, county Warwick.

476.

SEE THE LITTLE DAYSTAR MOVING—
LIFE AND TIME ARE WORTH IMPROVING,
  SEIZE THE MOMENTS WHILE THEY STAY:
SEIZE AND USE THEM,
LEST YOU LOSE THEM,
  AND LAMENT THE WASTED DAY.

Mr. Howard Hopley has recorded this motto, without
naming the locality ; and he says, "The little daystar was a
spot of light falling through a hole in the pointer, to indicate
the hour."

477.

SEEK YE THE LORD WHILE HE MAY BE
FOUND.

Isaiah, cap. iv. 6.

On the south-west porch of Mattishall Church, Norfolk,
dated 1857, and probably a restoration of the older dial,
figured in Mr. Ladbroke's "Churches of Norfolk," 1825-30.

478.

SEGNO LE ORE SÌ, MA NON PIÙ QUELLE.

I mark the hours 'tis true, but no longer those gone by.

On a farmhouse in the neighbourhood of Lari, Tuscany,
and noted by a writer in "Macmillan's Magazine."

479.
SEGNO SOLO LE ORE SERENE.

I mark only the bright hours.

This motto is on a modern dial on the wall of the back of Villa Novello, at Genoa. A bank separates the house from the sea, which it faces, and is luxuriantly covered with aloes, prickly pear, and other plants so familiar along the Riviera. The strong north wind sweeps down, and prevents the same careful cultivation of this spot which prevails in the rest of the garden ; but its wild luxuriance is very charming.

480.
SEMITAM, PER QUAM NON REVERTAR, AMBULO.

Job. xvi.

I go the way by which I shall not return.

The reference is evidently to the words, " When a few years are come, then I shall go the way whence I shall not return," Job xvi. 22. The dial is modern, and without date. It is painted yellow, bordered with grey. It is placed south declining west, on the wall of the church at Lavagna on the Riviera di Levante. The gnomon comes from the mouth of the sun, as if it were the tongue with which he was speaking. Lavagna lies between Chiavari and Sestri Levante. It formerly belonged, together with the greater part of the east coast, to the Fieschi of Genoa, who bore the title of Counts of Lavagna—notably so to that Gian Luigi Fieschi, who was the author of the famous conspiracy against Andrea Doria. The dial is beside the great door of the church, to which a flight of marble steps leads up, and which faces the sea.

481.

SEMPRE A VOI SEGNI ORE TRANQUILLE IL SOLE,
QUASI RAGGIO DI LEI CHE QUI SI COLE.

May the sun always mark tranquil hours to you,
As it were a beam from Her who is honoured here.

At Villa Mylius, Genoa, there is a plaster cast of the
Madonna and Child, and immediately above the figures a
dial is painted on the wall with the above motto. It is also
on the Sanctuary at Graglia, near Biella.

482.

SENESCIS ASPICIENDO.

Thou growest older whilst thou lookest.

On a dial at Versailles. See Nos. 35, 128.

483.

SENSIM SED PROPERE FLUIT IRREMEABILIS HORA:
CONSULE, NE PERDAS ABSQUE LABORE DIEM.

Gently but swiftly flows on the hour that can never return.
Consider well, that thou lose not the day without its work.

On a hospital at Casamicciola, Ischia. The town was
destroyed by an earthquake in 1881.

484.

SENSIM SINE SENSU.

Softly and no man knows.

Friston, or Bechyngton Place, now a farmhouse in a deep

dell, relieved with ancient elms, has features of antiquity, including a hall, the roof of which belongs to the fourteenth century. In the great window is a sun-dial, with the motto given above. (LOWER's "History of Sussex," 1870, vol. i., p. 193.)

485.

SENZA L' OMBRA NON DILETTO,
E PUR L' OMBRA È MIO DIFETTO.

Without a shadow I do not please ;
Nevertheless a shadow is my defect.

At Strevi, Monferrato.

486.

SENZA PARLAR IO SONO INTESO,
SENZA FAR RUMOR LE ORE PALESO.

Without speaking I am understood :
Without noise I reveal the hours.

On a wall by the roadside, near Pieve di Sori, Riviera di Levante ; also at Sordevole in Piedmont ; and at Bordighera. Dean Alford notes and translates this motto :—

"I speak not, yet all understand me well ;
I make no sound, and yet the hours I tell."

A gentleman walking from Como to Monte Generoso observed at Balerna a slightly different version, which is also at Balmuccia, Val Sesia ; and at Castasegna Val Bregaglia.

SENZA PARLAR DA TUTTI SON INTESO,
SENZA FAR RUMOR L' ORA PALESO.

Without speaking I am understood by all :
Without making a noise I reveal the hour.

487.

SENZA SOLE IO RIPOSO.
Without the sun I rest.

Traced on the wall of the Albergo del Gatto, a wayside
inn at Riva, Riviera di Ponente.

488.

SEPTEM SINE HORIS.
Seven without the hours.

The meaning of this bald inscription must be, that there
are, in the longest days, seven hours (and a trifle over) in
which the dial is useless. The motto is on a dial erected on
a gable at Packwood Hall, in the county of Warwick. See
No. 403.

489.

SEPTIES IN DIES LAUDEM DIXI TIBI.
Seven times a day do I praise thee.—Ps. cxix., 164.

Over the north door of the Cathedral at Padua.

490.

SET ME RIGHT AND USE ME WELL,
AND I Yᴱ TIME TO YOU WILL TELL.

Is engraved on an old pocket dial, which its owner thus
describes :—" It is a ring of brass, much like a miniature
dog-collar ; and has, moving in a groove in its circumference,
a narrower ring with a boss, pierced by a small hole to admit

a ray of light. The latter ring is made movable to allow
for the varying declination of the sun in the several months
of the year, and the initials of these are marked in ascending
and descending scale on the larger ring which bears the
motto. The hours are lined and numbered in the opposite
concavity." A similar dial belonging to a cottager at Pelynt,
Cornwall, is described and figured in " The Reliquary."

Mr. Lewis Evans has a ring dial, made by Proctor, with a
slightly different version of the above inscription; it is arranged
thus :—

SET ME	USE ME	AND I
RIGHT	WELL	TIME TELL.

491.

SHADOWS CAST UPON THE DIAL SHOW
THE PRESENCE OF THE SUN ABOVE;
SHADOWS CAST UPON OUR LIFE BELOW
TRUE TOKENS ARE THAT GOD IS LOVE.
April 6, 1882.

On a dial in Ovingdean churchyard, Sussex.

492.

SHADOWS WE ARE, AND
LIKE SHADOWS DEPART.

In Pump Court, Temple; and at Menwith Hill, Darley,
Ripley, Yorkshire. See No. 220.

493.

SHOW ME THE LIGHT OF THY COUN-TENANCE.

From Psalm lxxx., is engraved below a handsome vertical

dial, erected in 1883 at Abbeyfield, Sheffield, by Bernard Wake, Esq. Above the dial is the verse—

MY TIME IS IN THY HAND.

494.

SI CULPARE VELIS, CULPABILIS ESSE CAVEBIS.
NEMO SINE CRIMINE VIVIT: IDCIRCO NE TEMERE
    JUDICATO.

If thou wouldst blame, thou wilt beware of being blameworthy.
No one lives without reproach ; therefore judge not rashly.

At Moccas Court.   See Nos. 635 and 331.

495.

SI NESCIS, HOSPES, SUNT HIC ORACULA PHOEBI,
CONSULE, RESPONDENT HOC TIBI, DISCE MORI.

Stranger, here the sun's oracles reply :
Ask them, they give thee answer : Learn to die.

Contributed by the Rev. R. F. Littledale, LL.D., locality
not known.

496.

SI SOL DEFICIT, NEMO ME RESPICIT.

If the sun fails, no one regards me.

In the cloisters at Chambery.   See No. 366.

497.

SIC LABITUR AETAS. 1778.

GARGRAVE FECIT.

Thus life slips away.

Formerly on the tower of Middleham Church, Yorkshire,
but it was removed about the year 1876, when the church
was rebuilt, and has not yet (1888) been replaced. The
motto also occurs at Darlington.

498.

SIC MEA VITA FUGIT.

So my life flies.

This is at Asti, an ancient town between Turin and Alessandria.

499.

SIC PETIT OCEANVM PHOEBUS, SIC VITA SEPULCRVM
DUM SENSIM TACITA VOLVITUR HORA ROTA:
SECULA SIC FUGIUNT, SIC LUX, SIC UMBRA, THEA-
TRUM
DONEC STELLIGERUM CLAUSERIT UNA DIES.

So Phœbus seeks the ocean, life the urn,
While on still wheels the hours softly turn,
So fly the ages, light and shade shall fly,
Till one day close the starry scene on high.

Contributed to the "Gentleman's Magazine," Sept., 1802, vol. lxxii., p. 855, as an "Inscription on a dial in a circle." See No. 473.

500.

SIC PRAETERIT AETAS.

So doth time pass.

Formerly on the Market Cross, King's Lynn. See No. 316.

501.

SIC SUA CUIQUE DIES.

So is his day to each one.

PARAPHRASE.

"Thus every passing life is found
A passing shadow on the ground."

On a dial in a village between Lugano and Como.

502.

SIC TRANSIT GLORIA MUNDI.

So passes the glory of the world.

This may be read on Fountains Hall, near Ripon. The
hall was built out of the ruins of the adjacent abbey by

Stephen Proctor, one of the esquires to James I. The same
motto is over the church porch at St. Just, Cornwall, where

the dial is made of slate ; and over it is a representation of an angel holding an hour-glass, with the sun half-risen ; below is the name of Nicholas Raleigh.   The motto is also on Louth Church, Lincolnshire ; on the Convent of Pomier, near Geneva ; on the church tower of Brandon, Suffolk ; on the Cross-dial at Elleslie, near Chichester, see No. 48 ; on a plain horizontal dial at Bridlington Quay, dated 1844; on the gnomon of a similar one at Chapel House, Raughton-Head, Cumberland, 1778 ; and on a vertical stone dial formerly on Foulden Church, Norfolk, which was unfortunately blown down some years ago, and now lies in ruins ; it bore below the motto, a carved representation of the sun, and date 1727.   E. Horren, W. Cooper, Church wardens.   There is now (1888) a dial plate lying against the wall of Inveresk Church, near Edinburgh, which bears the same motto, and it is further inscribed " Archibald Handasyde Piscatorii fecit. MDCCXXXV."

In 1801 the same words were on a window dial at Northhill Rectory, Bedfordshire, dated 1664; and in 1869 they were still to be seen on a seventeenth century dial on a house at Heigham, near Norwich.   Mrs. Frances Clarke Fraser, writing from Ceylon in 1888, says that the motto is engraved in quaint characters (the capital letters being shaped like animals) upon a brass dial at Baudarapolla, Màtalè, Ceylon. A similar dial used to exist in front of the Rest House, Avisawellè, Ceylon, a building which belongs to the Dutch period, and bears an inscription in Dutch upon its walls.

503.

SIC TRANSIT HORA.

1697.

So passes the hour.

On a stone dial over an old doorway at Farnley Hall, Yorkshire.

504.

SIC UMBRAE DECLINAVERUNT.

So have the shadows gone down.

On the high campanile of a church near Lugano.

505.

SIC VITA.

So is life.

QUA REDIT NESCITIS HORAM.

You know not the hour in which HE returns.

On a horizontal dial at the Chantry, Newark.

506.

SIC VITA DUM FUGIT STARE VIDETUR.

So life while it flies seems to stand still.

On a house at Bourges. See No. 255.

507.

SIC VITA FUGIT.

So life flies.

At Sestri Levante on the Riviera, and at Abriès, in Dauphiné, dated 1859, Zerbola, G. F.

508.

SIC VITA TRANSIT.

So passes life.

The traveller who penetrates to the sequestered spot, may read this dial motto on the old house of Compton Wynyates, near Edgehill, in Warwickshire, which belongs to the Marquis of Northampton, and is sometimes called "Compton in the Hole" from its position, as it stands in a deep hollow

surrounded by hills and woods, and seemingly shut in to perpetual loneliness. It is a grand old hall, and was built by Sir William Compton (temp. Henry VIII.), who is said to have brought the curious chimneys from the Castle of Fulbrook, which he demolished. He stood in the favour of his king, and may be said to have founded the Compton family, as noble. His grandson was created Earl of Northampton by James I., and was father of the "loyal Earl" who followed Charles I., and grandfather of Compton, Bishop of London, who opposed James II. The old house suffered much in the civil wars, and is now dismantled. It is built round a court, and surrounded by a moat. The roof and ceilings are in good repair. It contains a small chapel for secret celebration of the mass, with private staircases. The dial hangs on the east side of the house, overlooking what was formerly the pleasaunce. Mr. Howitt writes : " When about a furlong from the house, I turned and saw that it was already hidden in its deep combe, and shrouded by its wooded hills ; and I was deeply sensible of the utter loneliness and silence of the scene. I never on the moors of Scotland or Cornwall felt such a brooding sense of an intense solitude."

509.

SIC VITAE CERTA RATIO :
TEMPUS FUGIT, MORS VENIT.   1747.

Thus is the sure reckoning of life :
Time flies : death comes.

At Brough, Westmoreland, fixed on a tombstone-shaped stone.

510.

SICUT UMBRA.

As a shadow.

On a small square dial, fixed at an angle to the wall over the arch of the doorway of the south porch of Maker Church near Devonport.

511.

SICUT UMBRA DECLINANT DIES NOSTRI.

F.A.D. MDCCCXXII.

Like a shadow our days go down.

On the villa Quiete, Varese.

512.

SICUT UMBRA TRANSEUNT DIES.

As the shadow pass the days.

On the church porch of St. Levan, one of the most westerly parishes of West Cornwall. The church is rich in old oak, and also possesses a fragmentary copy of King Charles I.'s letter of thanks to his people of Cornwall for their fidelity, dated from his camp at Sudeley Castle, 1643, and ordered to be printed, published, and read in every church or chapel in Cornwall, and to be kept for ever as a record of their king's gratitude.

513.

SINE FEBO . . . EST NIHIL.

Without the sun (Phœbus) . . . is nothing.

At Casal dei Pazzi, near Rome; the inscription is almost entirely defaced.

514.

SINE LUMINE INANE.

Without light all is useless.

Formerly on a finely painted dial, south declining west,

formerly in a window of the Church of St. Bennet Fink, Threadneedle Street, now destroyed. The foundation of this church was very ancient, but it was rebuilt by Robert Fink the elder in 1633, and after being burnt down was again rebuilt in 1673. The following extract from the "Saint's Nosegay," by Mr. Samuel Clark, minister of this church from 1642-66, may serve to illustrate the motto:— "If the sunne be wanting it will be night for all the stars; so if the light of God's countenance be wanting a man may sit in the shadow of death for all the glyster of worldly contentment. As light continues not in the house, but by its dependance on the sun: shut out that and all the light and beauty is presently gone: so we can see nothing but by the constant supply of the Spirit of Christ. Hee that begins must finish every good work in us."

515.

SINE NUBE PLACET.
1869 Z. G. F.
When there is no cloud (the dial) pleases.

At Vallouse, Dauphiné. Z. G. F. are the initials of the maker. See No. 507.

516.

SINE SOLE NIHIL SUM.
Without the sun I am nothing.
Cum sole medium Recti indico. F. G. A. 1, 1870.

At Vevey; and on a church at Ornavasso, near the Lago Maggiore. The situation is fine, commanding a view of the Lake of Nargozio and over hill-sides covered with vines, chesnut, and mulberry trees, with grey rocks peeping out between them. The dial is painted on the church wall.

The motto SINE SOLE NIHIL is at Puisseaux, in France.

517.

SINE SOLE SILEO.

Without the Sun I am silent.

On the chapel of St. Philippe, Nice; at Vevey; at Pino in Piedmont; and at Alghero in Sardinia; also on the church tower at Hoole, Lancashire, with the date 1815; and on a house at Ashwicke, near Bath.

518.

SINE UMBRA NIHIL.

Without shadow there is nothing.

On one of the dial faces on West Pier, Brighton. See No. 206.

519.

SIT NOMEN DOMINI BENEDICTUM IN SAECULA. 1821.

Blessed be the name of the Lord for all ages.

On a dial at Abriès, Dauphiné.

520.

SIT PATRIAE AUREA QUAVIS.

May there be for our country in some wise a golden (hour.)

There is a dial carved in stone above the façade of the

Maison du Roi, or Broodhuys, at Brussels, which bears this motto. It is on the fine old building, opposite the Hotel de Ville, in the square where the executions of Counts Egmont and Hoorn took place. The Broodhuys seems to have undergone many alterations. It was built about 1525, and in it the two noblemen passed the night before their execution, but it seems to have been rebuilt in 1668, by order of the Archdukes Albert and Isabella, and again altered in 1757. Until a recent restoration it bore on its façade the following inscription, which contains a chronogram of the date 1624:

A PESTE, FAME, ET BELLO, LIBERA NOS MARIA PACIS.
HoC voTVM paCIs pVbLICae eLIsabeth ConseCraVit.

From plague, famine, and war, deliver us, peaceful Mary.
This offering for the national peace was dedicated by Elizabeth.

A statue of the Archduchess was placed above. The dial probably dates from the last rebuilding, 1757. [It has now, 1888, disappeared.]

521.

SIT SINE LITE DIES.
Let the day be without strife.

On Darlington church. The dial is placed high on the south wall; the face is black, the lines and lettering gold.

522.

SO FLIES LIFE.

On an old house at Southall, Middlesex.

523.

SO FLYS LIFE AWAY. 1738.

On the church tower at South Stoneham, Hampshire,
" Jo. Sharpe, Ro. Houghton, Churchwardens ; " also on " The
Old Windmill" Tavern at Turnham Green, Middlesex,
with date 1717.

524.

SO MARCHES THE GOD OF DAY.

At Hartington church, Derbyshire, on a dial over the
south porch. The inscription is probably taken from Leadbitter's absurd translations of Latin mottoes.

525.

SO PASSETH AWAY THE GLORY OF THE WORLD.

On the church at Chipping Sodbury, Gloucestershire.

526.

SO ROLLS THE SUN, SO WEARS THE DAY,
AND MEASURES OUT LIFE'S PAINFUL WAY:
THROUGH SHIFTING SCENES OF SHADE AND LIGHT,
TO ENDLESS DAY OR ENDLESS NIGHT.

FOR THE LADY ABNEY AT NEWINGTON, 1735.

These lines were written by Dr. Watts as the motto on a
handsome solid pillar-dial which formerly stood in the garden

of Lady Abney at Stoke Newington, Dr. Watts being resident there as tutor in the family of Sir J. Hartopp. Sir Thomas Abney was Lord Mayor of London in 1700, and died in 1722. The dial has been removed to Edmond Castle, near Carlisle, the residence of J. H. Graham, Esq. Mr. H. Hopley has noted a different version of the lines, without recording any locality :—

> "So glide the hours, so wears the day,
> These moments measure life away,
> With all its trains of Hope and Fear ;
> Till shifting scenes of Shade and Light.
> Rise to Eternal Day, or sink in endless Night."

Dr. Watts' lines are also on a dial placed, in 1880, on the village school, Carthorpe, Yorkshire.

527.

SO SOON PASSETH IT AWAY.

Ps. xc., ver. x. 1782.

On the church of St. Martin's by Looe, Devon ; and on St. Matthias, Liskeard, with the names of Wm. Hony, LL.B., Vicar, Neh. Williams, and Frans. Croker, Churchwardens.

528.

SO TEACH US TO NUMBER OUR DAYS
THAT WE MAY APPLY OUR HEARTS UNTO WISDOM.

On a vertical stone dial on the porch of St. John's Church, Leeds, put up after the restoration of the church, about A.D. 1868, in place of one removed forty years previously. Also in Trefnant Churchyard, see No. 555. The verse is from Psalm xc. 12.

529.

SOL EST LUX ET GLORIA MUNDI.

The sun is the light and glory of the world.

One of the mottoes at Moccas Court.   See No. 635.

530.

SOL EST REGULA.

The sun is the rule.

On a house at Briançon.   See No. 463.

531.

SOL GLORIA MUNDI.

The sun the glory of the world.

On a house in Whitehorse Yard, Wellingborough.   It is a square wooden dial, without date.

532.

SOL ME, VOS UMBRA.

The sun (guides) me, the shadow you.

On a farmhouse at Coldthorpe, Gloucestershire.

533.

SOL ME VOS UMBRA REGIT.

The sun guides me, the shadow you.

On the church of St. Stephen by Saltash, which is the original parish church of Saltash.   The names Joseph Avery and Savell Doidge, 1783, are also engraved on the dial.

534.

SOL MINISTRAT UMBRAM.

The sun provides the shadow.

On a dial in the churchyard of Prees, Salop, with the date 1824, and the words, "John Calcott, fecit. George Ore, Samuel Worthen, Churchwardens."

535.

SOL NON OCCIDAT SUPER IRACUNDIAM VESTRAM.

Ephes. iv. 26.

Let not the sun go down upon your wrath.

HORAS NON NUMERO NISI SERENAS.

I count the bright hours only.

Lat. 51. 31. North.   Richard Melvin fecit from London.

On a handsome pillar bearing a horizontal dial of slate, at Ember Court, Surrey. The inscriptions are somewhat defaced. Besides the centre gnomon there are smaller ones at the four corners, showing the time of day at various places on the earth's surface. The text is on a dial at Ninane, near Chaudfontaine, Belgium; at La Fiera di Primiero, see No. 198; at Areley Kings (No. 34); and in English on Bishop Copleston's dial (No. 264); also on a pedestal dial in a garden near Esher, Surrey.

536.

SOL TEM[P]O DI SATURNO IL DENTE EDACE
E DEL PALLONE IL GIOCATOR FALLACE. 1826.

Nothing save Time's destructive tooth I dread,
And the ball by unskilful player sped.

At Chieri, in Piedmont. Two or three Italian scholars
have tried to make sense of this obscure motto, and have
failed. The first allusion to the mythological legend of
Saturn devouring his children will be recognized ; and the
accompanying simile can only be explained by a reference to
the favourite Italian game of *pallone.* This game somewhat
resembles *tennis,* and still remains a living representative of
the old Roman game of *pila.* The manner of playing it has
been thus described by Mr. Story ("Roba di Roma," vol. i.) :
"It is played between two sides, each numbering from five
to eight persons. Each of the players is armed with a *brac-*
ciale, or gauntlet of wood, covering the hand and extending
nearly up to the elbow, with which a heavy ball is beaten
backwards and forwards, high into the air, from one side to
another. The object of the game is to keep the ball in constant flight, and whoever suffers it to fall dead within the
bounds loses. The game is played on an oblong figure,
marked out on the ground, or designated by the wall around
the sunken platform on which it is played, and across the
centre is a transverse line dividing the two sides ; and as the
ball falls here and there, now flying high in the air, and
caught at once by the *bracciale* before touching the ground,
now glancing back from the wall which generally forms one
side of the lists, the players rush eagerly to hit it, calling
loudly to each other, and often displaying great agility, skill,
and strength." Allusions to the game of *pallone* may be

U

found in the works of the modern Italian poets. Leopardi and Aleardi have both made use of it as a subject for their verse.

. The above motto was ultimately shown to Antonio Maschio, a gondolier in the service of the National Bank at Venice, well known for his interpretation of Dante's *Divina Commedia.* He said at once that the word *tempo* should be *temo,* and then the meaning would be, " I fear only the devouring tooth of Saturn, and the inexpert player with the ball." That is, the gnomon fears alike Saturn's wet weather which corrodes iron, and the bad pallone player who may throw his ball against and break it.

537.

SOL TIBI SIGNA DABIT: SOLEM QUIS DICERE FALSUM AUDEAT?

The sun will give thee the signs : who will dare to say the sun is false?

From Virgil's first Georgic, line 463. This is the motto of a sun-dial on one of the terraces at Bramshill Park, Hampshire, the seat of the Rev. Sir William H. Cope, Bart. At the same place are three other dials, but only the family arms with date and initials are engraved on them. It was the motto of the old " Sun " newspaper. Dryden's translation of the line runs :—

" The sun reveals the secret of the sky ;
And who dares give the source of light the lie ? "

The first part of the above motto, SOL TIBI SIGNA DABIT, was until 1882 on a dial on the Bridge Trust Building, Bideford, erected in 1758. It is still on the wall of the cloister of S. Stefano Belluno, now used as a public office.

538.

SOLE ORIENTE, FUGIUNT TENEBRAE.

With the rising sun the darkness flies.

On a dial in a garden in the diocese of Connor.
Bishop Mant, in his Latin and English poem, " The Sun-
dial of Armoy," writes thus :—

" Night flies before the orient morning,
    So speak the Dial's accents clear ;
So better speaks the Prophet's warning
    To ears that hear.

" Night flies before the Sun ascending ;
    The sun goes down, the shadow spreads—
O, come the day which, never ending,
    No night succeeds.

" And see a purer day-spring beaming,
    Unwonted light, nor moon nor sun ;
But Light itself, with glory streaming,
    God on His throne ! "

539.

SOLE ORIENTE ORIOR,
SOLE PONENTE CUBO.

With the rising sun I wake,
With the setting sun I sleep.

Believed to be in Malta.

540.

SOLEM QUIS DICERE FALSUM AUDEAT?

Who will dare to say the sun is false?

On a dial at Newbiggin, near Carlisle, with date A.D.
1722. " Carolus Eades delineavit, Johannes Gosling, Sculpt."
Also on St. Mary's Church, Penzance, with the addition of
TEMPUS EDAX RERUM. The present church is modern,
but the dial was removed from the wall of the former church,
built in 1680. A figure of Time with his scythe is represented on the dial. The motto is from Virgil, Georg. i.,
463. See No. 537.

541.

SOLES PEREUNT ET IMPUTANTUR.

Days (literally, *suns*) *depart and are reckoned.*

Outside the Dean's kitchen, at Durham, is a square dial,
gold-lettered, which bears this inscription. It is now (1888)
much decayed.

542.

SOLI DEO GLORIA.

To God alone be glory.

This inscription is carved on several stones in Nuremburg,
and may have belonged to dials which have been removed.
It is also on an ivory portarium in the Nuremburg Museum,
with the name of Paulus Reinnan, 1652, and on one in the
British Museum, " Paulus Reinman zu Normberg faciebat
1578," and on two others marked Nicolavs Miller, 1645.
(See No. 562.),

543.

SOLI, SOLI, SOLI. 1756.

On a simple south dial, with the motto and date on a scroll above, and the face of the sun made a central point to which the gnomon is fixed, is the word " Soli " thrice given. It occurs at Monthey, in the Canton du Valais. The same may also be read at Bonneville.

The representation of the sun's face on a dial has been frequently noted already, but to this motto and the preceding one, it is particularly appropriate. The design, a human face, with rays all round, is of very ancient origin. It was found carved in relief in a cavern near Babain in Upper

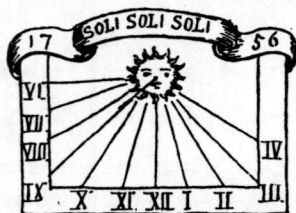

Egypt, together with two priests adoring and offering sacrifices below. In this manner the Persians also represented the Sun God, as well as in the form of a young man, Mithras. It is quite likely that the words *Soli, Soli, Soli*, and *Deo Soli Gloria* (which may bear a double meaning) were originally Mithraic inscriptions. Under the Roman Empire there were altars set up to Mithras with the inscription, *Deo invicto Mithrae.* Several have been found in England inscribed, *Deo Soli*, To God the Sun, *Deo Soli invicto*, To God the Sun unconquerable. That the trace of this ancient worship should still be found on sun-dials need surprise no one. [If *Soli Soli Soli*, be indeed a Mithraic inscription, it probably should be translated "To the peerless Sun, we only," *i.e.*, the secret society of Mithraists. R. F. L.]

544.

SOLIS ET ARTIS OPUS,
A MAI CESSAR D' OPRAR SEMPRE C' INVITA.
il Giorno 23 Maggio 1867.

The work of the sun and of art,
It ever incites us never to cease working.

On a farmhouse near Varese. The first line is the
motto on a house-dial at Grasse, France; the dial is a large
oblong, plain in pattern, and painted on the wall with the
motto at the top. The same may also be seen at Milan on
a modern dial, south declining west; and on a white marble
dial on a house between Palermo and Monreale, dated 1882.

545.

SOLIS ADIT LUX,
HIC DOCET UMBRAE CRUX,
DATUR HORA.
UMBRAM ADDIT NOX,
HINC ABIT UMBRAE VOX,
ABIT HORA ABSIT MORA.

The sun's light shineth here,
The shade's cross teacheth clear,
Told is the hour of day.
Night makes the shade more dense,
The shade's voice goeth hence,
The hour goes, be there be no delay.

These lines are engraved on the eight sides of a shaft in
the Vicarage garden, Shenstone, near Lichfield, upon the

top of which is a cross dial, similar to No. 221, which stands
in Shenstone churchyard. Both of these dials were erected
by the Rev. R. W. Essington, Vicar, who took their pattern
from one in the gardens at Highlands, near Calne, Wilts,
which, however, has no motto.

The dial at Shenstone Vicarage has also a Greek, and a
Hebrew motto, engraved on a slate step at the base of the
shaft in front of the cross. The first is:

$$\text{ὥραν δίδωσι} + \text{ὄντος ἡλίου.}$$

(the word σταῦρος, *a cross*, being supplied by +).

The cross gives the hour in sunshine.

and the second,

נְהִי אוֹר

Let there be light.

See No. 599. A copy of this cross dial has been
erected at Hamstall-Ridware, near Rugeley, but it has no
motto. It is in the churchyard, and stands on a pavement
made partly from smooth river stones, and partly from some
beautiful old tiles found in the church. The cross is of
white marble, the pedestal of alabaster, and till 1868,
supported a font, which was placed in the church about
1780.

Two other translations have been made of the Latin lines
on the dial at Shenstone Vicarage, but the one given above
seems to follow the original more closely than the rest.

(1) *Sunlight falls, and lo! the Cross's shadow fain would teach*
To us the present hour by heaven is lent!
Night darkens, and then no longer can the shadow preach,
Avoid delay, your time is almost spent.

(2) *Light falls from heaven !*
Then doth the Cross's shade
This lesson sweetly teach :
Thy time—Heaven's grace !
Night's deeper shades
Close round ! The voice is hushed,
So soon that grace is spent,
It flies apace,
Hold on thy race.

546.

SON FIGLIE DEL SOLE, EPPURE SON OMBRE.

They (the hours) are daughters of the sun, and yet are shadows.

So we venture to print this motto, for, as it stands in Dean Alford's book, there is clearly some mistake in the wording; and we have now, by the alteration of a single letter " figli*e* " for " figli*a*," made what appears to us better sense of the whole. The Dean gives the following paraphrase :

" I the sun my father call,
Yet am shadow after all."

547.

SON POCHE LE ORE MIE, LE TUE SON MOLTE.

My hours are few, thine are many.

At San Remo ; also on a house at Ventimiglia.

548.

SONO BARRA OSCURA E FISSA
EPPURE SONO SERVO DEL SOLE
E SCHIAVO AL MOTO.

I am a bar dark and immovable,
Yet I am a servant to the sun,
And a slave to motion.

On a dial on the tower of the Grand Hotel, Pegli, placed there in 1874, and the motto added by the Marquis de Nicolay.

549.

SPECTATOR FASTIDIOSUS, SIBI MOLESTUS.

He that looks too proudly is a trouble to himself.

At Bywell Abbey, near Newcastle-on-Tyne. It is difficult to understand what this motto means; we have translated it literally. It may either point to a spectator bending over the dial so as to intercept the sunshine; or to a passer-by who is too proud to use this humble means of learning the time.

550.

STA PROMISSIS.

Stand to your promises.

On the stone pedestal of a dial at Niddrie Marischall, near Edinburgh, the seat of the Wauchops. The arms of the family are engraved on the bronze dial face, and also on the pedestal, but the motto is not their heraldic one. The words *Wachop of Niddrie* are inscribed beside the shield on the face; and also *Jacobus Clark, Dundee, fecit*. There is no date.

551.

Diall. (*loq.*) STAIE, PASSINGER
TELL ME MY NAME
THY NATURE.

Pass. (*resp.*) THY NAME IS DIE
ALL. I AM A MORTALL
CREATURE.

Diall. (*loq.*) SINCE MY NAME
AND THY NATURE
SOE AGREE,
THINK ON THY SELFE
WHEN THOV·LOOKS
VPON ME.

There is an ancient dial, having four sides, at Millrigg, in the parish of Culgaith, near Penrith.   The opening dialogue

betwixt Dial and Passenger is inscribed on one side of the square, and on the other side is Dial's moral deduction from it.   The two remaining sides of the square are occupied by the armorial bearings of the Dalston family, with the initials

" I. D "; and those of the Fallowfields with " H. F." John
Dalston resided and died at Millrigg in 1692. He was the
son of Sir Christopher Dalston, of Acorn Bank, who was
knighted by James I. in 1615. This latter place was the
chief residence of the family. The manor of Temple
Sowerby, immediately adjoining, was granted by Henry VIII.
to Thomas Dalston, Esq., on the dissolution of religious
houses. It belonged originally to the Knights Templars,
and afterwards to the Hospitallers. Millrigg is now occupied as a farm house.

552.

STEH' BEY UNS IN ALLER NOTH,
HIER IN LEBEN UND IN TOD.

Stand by us in all need, here in life and in death.

At Salzburg. The dial contains a fresco of the Virgin
and Child.

553.

SUB UMBRA QUIESCUNT,
SUB LUCE GAUDENT. 1770.

Under the shade they rest,
Under the light they rejoice.

On the Hôtel des Invalides at Paris.

554.

SUMUS UMBRA.
1691.

A shadow are we.

On the south wall of an old house in Lower Tottenham.
" Notes and Queries," 4th Series, iv. 188.

555.

SUNS RISE AND SET
TILL MEN FORGET
THE DAY IS AT THE DOOR,
WHEN THEY SHALL RISE NO MORE.
O EVERLASTING SUN,
WHOSE RACE IS NEVER RUN,
BE THOU MY ENDLESS LIGHT
THEN SHALL I FEAR NO NIGHT.

SO TEACH US TO NUMBER OUR DAYS, THAT WE MAY
APPLY OUR HEARTS UNTO WISDOM.

Psalm xc. 12.

On a dial in Trefnant Churchyard, county Denbigh, erected by Mrs. Whitehall Dod, of Llannerch. Three devices are also engraved on the dial.

556.

SUPREMA MULTIS HORA, FORSAN TIBI.

The last hour to many, perhaps to thee.

On the Riviera.

557.

SWIFT RUNS Yᴱ TIME
THIS DIALL FACE DOTH SHOWE,
YE HOURES ARE FEWE
THAT YE SHALL PASS BELOWE.

Mr. Harry Hems writes in the " Building News : " " It

is twenty-five years or more ago that, at that time an appren-
tice lad in Yorkshire, I recut an inscription upon an old sun-
dial as above."

558.

TACITO PEDE LABORO.
I toil with silent foot.

This dial motto is on the outside wall of the old palace of
the Princes of Masserano (La Marmora) at Masserano in the
province of Novara in Italy. Lamartine expresses a similar
idea :—

" L'ombre seule marque en silence
Sur le cadran rempli, les pas muets du temps."

559.

TA NY LAGHYN AIN MYR SCAA.
Our days are like a shadow.

TEMPUS FUGIT.
Time flies.

On a marble dial at Kirk Braddan, Isle of Man, dated
1860. Over the dial face are the arms of the island, three
legs conjoined on the fess point, and beneath it are the
mottoes.

560.

TA NYN LAGHYN ER Y THALLOO NYR
SCADOO. (1 Chron. xxix. 15.)
1835.
Our days on the earth are as a shadow.

On a white marble vertical dial, which is placed against the
south wall of Malew Church in the Isle of Man.

561.

TAK TENT OF TIME ERE TIME BE TINT.

Was inscribed round the top of a handsome pillar that stood in front of the Exhibition Buildings, Edinburgh, and was called Prince Albert Victor's dial. It bore an inscription to the effect that the Exhibition was opened by Prince Albert Victor in May, 1886. The pillar was octagonal, and surmounted by eight vertical dials, each of which had a motto.

1. Time and tide tarry for no man.
2. Light is the shadow of God.
3. Time is the chrysalis of Eternity.
4. As a servant earnestly desireth the shadow.
5. Time as he passes us, has a dove's wing,
   Unsoiled and swift, and of a silken sound.
6. Man's days are as a shadow that passeth away.
7. Well arranged time is the surest sign of a well arranged mind.
8. I mark but the hours of sunshine.

The Exhibition Buildings were only temporarily erected, and the dial was removed when these were taken down. The motto " Tak tent of time, ere time be tint " is also on the clock tower at Keir, Perthshire, placed there by the late Sir William Stirling Maxwell, with the two following lines :—

IT IS LATER WITH THE WISE THAN HE IS AWARE.

HOURS ARE TIME'S DARTS, AND ONE COMES WINGED WITH DEATH.

The lines " Time as he passes us," &c., are from Cowper's " Task," Book iv.

562.

TEMPORA LABUNTUR, TACITISQUE SENESCIMVS ANNIS,
ET FUGIT FRENO NON REMORANTE DIES. ﹐
SOLI DEO GLORIA.

1599.

Paulus Reinman. Nurembergæ fac.

Time glides by, and we age with the silent years,
And our day flies, with no rein to hold it back.
To God alone be glory.

On an ivory portarium in the British Museum. The
beginning is a quotation from Ovid, Fasti, 6, 771.

563.

TEMPORA MUTANTUR, NOS ET MUTAMUR
IN ILLIS.

The times change, and we too change with them.

On a pillar dial in the garden at Brockhampton Park, near
Cheltenham. This well-known line is not classical, but is
by Matthew Borbonius, a Latin poet of the sixteenth
century. The true reading of the sentence is *Omnia
mutantur,* &c.

564.

TEMPORA TEMPORE TEMPERA.

Seasonably seize the seasons.

It is very difficult to reproduce the alliteration of the

original. The motto is on the church at Vian, in Pied-mont. The two first words of the same inscription were read on a portarium in Munich Museum by Charles T. Gatty, and he saw that a third word was engraved after them, but he could not decipher it, as it was covered by the handle attached to the dial.

565.

TEMPORE NIMBOSO SECURI SISTITE GRADUM,
UT MIHI SIC VOBIS HORA QUIETIS ERIT.

In time of clouds stay your step, in safety,
As to me, so to you, it will be an hour of rest.

This pretty and appropriate inscription is placed above a plain dial, south declining west, which is painted on the side wall of an Inn near one of the stations on the Mont Cenis railway line, just before reaching St. Michel, and nearly at the foot of the mountain. It will be seen that the word *gradum* will not scan where it stands.

566.

TEMPORIS MEMOR MEI, TIBI POSUI
MONITOREM.

Christian.   1681.   De Whitehouse.

Mindful of my time, I have erected a warning for you.

This inscription is said to have existed on a dial in the churchyard of Kirk Michael, Isle of Man. The dial was horizontal, erected upon a square stone, with a granite shaft below. The motto was engraved upon the south and west sides of the stone, and these are now so much broken away that only the two first letters of each of the three first words remain—TE, ME, ME—one below the other, on the west side. On the east side are the arms of the island, *three legs conjoined in the fess point;* and on the north side there is the name *Christian,* which was probably either that of the donor, or the maker. Whitehouse is the name of an estate in the parish where Christian may have lived. The remains of this dial stand close to the entrance of the church, and to the grave of Bishop Wilson. At Maughold there is a dial outside the church gates, erected on a pillar which seems to be part of the shaft of an ancient cross, and on the metal plate is inscribed " Ev. Christian *fecit.* 1666 ;" whilst on a dial which once stood at Lewaigue House, which is also dated 1666, the name of "Ewan Christian" appears as the donor, and " Edm. Culpeper" as the maker.

567.

TEMPUS AD LUCEM DUCIT VERITATEM.

Time brings truth to light.

Noted by Mr. Howard Hopley, but no place named.

558.

TEMPUS EDAX RERUM. 1834.

Time the devourer of (all) things.

This phrase from Ovid, Metam. 15, 234, is on the plate of a pillar-dial in Easby Churchyard, which is picturesquely situated close to the ruined abbey by the river side, about a mile from Richmond, in Yorkshire. It was formerly on the dial at Park Hill (see No. 422); as well as on Dewsbury Church, with the date 1816; and on the porch of Gulval Church,

Cornwall, dated 1810. Time is here represented walking above the dial face, and holding both a scythe and hour glass. It is on St. Mary's Church, Penzance, with No. 540; also on a house in the village of Cutcombe, near Dunkery Beacon; in the Albert Park, Middlesborough, No. 613; and at Rye, see No. 583.

Quarles says, *Book* iii. *Emblem* 13,

> " Read on this dial, how the shades devour
> My short-liv'd winter's day ; hour eats up hour ;
> Alas ! the total's but from eight to four."

569.

TEMPUS FUGIT.

Time flies.

Is on a florid pillar-dial in Handsworth Rectory garden, Yorkshire; also on the old Priory church at Bridlington. It is inscribed on a marble dial at Kirk Braddan in the Isle of Man, with the date 1860. See No. 559. At Ossington, Nottinghamshire, the seat of the late Lord Ossington, there still stands a dial bearing this motto. In Thoroton's " History of Notts," it may be seen figured in the same plate with the church and hall as they stood in the time of Charles I. ; but both of these have since been rebuilt. The sun-dial alone remains.

The same motto, " Tempus fugit," is on the church of Holy Cross, Crediton; over the porch of East Horndon Church, Essex, with the date 1728 ; on the churches of Leighton Buzzard, (see No. 46); of St. Mary the Virgin, Wiggenhall, Norfolk, dated 1748, John Rockley, Church-warden ; of Easton, Norfolk, E. H. 1694; of Ellastone,

Derbyshire, (see No. 695); of the parish church, Reigate; on the porch of Stalham Church, Norfolk, 1801; and the Wesleyan Chapel, Thorpe Hesley, Yorkshire, 1797. It is also on a plain horizontal dial in the garden of the Corn-mill, Ecclesfield, Yorkshire; and at Borranshill House, near Carlisle, see No. 301; on the south wall of the tower of Brampton Church, Huntingdonshire; on the south transept of Bourn Abbey Church, Lincolnshire; and in the church-yard of Astbury, Congleton, upon a pedestal which seems to be the base of an ancient cross.

> " The dial above the doorway
> (His face was hoary gray)
> As in a dream did measure
> The sultry summer day.
> And ever " Tempus fugit : "
> " Hoc age," said the stone ;
> But who should mind his warning,
> The preacher preached alone."
>
> ANNE EVANS.

570.

TEMPUS FUGIT, MEMENTO AETERNITAS.

(*sic*).

Time flies, remember eternity.

Ricardus Melville fecit.   Glasgow, 1848.

This Latin motto, if it can be so described, is engraved on the plate of a horizontal dial which stands in the garden of the Royal Hotel, Bridge of Allan, Perthshire.

571.

TEMPUS FUGIT, MORS VENIT.

Time flies, death comes.

UT HORA SIC VITA.

As the hour, so is life.

On a pedestal dial in Acton Churchyard, Cheshire. The first motto is also at Brough, Westmoreland, see No. 509; and on a stone pillar dial in Matlock Churchyard. The dial at Matlock has been ill-treated, and in 1874 the gnomon had disappeared.

572.

TEMPUS FUGIT PER UMBRA(M).

Time flies by the shadow.

Russell Casson fecit, 1727. Thomas Hutton.

In the churchyard of Cartmel, Lancashire. A previous dial evidently existed here, as the following entry appears in the transactions of " Twenty-four sworn men," in connexion with Cartmel Priory Church : " 1630, Paid, Itm for setting up the Sunne dyell, iij^s vj^d."

573.

TEMPUS FUGIT UT UMBRA.

Time flies as a shadow.

On Bradfield Church, Yorkshire, with No. 428.

574·
TEMPUS LABANTUR.

Formerly on the old Custom House at Ipswich, but both building and dial have been taken away.   Evidently *labantur* is a corruption of *labitur*, meaning *Time glides away*.

575·
TEMPUS LABILE.
Gliding time.

This is on a dial, facing south, over the kitchen-garden door at Esholt Hall, near Leeds.   There was originally a nunnery at " Esteholt," as Dugdale writes it, which was a cell to Sinningthwait, and of the Cistercian order.   Pope Alexander III. took this nunnery into his protection in 1172. The present hall was built in the early part of the last century by Sir Walter Calverley, Bart., and in 1754-5 it was sold to Robert Stansfield, Esq., to whose representative it now belongs.   The same motto is on an old, nicely-carved stone dial, which is fixed against the front of a cottage house in Bishopthorpe, near York; and below is a small, apparently marble slab, let into the wall, with the date 1691.   They have possibly no connection with each other, and may be relics of some former archiepiscopal buildings.

576.
TEMPUS ABIT, MORS VENIT.
Time passes away, death comes.

On a dial formerly in the Isle of Man.   See No. 331.

577.

TEMPUS OMNIUM PARENS.
Time the parent of all things.

On the dial at Park Hill, Oswestry. See No. 423.

578.

TEMPUS TERIT OMNIA.
Time wears away all things.
1612.

On an ivory portarium in Nuremburg Museum.

579.

TEMPUS UT UMBRA PRAETERIT.
Time passes by as a shadow.

At Brougham Hall. See No. 379.

580.

TEMPUS VINCIT ET DIRIGIT OMNIA.
An° 1773.
Time conquers and rules everything.

On a vertical dial of metal, placed over the front door of one of the masters' houses at St. Paul's College, Stony Stratford, Bucks. The two last words are contracted on the dial.

581.

TEMPUS VITAE MONITOR.
Time the warning of life.

Over the south porch doorway of St. Peter's, Wolverhampton, with the date 1778.

582.

TENERE NON POTES, POTES NON PERDERE DIEM.
Thou canst not hold, thou canst not destroy a day.

At Ripley, Surrey. See No. 429.

583.

THAT SOLAR SHADOW, AS IT MEASURES LIFE, IT LIFE RESEMBLES TOO.

TEMPUS EDAX RERUM.
Time the devourer of (all) things.

These mottoes are on a vertical dial which used to be on the front of Rye Grammar School. The building was erected in 1636. The dial was presented to the school by Colonel de Lacy Evans when he was one of the representatives of the borough in Parliament, and it remained upon the school until 1887, when the building was re-pointed, and new windows were put in to commemorate the Queen's Jubilee; and as it was found that the dial obscured one of the windows, it was removed and placed upon the Town Hall.

The first motto is from Young's "Night Thoughts," Night ii. See No. 56.

584.

THE EARTH IS THE LORD'S AND THE FULNESS THEREOF.

In the Albert Park, Middlesbrough. See No. 613.

585.

THE DAY IS THINE.
1790 . . . . 1880.

On Market Deeping Church, Northamptonshire. The dial is on the south wall of the tower; and there is a second dial on the north wall. See No. 598.

586.

THE GREATER LIGHT TO RULE THE DAY.
Gen. 1.

On a remarkable dial formerly on the church of St. Mary le Tower, Ipswich. It was of large size, and filled the whole space of a window within an arch which had apparently been plastered up to admit of the dial being placed there. On the dial face were painted the twelve signs of the Zodiac in their proper colours. Below, at the left-hand corner, a figure of Atlas bearing the terrestrial globe on his shoulders, and on the right, Science regarding the celestial globe. Above, at the left-hand corner, Time, with his scythe and hour-glass, and at the right, Death. This dial was removed about 1860, and cannot now be traced. It probably dated from the eighteenth century. The same text is on Copdock Church, Suffolk ; and on the tower of Thorp Arch Church, Yorkshire, there is a square stone dial inscribed, " 1. Gen : 16 " which no doubt also refers to the text.

587.
THE HOUR COMETH.
A.D. 1826.

On the porch of Saxthorpe Church, Norfolk. The dial is square and the inscription is above the hour lines. It was put up in 1826 by Lieut. Davies, R.N.

588.
THE HOUR IS COMING IN THE WHICH ALL THAT
ARE IN THE GRAVES SHALL HEAR HIS VOICE.
MDCCCXXXIII.

On a dial in the churchyard at Stretton, Cheshire.

589.
THE HOUR NOW SHOWN PERHAPS MAY BÈ THY
LAST,
REPENT AND PRAY BEFORE THAT HOUR BE PAST.
1733. Ex dono Johannnis Wilder.

On a horizontal dial in Sulham Churchyard, Berks.

590.

THE HOURS PART US,
BUT THEY BRING US TOGETHER AGAIN.

This motto was devised by the late Juliana Horatia Ewing,
with the intention of placing it on a sun-dial which she and
her husband offered to erect, as a parting gift, upon the Mess
Hut of the Royal Engineers, South Camp, Aldershot, 1877,
" In grateful record of happy hours spent there."   The dial
was not erected, however, as another offering was preferred
in its place, but the motto is inserted here as an illustration
of one of the lessons which the devisor learnt from the shifting scenes of life amongst which she lived for seven years in
Aldershot Camp.   The same thought was more fully set
forth in her " Story of a Short Life " (p. 75).   " True to its
character as an emblem of human life, the Camp stands on,
with all its little manners and customs, whilst the men who
garrison it pass rapidly away.   Strange as the vicissitudes of
a whole generation elsewhere, are the changes and chances
that a few years bring to those who were stationed there
together.   To what unforeseen celebrity (or to a dropping
out of one's life and even hearsay, that once seemed quite as
little likely) do one's old neighbours sometimes come !   They
seem to pass in a few dull seasons as other men pass by life-
times.   Some to foolishness and forgetfulness, and some to
fame.   This old acquaintance to unexpected glory; that
dear friend—alas !—to the grave.   And some—GOD speed
them !—to the world's end and back, following the drum till
it leads them Home again, with familiar faces little changed
—with boys and girls, perchance, very greatly changed—and
with hearts not changed at all.   Can the last parting do

much to hurt such friendships between good souls who have so long learnt to say farewell; to love in absence, to trust through silence, and to have faith in reunion?"

591.

THE HOURS, UNLESS THE HOURS BE BRIGHT,
    IT IS NOT MINE TO MARK:
I AM THE PROPHET OF THE LIGHT,
    DUMB WHEN THE SUN IS DARK.

From a note-book. No locality recorded.

592.

THE LAST HOUR TO MANY, POSSIBLY TO YOU.

On the church at Hartlepool, co. Durham.

593.

THE LORD BY WISDOM HATH FOUNDED THE EARTH,
BY UNDERSTANDING HATH HE ESTABLISHED THE
    HEAVENS.

In the Albert Park, Middlesbrough. See No. 613.

594.

THE LOVE IS TRUE: THAT I O V:
AS TRUE TO ME: THEN C V B.

On the exterior of a ring dial, which is an inch and a half

in diameter. The initial letters of the twelve months are also engraved on the exterior ; the numerals of the hours are within. The present owner of this dial is not known.

595.

THE MOMENT PAST
LAID MANY FAST.

Near Dennington, Suffolk.   See No. 319.

596.

THE MORNING COMETH, AND ALSO THE NIGHT.

In the Albert Park, Middlesbrough.   See No. 613.

597.

THE NATURAL CLOCKWORK BY THE MIGHTY ONE
WOUND UP AT FIRST, AND EVER SINCE HAS GONE ;
NO PIN DROPS OUT, ITS WHEELS AND SPRINGS ARE
      GOOD,
IT SPEAKS ITS MAKER'S PRAISE THO' ONCE IT STOOD ;
BUT THAT WAS BY THE ORDER OF THE WORKMAN'S
      POWER ;
AND WHEN IT STANDS AGAIN IT GOES NO MORE.

JOHN ROBINSON, RECTOR.   ⎫
A. DOUGLASS, CLERK FECIT. ⎬ A.D. 1773.
                           ⎭
THOMAS SMITH   ⎫
SAMUEL STEVENSON   ⎬ CHURCHWARDENS.
                           ⎭
      SEAHAM IN LATITUDE 54D. 51M.

On the south porch of Seaham Church, co. Durham. The motto is above the dial, and cut in a heavy stone of ungainly shape.

598.

THE NIGHT COMETH. 1800.

Formerly over the church door at Melsonby, Yorkshire, but removed probably during the restoration of the church in 1871. It is also on the tower of Barnes Church, Surrey, undated. The same motto is found upon a dial on the tower of Market Deeping Church, Northamptonshire, which is specially remarkable for being placed on the *north* side of the building. The gnomon instead of being parallel to the polar axis of the earth, is placed in an exactly opposite direction on account of the unusual aspect of the dial. See No. 585.

599.

THE PASSING SHADOWS WHICH THE SUNBEAMS
    THROW
ATHWART THIS CROSS, TIME'S HASTENING FOOT-
    STEPS SHOW;
WARNED BY THEIR TEACHING WORK ERE DAY BE
    O'ER,
SOON COMES THE NIGHT WHEN MAN CAN WORK
    NO MORE.

These lines are engraved upon a plate which support a cross sun-dial, similar in construction to No. 545. It stands on a stone pedestal upon the terrace of the hospital of S. Cross, Rugby. The building was erected in 1882, chiefly by the liberality of a gentleman and his wife who live in the town. There are mottoes in the wards and over some of the doorways ; that over the porch is " Deus nobis haec otia fecit —anno salutis 1882." Over the out-patients' entrance is one which is often used as a dial motto, " Post tenebras spero lucem." The lines on the cross dial were written by R. E. Egerton-Warburton, Esq. (see No. 298). The dial was designed by Henry Wilson, Esq., of Grays Inn Square, London, who was the architect of the Hospital, and he selected the fine old characters in which the lines of the motto are engraved.

600.

THE SMALL AND THE GREAT ARE THERE: AND THE SERVANT IS FREE FROM HIS MASTER. Job iii. 19.

One of three mottoes on St. Patrick's Church, Patrick, Isle of Man. See No. 372.

601.

THE SUNLIT DIAL SHOWS
THE FLEETING HOURS OF DAY,
THE CROSS FORESHADOWETH THOSE
WHICH NEVER PASS AWAY.

On the wall of the new church at Warburton, Cheshire.

602.

THE TIME IS AT HAND.

Noticed in the "Gentleman's Magazine," November, 1765. No locality given.

603.

THE TIME IS SHORT.

From 1 Cor. vii. 24, and placed in 1882 on the church of Kilnwick, Yorkshire, instead of No. 174, which had become illegible. The dial is a large wooden one, undated.

604.

ΘΕΟΣ ΓΕΩΜΕΤΡΕΙ.

God measures the earth.

MIhI DeVs LVX et saLVs.

God is my light and salvation.

WHERE NOW YOU STAND THE TIME TO SPY
WHO KNOWS HOW SOON YOU THERE MAY LYE.
BOTH TIME AND PLACE ARE MONITORY,
THAT YOU AND THEY ARE TRANSITORY.
HEAVEN IS OUR TEMPLE, DEATH'S THE PORCH,
CHRIST IS THE WAY, HIS WORD OUR TORCH.
HERE LET US WALK WHILE WE HAVE LIGHT,
TOO LATE BEGINS OUR WORK AT NIGHT.

A dial which bore these mottoes was until 1858 on Hadleigh Church, Suffolk. The Latin motto forms the chronogram 1627. A MS. history of Hadleigh by Dr. Wilkins, quoted by Mr. Philip Parsons, in the "Monuments of Kent," 1794, gives a description of the dial which was placed over the porch, the gnomon standing over the figure XI and above this the Greek motto was written in golden letters, the Latin one was inscribed within the hour lines and the

English verse below the dial, in letters of gold on a black ground, the dial itself being painted in blue with gold lettering. The Greek motto is taken from the saying attributed to Plato: " The God always geometrises," ὁ θεὸς ἀει γεωμέτρει. See Plut. Sym. viii. 2. Milton thus describes the Son of God employed in the works of Creation :—

> " In his hand
> He took the golden compasses, prepared
> In God's eternal store, to circumscribe
> The Universe, and all created things :
> One foot He centred, and the other turned
> Round through the vast profundity obscure,
> And said : Thus far extend, thus far thy bounds,
> This be thy just circumference, O world ! "

Milton's conception was derived from Proverbs viii. 27, " When He prepared the heaven, I was there, when He set a compass upon the face of the deep."

605.

THESE SHADES DO FLEET
FROM DAY TO DAY :
AND SO THIS LIFE
PASSETH AVVAIE.

In front of Marrington Hall, Shropshire, on the lawn, is a curious old four-sided dial, thus inscribed round the pillar, near the top. It is coeval with the house, and dated 1595. The shaft of the dial is set in a solid square stone at the base, round the chamfer of which runs the legend :—

FOR CHARITI BID ME ADW (ADIEU ?) WHO WROUGHT THIS STONE FOR THEE TOMB OF R L L.

These letters are the initials of Richard Lloyd. On the sides of the shaft are various heraldic bearings, emblems, and devices—the arrow, death's head, cross bones, oak branches, two serpents intertwined, a plant in a pot, an owl on an oak branch, &c., mingled in arrangement, and showing the arms of families who have owned the property. Amongst these are those of Newton, to which family, it is believed that Sir Isaac Newton belonged. In out-of-the-way corners of the stone there are many dials curiously inserted. The other inscriptions are :—

DEUS MIHI LUX.

God is my light.

FINIS ITINERIS SEPULCHRUM.

The grave is the end of the journey.

FUI UT ES, ERIS UT SUM.

I was as thou art, thou wilt be as I am.

UT HORA SIC VITA.

Life is as an hour.

The dial seems to be the sepulchral monument of Richard Lloyd, either erected during his lifetime or placed over his remains. Amongst the devices before mentioned, there is an effigy of Richard Lloyd.

Y

606.

THIS FOURFOLD INDEX OF SWIFT TIME,
ON WHICH $\frac{E}{Y}$ SHADOW VEERETH ROUND,
SHOULD MAN EXCITE TO THEMES SUBLIME,
SINCE NOU^T BUT SHADOWS HERE ARE FOUND.

UT HORA SIC VITA.　　　　UT VITA SIC UMBRA.
As the hour, so is life.　　　*As life, so is the shadow.*

DUM SPECTAS FUGIO.　1747.
While thou lookest, I fly.

Made for Saddlebow, whose Lat. is 54 : 45.

A solid block of stone, bearing three dials on the sides, and

one on the top, now stands, mounted on steps, in the garden
of Thorp Perrow, Yorkshire.　It was formerly at a farmhouse called Saddlebow, in Lunedale, and was bought by
Sir Frederick Milbank, Bart., and set up at first at Wemmer-
gill Lodge, and afterwards at Thorp Perrow.　The lines,
figures, and mottoes are all carved in the stone.

607.

THUS ETERNITY APPROACHETH. G. Holden, 1766.

Over the south porch of the church of St. John the Baptist, Pilling. The Rev. G. Holden, a well-known mathematician, was incumbent at the time when the dial was erected; and the portrait of a man in clerical costume, which was painted in one corner of the dial face, no doubt was meant to represent Mr. Holden.

608.

THUS THE GLORY OF THE WORLD PASSES AWAY. 1807.

Over the door of the church at Willerby, near Scarborough. The dial is plain and circular in form.

609.

THY DAYS ARE LIKE A SHADOW THAT DECLINETH.

On the porch of St. Madron's Church, near Penzance. The dial has no date, and is much worn by weather. The words are almost those of Psalm cii. 11. See No. 323.

610.

TIME AND TIDE STAY FOR NO MAN.

On the dial of St. Mary's Church, Putney, overlooking the Thames.

611.

TIME AND TIDE TARRY FOR NO MAN.

This motto is on a dial in Brick Court, Middle Temple, which has been recently restored, and replaced on the new buildings. The dates on the Temple dials are altered every time they are repainted, so are no guide to the time of their first erection. Probably they belong to the eighteenth century, and may have been seen by Goldsmith, who bought chambers in Brick Court for £400, and died there in 1774. The Templars' device of the Holy Lamb and staff or flag with a red cross is on all the dials. The motto may be read with reference to the time when the lawyers went from their chambers to the courts at Westminster by boat, and the favouring tide in the river was an important element in conveying them in time for business. The same inscription on a large vertical dial was formerly to be seen in the hall of New Inn, Wych Street, but the dial has long been removed. It was also on one of the two dials on Nonsuch House, one of the most curious and picturesque buildings of old London Bridge. These dials are said to have been put up in 1681, in the mayoralty of Sir Patience Ward. The houses on London Bridge were taken down in 1757 ; and the bridge was destroyed by fire in the following year.

The above motto, with eight others, was on Prince Albert Victor's dial at Edinburgh Exhibition in 1886. See No. 561.

612.

TIME AS HE PASSES US, HAS A DOVE'S WING, UNSOILED AND SWIFT, AND OF A SILKEN SOUND.

On Prince Albert Victor's dial at Edinburgh Exhibition, with eight other mottoes. See No. 561.

613.

(1.) TIME BY MOMENTS STEALS AWAY, FIRST THE HOUR AND THEN THE DAY.

(2.) ΕΞΑΓΩΡΑΖΟΜΕΝΟΙ ΤΟΝ ΚΑΙΡΟΝ ΟΤΙ ΑΙ ΗΜΕΡΑΙ ΠΟΝΗΡΑΙ ΕΙΣΙ.

Redeeming the time because the days are evil.

(3.) TEMPUS EDAX RERUM.

Time the devourer of (all) things.

(4.) BOAST NOT THYSELF OF TOMORROW—FOR ON THINE EYELIDS IS THE SHADOW OF DEATH.

(5.) THE MORNING COMETH AND ALSO THE NIGHT.

(6.) THE LORD BY WISDOM HATH FOUNDED THE EARTH, BY UNDERSTANDING HATH HE ESTABLISHED THE HEAVENS.

(7.) THE EARTH IS THE LORD'S, AND THE FULNESS THEREOF.

> " How grand the orbs of light on high,
> With all the blue ethereal sky,
> And spangled heavens a shining frame,
> Their great Original proclaim !
> In reason's ear they all rejoice,
> And utter forth a glorious voice,
> For ever singing as they shine
> " The Hand that made us is divine."

These seven mottoes, and the eight lines from Addison's paraphrase of Psalm xix., are engraved upon the face of a vertical south dial, erected in the Albert Park, Middlesbrough, by the gift of H. W. F. Bolckow, M.P. The design and workmanship were done by Mr. John Smith, of South

Stockton, who was seventy years of age when he executed the commission, but he has been deeply interested in the art of dialling since his boyhood. He was born at Beilby, near Pocklington, in 1807, and brought up as a farmer, but his taste for mechanical art was so strong that by the time he was eighteen he had constructed a wooden sun-dial which indicated the time in England and New York, and he erected it in his father's garden. In 1830 he constructed a machine which seems to have foreshadowed the pedometer of later years. This he fastened to his father's waggon, and by means of it he could measure the number of miles that the cart traversed. It was thus described in the "London Mechanic's Magazine":—"It is a species of clock-work, . . . and receives its motion from one of the hind wheels. It has two pointers attached to it, one of which revolves round in one mile, and the other in thirty-six miles, and a hammer strikes at every revolution of the former. The dial-plate is also ornamented with a diagram of the heavens representing the earth and moon revolving round the sun."

Mr. Smith placed a vertical sun-dial upon the Wesleyan chapel at Beilby, in 1837, which has no motto. He has since constructed many other dials, including one which he calls his "Art Sundial," a horizontal one, on which the same mottoes appear that are on the Middlesborough dial, and in addition to these the questions, "What is Deity? What is Eternity?" which are answered by the following inscription round the margin of the plate: "Deity is the King Eternal, Immortal, Invisible, the only Wise GOD our Saviour. Eternity is endless duration. Reader, That GOD will be thy Judge, and Eternity thy portion, Prepare in Time and be for ever blest."

This Art Sundial can be obtained from Messrs. Craig and Mackenzie, Stockton on Tees.

In the year 1873 Alderman Mathew Smith presented a large dial to the People's Park at Halifax. It was constructed by Mr. John Smith, and bears the first four mottoes which are on the Middlesbrough dial. Alderman Mathew Smith was elected Mayor of Halifax in 1879.

614.

TIME CAN DO MUCH. 1777.

On a dial in the garden of Leventhorpe Hall, near Leeds.

615.

TIME FLIES. 1781.

On a white house near the wall of the sea at Hartlepool. In the sixth book of Wordsworth's " Excursion" there is a pleasant episode showing how two political opponents, " flaming Jacobite and sullen Hanoverian," used to meet and discuss in " The churchyard among the mountains ; " and finally agreed to lie after death in one spot to be marked by a dial, which was thus inscribed :—

TIME FLIES; IT IS HIS MELANCHOLY TASK
TO BRING, AND BEAR AWAY, DELUSIVE HOPES,
AND REPRODUCE THE TROUBLE HE DESTROYS.
BUT, WHILE HIS BLINDNESS THUS IS OCCUPIED,
DISCERNING MORTAL ! DO THOU SERVE THE WILL
OF TIME'S ETERNAL MASTER, AND THAT PEACE
WHICH THE WORLD WANTS, SHALL BE FOR THEE CON-
FIRMED.

It must be acknowledged that these lines partake a little of the prosiness of which the poet is so often accused.

616.

**TIME FLIES, DEATH HASTES, A MOMENT MAY BE
    WISHED
WHEN WORLDS WANT WEALTH TO BUY.**

On a Sun-dial at Newlyn West, Cornwall. The lines
have been adapted from Young's "Night Thoughts;" Night
ii. 292.

> "Time flies, death urges, knells call,
> Heaven invites:"

and 306, 7.

> "A moment we may wish
> When worlds want wealth to buy."

617.

**TIME FROM THE CHURCH TOWER CRIES TO YOU
    AND ME,
UPON THIS MOMENT HANGS ETERNITY:
THE DIAL'S INDEX AND THE BELFRY'S CHIME
TO EYE AND EAR CONFIRM THIS TRUTH OF TIME.
PREPARE TO MEET IT; DEATH WILL NOT DELAY;
TAKE THEN THY SAVIOUR'S WARNING—WATCH AND
    PRAY!**

These lines, by James Montgomery, were, in 1883,
placed beneath a vertical dial which replaces an old one
without motto, on Robinson's Hospital (or Almshouses) at

Burneston, Yorkshire. The hospital, founded in 1680, is separated only by a road from the churchyard, and lies

almost under the shadow of the belfry. The dial was put up by G. J. Serjeantson, Esq.

618.

TIME IS THE CHRYSALIS OF ETERNITY.

One of nine mottoes on Prince Albert Victor's dial at Edinburgh Exhibition. See No. 561.

619.

TIME IS, THOU HAST: SEE THAT THOU WELL EMPLOY;
TIME PAST IS GONE: THOU CANST NOT THAT ENJOY.
TIME FUTURE IS NOT, AND MAY NEVER BE;
TIME PRESENT IS THE ONLY TIME FOR THEE.

Over the door of a schoolmaster's house at Leyburn, Yorkshire. Another version gives the two first lines thus :—

"Time was, is past: thou canst not it recall;
Time is, thou hast: employ the portion small."

620.

TIME IS ON THE WING, AND THE MOMENTS
OF LIFE ARE TOO PRECIOUS TO BE
SQUANDERED AWAY ON TRIFLES.

AH, WHAT IS HUMAN LIFE!
HOW LIKE THE DIAL'S TARDY MOVING SHADE:
DAY AFTER DAY GLIDES BY US UNPERCEIVED,
YET SOON MAN'S LIFE IS UP, AND WE ARE GONE.

At Hesketh, in Lancashire.

621.

TIME'S GLASS AND SCYTHE
THY LIFE AND DEATH DECLARE;
SPEED WELL THY TIME,
AND FOR THY END PREPARE.

Suggested motto for a dial, communicated by Mr. W. Osmond, of Salisbury.

622.

TIME'S ON THE WING,
DEATH'S APPROACHING,
THE HOUR'S UNCERTAIN.

1787.

On the church, Botus Fleming, Cornwall.

623.

TIME TIDE
DOTH WAIST
THEREFORE
MAKE HASTE
WE SHALL—

On a dial which originally stood in the garden at Carville
Hall, the teaching of the motto being enforced by the
position of the house, which stands midway between Newcastle and the sea, overlooking the Tyne. Carville Hall is
now the property of Wigham Richardson, Esq., and he has
presented the dial to the members of the Newcastle Society
of Antiquaries, who have placed it upon the roof of the
Norman keep of the Castle. The following description of
the dial has been given by the Rev. J. R. Boyle: "The
dial stone is an oblong slab, two sides of which are parallelograms, and two are rhomboids. This rests upon an
upright pillar. The dial slab lies in the plane of the earth's
equator. On its upper surface is a north polar dial, which
will show the time from the vernal to the autumnal
equinox. On its under surface is a south polar dial, which
will show the time from the autumnal to the vernal equinox.

On the vertical sides of the dial are four erect direct dials, facing exactly the four quarters of the earth. The dials are all graduated to half hours. I have placed the dial in the meridian of the castle of Newcastle. It will therefore show, when the equations of time are applied, not Greenwich, but local time. On the north side of the stone is a shield bearing *two bends and a crescent for difference, impaling, ermine, a chevron engrailed."* The latter are the arms of John Cosyn, who built Carville Hall, and died in 1662. He was buried at All Saints, Newcastle. The Hall is also called Cosyns House. The date 1667 is engraved on the pillar of the dial, and it was probably erected by John Cosyn's son-in-law, to whom the coat of arms evidently belonged. The motto is placed just above the north polar dial ; the word "dial" being of course required to complete the sense of the inscription." See No 725.

624.

TIME WASTED IS EXISTENCE, USED IS LIFE.

1826.

These lines from Young's "Night Thoughts" (Night II.) are over the porch entrance of the church at Hutton Buscell, Yorkshire, on an oval-shaped dial. The same idea is expressed by Herrick :

> " Long have I *lasted* in this world 'tis true,
> But yet these years that I have *lived*, but few.
> Who by his grey hairs doth his lustres tell,
> Lives not those years, but that he lives them well.
> He lives, who lives to virtue, men who cast
> Their lives to pleasure do not *live*, but *last*.

625.

TIME WASTES OUR BODIES AND OUR WITS,
BUT WE WASTE TIME AND SO WE'RE QUITS.

These lines, altered to fit the size of the stone, are on a vertical dial placed, in 1880, on the farm buildings at Camphill, Yorkshire, by G. J. Serjeantson, Esq. The original couplet runs thus:

Time wastes us, our bodies and our wits,
And we waste Time, so Time and we are quits.

The old proverb:

A STITCH IN TIME SAVES NINE.

is cut on the same dial.

626.

TIME WILL SHOW.

On a house at Down, in Kent, near the one in which Charles Darwin used to live.

627.

ΤΟ ΣΗΜΕΡΟΝ ΜΕΛΕΙ ΜΟΙ,
ΤΟ Δ'ΑΥΡΙΟΝ ΤΙΣ ΟΙΔΕ;

To-day is my care, but of to-morrow who knows?

Inscribed on the base of the pedestal of a pillar dial at Watton Abbey, near Driffield. The lines are from "Anacreon," Ode xv., l. ix.

628.

TRANSIT HORA MANENT OPERA.

The hour passes, the deeds remain.

DUM TEMPUS HABEMUS OPEREMUR BONUM.

While we have time let us do good.

In the courtyard of the monastery at Blois is a large vertical dial fronting the Evêché, which bears these mottoes.

629.

TRIFLE NOT, YOUR TIME'S SHORT. 1775.

At Milton, near Gravesend. So says Sir Walter Scott.

" Nay, dally not with Time, the wise man's treasure,
Though fools are lavish on't—the fatal Fisher
Hooks souls, while we waste moments."

630.

TRUE AS THE DIAL TO THE SUN,
ALTHOUGH IT BE NOT SHONE UPON. 1808.

The lines are from " Hudibras," and the dial is placed on the south aisle of Halifax Church, Yorkshire. The names of William Roberts, John Illingworth, Robert Abbott, and John Sutcliffe, churchwardens, are inscribed upon it, and the date 1808. Another dial, probably, older than this one, but of stone, and without a motto, crowns the gable of the south porch.

631.

TU NUMERI L' ORE MA NON SAI L' ORA DELLA MORTE.

Thou countest the hours, but thou knowest not the hour of death.

At Vigo, near Pinzola.

632.

TUA HORA RUIT MEA.

The hour which is mine, destroys what is thine.

In the cloister of the old Franciscan convent at Cimièz, near Nice. The Latin of the motto is monkish; *ruo* is treated as an active verb, and the dial, as usual, is supposed to speak. See No. 112.

633.

TVAM NESCIS.

Thou knowest not thine (hour).

On a house in Palermo; and also on the cathedral clock at Monreale.

634.

TVVS EST DIES, ET TUA EST NOX,
TV FABRICATVS ES AVRORAM ET SOLEM.

The day is Thine, and the night is Thine,
Thou hast prepared the light and the sun.

A vertical dial on Maxey Vicarage, Northamptonshire, which was erected by the Rev. W. D. Sweeting. His initials, W. D. S., and the date 1881, are perforated in the copper support of the gnomon; so that the latter can be read backwards or forwards, and both in the forenoon and afternoon the shadow gives the date of the erection of the dial.

635.

TYME PASSETH AND SPEKETH NOT,

DETH COMETH AND WARNETH NOT,

AMENDE TO-DAY AND SLACK NOT,

TO-MORROW THYSELF CANNOT.

The above lines are inscribed round the four sides of a very beautiful old dial pillar, at Moccas Court, Herefordshire. It

bears several dials of various shapes, circular and heart-shaped, concave ones, triangular, &c.; between and around these faces, the following Latin mottoes are sculptured. The first is from the Vulgate, Ps. xix. 1.

(1) Coeli enarrant gloriam Dei et Operationem manvvm eius annvnciat firmamentum.

The heavens declare the glory of God, and the firmament showeth His handywork.

(2) Si culpare velis, culpabilis esse cavebis; Nemo sine crimine vivit; id circo ne temere judicato.

If thou wouldst blame, thou wilt beware of being blameworthy. No one lives without reproach, therefore judge not rashly.

(3) Instar globi stat machina mundi.

Like a ball stands the framework of the world.

This is round a circular concave face, and round a heart-shaped one is:

(4) Dilige Dominum Deum toto corde.

Love the Lord thy God with all thy heart.

(5) Sol est lux et gloria mundi.

The sun is the light and glory of the world.

This is round another circular face. On the north side, beneath the signs of the planets, is "Domus Planetarum. Philippus Jones."

The dial pillar which now belongs to the Rev. Sir George Cornewall, Bart., is thought to have been made in the reign of Charles II., and was first set up at Mornington Court (on the opposite side of the Wye), the property of the Tompkins family. When this property came into possession of the Cornewalls, the dial was brought to Moccas. A similar one is at Kinlet, near Bewdley, but it is not in such good preservation as the one at Moccas.

z

636.

TYME TRYETH TROTHE.

On a dial in the village of Cradley, near Malvern.

637.

ULTIMA DECIDET.

1848 B. A. F.

The last (hour) will determine.

On a house at Ventimiglia.

638.

ULTIMA FORSAN.

Perhaps the last (hour).

This motto was observed in Switzerland. The dial was
round in shape and modern ; it faced south and was painted
blue and grey on a wall.

639.

ULTIMA LATET.

The last (hour) is hidden.

At an angle of the cloister beneath the belfry of the
Franciscan convent at Cimièz, near Nice, which has been
already mentioned, No. 112. Mr. Hopley read this inscription, and says that "when the old monks tolled the Angelus,
this dial was half in gloom, and the evening hours were
shrouded in shade." The motto is also at Alagna.

640.

ULTIMA MULTIS.
The last (hour) to many.

On an old Romanesque church at S. Beat, Hautes
Pyrenées.   The dial is on the belfry tower, beside a clock.

641.

ULTIMA NECAT.
The last hour kills.

At Spotorno.

642.

ULTIMAM TIME.
Fear your last hour.

At Rouen.

643.

UMBRA DEI.
The Shadow of God.

On the cross-dial at Elleslie, near Chichester, see No.
48 ; and on Dymock Church, Gloucestershire.

644.

UMBRA DOCET.
The shadow teaches.

On one of the four faces of the dial on Brighton pier, (see
No. 206).   The same thought is in No. 111, and No. 91.

645.

UMBRA LABITUR, ET NOS UMBRAE.

The shadow glides away, and we are shadows.

Formerly on Glasgow Cathedral.　See No. 407.

646.

UMBRA MONET UMBRAM.

Shade warns shade.

That is—the dial warns man.　For a similar thought see
No. 650.　The above motto was communicated by Sir
Frederick Elliot.

647.

UMBRA SUMUS.　Lat. 50. 52.　1739.
PEREUNT ET IMPUTANTUR.

We are a shadow.
(The hours) perish and are reckoned.

These mottoes occur on the north and south sides of a
square pillar dial at Brympton, near Yeovil; there are dial
faces on all the four sides.　The pillar is made of stone, and
surmounted by a ball.　It has been placed upon the terrace
by the present owner of Brympton, Sir Spencer Ponsonby
Fane, but was found by him on the top of the kitchen-
garden wall, when he came into possession of the place.

The first of the above mottoes is on the churches of St.
James', Parkham; SS. Mary and Gregory, Frithelstock,
Devon; and the parish church, Maidstone.

648.

UMBRA SUMUS—TAMEN HIS AEVUM COMPO-
NITUR UMBRIS.

We are a shadow—yet time is made up of such shadows.

Mr. Spencer Butler, Seaford, Surrey, writes : " I wanted to combine in one line the two ideas, that though we are fugitive like the dial shadow, yet like the dial shadows, in the aggregate we make up the space of time or eternity. The best shape I could give to the idea was the above line. I had on a south wall an ugly patch of cement where a summer-house had been. A friend suggested fixing an iron rod against it in a line pointing to the north pole. The dial was painted grey with a black border, the figures red.

649.

UMBRA TEGIT LAPSAS PRAESENTIQUE IMMINET
HORAE,
DUM LUX DUM LUCIS SEMITA VIRTUS AGAT.

Ere yet the threatening shade o'erspreads the hour,
Hasten, bright virtue, and exert thy power.

On a dial in the garden at Bryn Bella, near St. Asaph, where Dr. Johnson stayed, on the occasion of his visit to Wales. The motto and paraphrase were sent to us together.

650.

UMBRA VIDET UMBRAM:
VIVE HODIE.

A shadow marks the shadow,
Live to-day.

On a pillar dial at Bradford, Peverell House, near Dorchester. The inscription is somewhat defaced by time. It was possibly erected by George Purling, Esq., about 1815-20, when the garden was laid out. The correspondent who sent the motto points out that the " umbra" spoken of is evidently the man whose " days are as a shadow," and Pindar's σκιᾶς ὄναρ ἀνθρωπος (Pythia, viii. 95). A similar motto occurs on the tower of Broughton-Gifford Church, near Melkesham, but there the two last words are written : " Hodie vivo "—*To-day I live.*

651.

UMBRAE TRANSITUS EST TEMPUS NOSTRUM.

S. Sykes, fecit. Decem. 22, 1790.

Our time is the passing away of a shadow.

On a house dial in Wentworth, Yorkshire ; also at Cuers in France; and on the church of S. Crocifisso, Pieve di Cadore, with three other mottoes. See No. 205.

652.

UMBRAE TRANSITUS EST VITA NOSTRA.

Our life is the passing of a shadow.

On a church near Palermo.

653.

UMBRAM DUM SPECTAS REFUGIT REVOLU-BILE TEMPUS.

Whilst thou lookest at the shadow, on-rolling time escapes.

In Alderley Churchyard, Cheshire.

654.

UNA DI QUESTE T' APRIRÀ LE PORTE DI VITA LIETA, O DI SPIETATA MORTE.

One of these hours shall open thee the gate
Of blissful life, or of relentless fate.

Between Nervia and Convento, on the Riviera. Dean Alford read and translated this motto.

655.

UNA EX HIS.

One out of these.

On a plate in Zurich Museum.

656.

UNA UMBRA ET VAPOR EST HOMINVM VITA.

Man's life is at once a shadow and smoke.

There is a curious device on this sun-dial, which stands in Helston Churchyard, Cornwall. It represents St. Michael, we presume, as the figure is robed, winged, and with rays of

glory round the head, standing betwixt two towers, and driving his spear into a dragon which is at his feet.

657.

UNA HARUM VITAE HORARUM ERIT ULTIMA. 1814.

One of these hours will be the last of life.

On a church near Queen Hortense's Château of Arenemberg. The dial is circular in form. Time with his scythe is in the centre, and over him, a sun, from which issues the gnomon.

658.

UNAM TIME.

Fear one hour.

On a house at St. Pierre, on the Great St. Bernard road; and also at Gap.

659.

UNAM TIMEO.

One hour I fear.

On the church of Stazzano in Piedmont.

660.

UNITED IN TIME, PARTED IN TIME,
TO BE REUNITED, WHEN TIME SHALL BE NO MORE.

On a fine pillar of dials, designed and erected by Lady John Scott, at Cawston Lodge, near Rugby, in 1863. (See Frontispiece.) It was partly copied from the dial in the King's garden at Holyrood, which Charles I. presented to Queen Henrietta Maria. The pillar is mounted on two steps, and near the base are the Scott arms and the Spottiswood arms—Lady John Scott being Alice, the eldest daughter of John Spottiswood, Esq., of Spottiswood, co. Berwick. In separate panels round the lower part of the pillar are engraved "John and Alice Scott;" "A Bellenden," the old Border war-cry of the Scotts of Buccleuch; "Amo," one of their mottoes; "Best riding by moonlight," their ancient Mosstrooping motto; and "Patior ut potiar," the Spottiswood motto. The dial mottoes, the crests of the two families, and the monograms of Lord and Lady John Scott are carved in corresponding panels at the upper part of the pillar, the top being encircled by a serpent, the emblem of eternity.

661.

USE THE PRESENT TIME
REDEEM THE PAST
FOR THUS UNCERTAINLY
THOUGH IMPERCEPTIBLY
THE NIGHT OF LIFE APPROACHES.

In Aldingham Churchyard, Lancashire.

662.

USE WELL THE PRESENT MOMENTS AS THEY FLEET
YOUR LIFE HOWEVER SHORT WILL BE COMPLETE
IF AT ITS FATAL ENDING YOU CAN SAY
I'VE LIVED AND MADE THE MOST OF EVERY DAY.

Engraved on a horizontal dial in the churchyard of Water-
fall, Staffordshire.

663.

USQUE HUC CRESCIT.
Even so far there is increase.

This is at Beziers, in France.

664.

**VT HORA PRAETERITA
SIC FUGIT VITA.**

1612. A. B.

*As the hour that is past,
So doth life fly.*

Engraved on a horizontal dial, now (1887) in the possession of Colonel Fishwick, at The Heights, Rochdale, Lancashire.

665.

UT HORA SIC FUGIT VITA.

1578.

As an hour, so doth life fly.

Painted on the wall of King's College Chapel, Cambridge,
beside the south entrance. The motto is in old English
letters, and rather defaced.

666.

UT HORA SIC VITA.

1727.

Life is as an hour.

This motto may be seen on a little white wooden dial
which formerly stood on the porch of Stanhope, co. Durham,
but has now been placed on the south wall of the chancel.
The register books show that the dial was put up by Bishop
Butler, then rector. His "Analogy" was written when he

lived at Stanhope. The same inscription is on a horizontal dial, supported by an octagonal pillar, in Adel Church-yard, near Leeds; it is engraved on a scroll on the dial plate, with the addition of " J. Munn. Ebor. fecit ex donatu. 1682." About the same time Mr. Munn made a vertical dial for Almondbury Church, which is now on the south wall, and bears his name, and date 1682, and a hori-zontal one for Woodsome Hall, in the same neighbourhood, in 1683. The same motto is on all these three dials. It is also on a dial plate in the churchyard of Wath, near Ripon, the pillar which supports it is a single stone, probably once the shaft of a cross. The names of " Tho⁹ Browne, Geo. Yeats, 1735," have been carefully cut on the side.

Ut hora sic vita is likewise on the porch gable of Felton Church, Northumberland, 1724; on the almshouse at Ormsby, Yorkshire, 1776; on the porch of Methwold Church, Norfolk, with the gnomon projecting from the sun's face, and the names of " Rich. Clarke, Rich. Younge, Junʳ Church wardens, 1721;" on St. Giles's Church, Sidbury, Devon; on St. Patrick's Church, Isle of Man (see No. 372); on Hatford Church (57); on the church porch, Chapel-en-le-Frith, Derbyshire, 1871; on a pedestal dial in Acton Churchyard, Cheshire (571); on Witton-le-Wear Church, dated 1773; on Jarrow Church, co. Durham; over the church porch at Heddon-on-the-Wall, Northumberland; at Menwith Hill, near Darley (220); at Brougham Hall (379); at Marrington Hall (605), and at Thorpe Perrow (606).

The Rev. R. V. Taylor stated in the " Yorkshire Post" that the motto, *Ut hora sic vita*, with the date 1672, was upon a dial which formerly stood at Wooldale, near Holmfirth, in front of an old house. The plate was fastened upon a curious pillar of rudely hewn stones, which bore some resemblance to a house clock, and it was known by the name of "Old Genu's dial," or "Genu's clock." An engraving of it occurs in Morehouse's "History of Kirkburton." The pillar has been removed, and the dial erected on the wall of an out-building. It bears the initials "H. G." and "S. H.," supposed to be those of "the sulptor and owner."

Lastly, the above motto is inscribed on the clock which was placed in 1859 on the tower of Hoole Church, Lancashire, as a memorial of Jeremiah Horrox, who discovered the transit of Venus when he was curate at Hoole in 1639.

667.

UT UMBRA DECLINAVERUNT.

They have gone down as a shadow.

This may be read at Trafiume, near Cannobio, Lago Maggiore.

668.

UT UMBRA SIC VITA.

As a shadow, so is life.

This motto, dated 1695, is on a dial at Morden College, Blackheath; also at Morvah Church, West Cornwall, with the date 1-29 partially defaced. It is engraved, too, on one of the four corner pinnacles of the churchyard wall at Sleights, near Whitby. Here the motto is below the dial, which faces south. On the east side of the same pinnacle is another dial, with the date 1761, and the initials R T B and and G. B. It was in this year that Robert and Tabitha Bower built the church. It may be read on a cottage in the village of

Fenny Compton ; also near Baslow (see No. 158); at Shaftesbury, Dorset ; at Derwent Hall, Derbyshire (see No. 13); and on a dial over the south porch of Hartest Church, Suffolk ; and was formerly in the Isle of Man (see No. 331).

669.

UT UMBRA, SIC VITA TRANSIT.

As a shadow so doth life pass.

This is on a glass dial in a window of Election Chamber, Winchester College. The shape of the dial is an oblong square, set in an oval frame of richly-coloured glass. The motto is on a scroll in the centre of the upper half of the pane which forms the plate, and at one corner is the mysterious fly already noticed, see No. 117. Bishop Henry King, writing in the seventeenth century, says :—

> " What is the existence of man's life ?
>
>   *   *   *   *
>
> It is a dial which points out
> The sunset as it moves about :
> And shadows out, in lines of night,
> The suble changes of Time's flight ;
> Till all obscuring Earth hath laid
> The body in perpetual shade."

670.

UT UMBRA SUMUS.

As a shadow are we.

Is the motto of the dial on Cordell's Hospital, Long Melford, Suffolk, with the date 1573. It also occurs on an old house at Edmonton, Middlesex.

671.

UT VITA SIC FUGIT HORA.

The hour passes away like life.

On a Sanctuary dedicated to St. Francis of Assisi, which is situated on a hill that rises above the lake and town of Orta.

672.

UT VITA SIC UMBRA. 1833.

As life so is the shadow.

On a house at Kirby Moorside, Yorkshire. Also on one of the dials at Thorp Perrow. See No. 606.

673.

UTERE PRAESENTI MEMOR ULTIMAE.

Use the present (hour) mindful of the last.

On the church of S. Crocifisso, Pieve di Cadore, with three other mottoes. See No. 205.

674.

VAE TERRAE ET MARI, QUIA DESCENDIT DIABOLUS AD VOS, HABENS IRAM MAGNAM, SCIENS QUOD MODI- CUM TEMPUS HABET. APOC. C. XII. V. 12.

Woe to the earth and to the sea, because the devil is come down unto you, having great wrath, knowing that he hath but a short time.

The locality in which we find this inscription, which is

from the Vulgate translation and the Douay version, is very interesting. The dial, which seems to be held by an eagle in a very startled condition, is over an archway which leads into the great convent square at the top of the Sacro Monte at Varallo in Piedmont; and through this opening pilgrims from all parts of Italy have been accustomed to pass and re-pass in order to pay their devotions at the "Nuova Gerusa-lemme nel Sacro Monte di Varallo."

The Sacro Monte was founded in 1486 by Bernardino Caimo, a Milanese nobleman, and it grew rapidly in riches and reputation; the visits paid to it by Archbishop Carlo Borromeo contributing no little to its renown. Forty-six chapels or oratories are dotted over the hill, in each of which there is a scene from the life of our Lord, represented by groups of life-sized terra-cotta figures, that are clothed and painted in imitation of the reality; whilst the walls are covered with frescoes, on which the Alpine artists have exercised their skill for many years. Among these are some of Gaudenzio Ferrari's finest works, but the screens and partitions which enforce that distance which "lends enchant-ment to the view" of these figure groups, are by no means favourable to an examination of the frescoes. There are, however, some very striking groups, notwithstanding the drawbacks of age, eccentricity, and excessive realism. Some-times a grand force and truth of expression are revealed, which must have made the sacred scenes come home to the hearts of the mountaineers. The Sacro Monte is crowned by the Convent, which overlooks the lovely Val Sesia, whilst the town of Varallo lies at the foot of its Mount Calvary.

The dial is large, painted on the wall, and much orna-mented. A kind of eagle's head and wings rises above the plane, and something of the same sort appears below; the whole being enclosed in a narrow border. The width of the dial exceeds that of the arch beneath. The lines on the face show the Italian hours only—from i to xxiv. The tropics of Cancer and Capricorn are described upon it, and the parallels of the sun's course at his entrance into the twelve signs of the Zodiac, together with the characters of the signs. The motto is on a spiral scroll on one side of the dial, and a corresponding scroll on the other side, somewhat defaced, has an imperfect Latin inscription, which refers to the mechanism of the dial. This is preceded by the figures -645, which may be a partially obliterated date of 1645.

675.

VASSENE 'L TEMPO, E L' UOM NON SE N' AVVEDE.

DANTE, Purg. c. iv.

Time passes on, and man perceives it not.

This is on a house in the Via Brondolo, Padua; and "Padova la dotta" may be said to maintain its character for learning, even in its dial; and to show its fidelity to the memory of Dante, who is reported to have lived there in 1306. Nevertheless, the present dial is modern, and is painted on a wall in a back street—south, declining east—just above the green shutters of the windows of the first story. The round arched doorway below, supported by a pillar on each side, opens into a carpenter's shop; but there lingers an air of departed grandeur about the building, which suggests that its owners in the last century were people of greater consequence than the present occupiers.

A A

676.

VEILLEZ SUR TOUTE, CRAIGNEZ LA DER-NIÈRE.

Watch over every (hour), fear the last.

This inscription is on a scroll over a dial which is painted on the wall of a house at Cannes.

677.

VENIO UT FUR.

I come as a thief.

Copied by Mr. Howard Hopley, but no place named.   In Shakespeare's 77th sonnet we read :—

" Thou by thy dial's shady stealth may'st know
Time's thievish progress to Eternity."

And in the " Comedy of Errors " (act iv. sc. 2)—

" Nay, he's a thief too, have you not heard men say
That Time comes stealing on by night and day ? "

678.

VERA LOQUI AUT SILERE.

To speak the truth or to be silent.

On Highgate Grammar School.

679.

VESTIGIA NULLA RETRORSUM.
No steps backward.

On the dial in Essex Court, in the Temple ; and on a
house at Brompton-on-Swale, Yorkshire. See No. 368.
The same phrase is found in Horace, Epist. i. 1. 74-5, in
allusion to the fable of the fox invited into the lion's den, but
astutely declining—

> " Quia me vestigia terrent
> Omnia te adversum spectantia, nulla retrorsum."

It is interesting to remember that this motto was adopted
by John Hampden, when he took up arms for the Parliament.
In " Amor Mundi," Christina Rossetti writes :—

" Oh, where are you going with your lovelocks flowing
On the west wind blowing along this valley track ?
The downhill path is easy, come with me an' it please ye,
We shall escape the uphill by never turning back.

*   *   *   *   *

" Turn again, O my sweetest, turn again, false and fleetest :
This way whereof thou weetest I fear is hell's own track,
Nay, too steep for hill-mounting, nay, too late for cost
          counting :
This downhill path is easy, but there's no turning back."

680.

VIA CRUCIS VIA LUCIS.
The way of the Cross is the way of light.

At Hurstpierpoint School there is a dial shaped as a re-

cumbent Cross, which bears this incription.   The hours are
indicated by the position of the shadow on the different points
of the Cross.

681.

VIA VITAE.

The way of life.

Over a large square stone dial which was placed between
pinnacles against the south side of the tower of Sheffield
Parish Church.   The dial was removed when a new clock
was erected, but happily the Vicar has taken care to have the
older time-keeper restored to very nearly its former position.
The same inscription is on the cross-dial at Elleslie (No. 48);
and was formerly on Himbleton Church, Worcestershire.
The dial was of wood, and placed on a small wooden turret,
but, having become dilapidated, it was removed between
1850 and 1860.   The motto was also on a large dial on
Cawthorne Church, Yorkshire, " S. H. fecit. 1798," but this
was taken down at the partial rebuilding of the church in
1876.

682.

VIDE, AUDI, TACE.

See, hear, and be silent.

The position of this dial motto is not identified.

683.

VIDES HORAM ET NESCIS FUTURUM.   1836.

Thou seest the hour, and thou knowest not the future.

The dial is a large erect one, painted, south declining

west, on the wall of a house at Pra on the Riviera, which forms part of what was once a little chapel, the tower and bell of which still remain. The small adjoining house was probably the priest's residence. The belfry tower is the oldest and most picturesque portion of the building, constructed in the true Genoese style, with alternate stripes of black and

white marble. All other traces of its former use have now disappeared. The windows on either side of the dial may usually be seen festooned outside with clothes after a washing day, and the tenants are poor people. It stands in the middle of the Piazza, which is the great rendezvous of all the inhabitants of Pra. This place is a large village, seven or eight miles west of Genoa, where both fishing and boat-building are carried on.

684.

VIDES HORAM NESCIS HORAM.

1853.

Thou seest the hour, thou knowest not the hour.

Over the door of the church at Alassio.

685.

VIDETE VIGILATE ET ORATE, NESCITIS ENIM DIEM NEQUE HORAM.

Take heed, watch and pray, for ye know neither the day nor the hour.

Over the south door of the Frauenkirche at Munich. The dial is very large and handsome, painted on a ground of blue with gold stars. A small seated figure in the centre of a glory of golden rays holds the Gnomon, a flying angel on each side bears up the scroll on which the hours are marked. Below, the equator, the circles of the earth, &c., are shown on a large surface, round the border of which are the signs of the Zodiac. The figures are gracefully drawn, and the dial seems to date from the seventeenth century.

686.

VIGILA, ORAQUE.

Watch and pray.

On a buttress of the south transept of the parish church, Leighton Buzzard. See No. 46.

687.

VIGILARE ET ORARE TEMPUS DIRIGIT.

To watch and pray, time ordains.

This motto, on a scroll, is engraved on a stone dial over the porch of Harewood Church, near Leeds. At the bottom are words, "Robert Smith fecit 1751." The motto is much worn, and the last word nearly illegible.

688.

VIGILATE ET ORATE.

Watch and pray.

Over the south porch of Rothwell Church, near Leeds, with the further inscription, "I Verity fecit. Lat. 53.15", and date 1821. The motto and figures are on a blue border. The same motto is on a wooden vertical dial on Bridge's almshouses, Thames Ditton, dated 1746 and 1720, the latter being the date of the building. "Ex dono Henrici Bridges, Gent." It is also at Reading, with date "1727, G. P."; at Warwick; and over the church porch, Clovelly.

689.

VITA FUGIT VELUT UMBRA. 1790.

Life flies as a shadow.

On the church at Sandal, Yorkshire. The dial was removed during the restoration of the building, but it is hoped that it will be replaced.

690.

VITA HOMINIS SICUT UMBRA FLUIT.
The life of man flows away like a shadow.

At Courmayeur.

691.

VITA QUASI UMBRA.
Life is as a shadow.

At Sproughton Rectory, near Ipswich.

692.

VITA SIC TRANSIT. 1817. LAT. 54.20 N. S. 20 W.
W. PUTSEY DELINEAVIT.
So life passes away.

This is on a square dial on Pickering Church, Yorkshire.

693.

VITA TUA SEMPER INCERTA.
Thy life is ever uncertain.

In the Chiostro del Noviziato, St. Antonio, Padua. The dial is traced on the wall above the arches of the cloister, and is nearly defaced; the first word can only be guessed at.

694.

VITA UMBRA. 1867.

Life is a shadow.

On Archbishop Abbot's Hospital, Guildford. The dial is nearly at the top of the entrance tower. The building dates from 1619: probably the date 1867 refers to the restoration or repainting of the dial.

695.

VIGILATE ET ORATE: TEMPUS FUGIT.

1781.

Watch and pray : Time flies.

High up on the tower of Ellastone Church, near Ashbourne, Derbyshire, are these mottoes. The dial is fixed over a small built-up window, or what seems like it, and below is the additional inscription, " KNOWE THYSELFFE," which looks of older date.

The same mottoes with the date 1797, are on a dial upon the Wesleyan Chapel at Thorpe Hesley, near Rotherham ; and they are likewise on the endowed school at Brampton Bierlow, with the date 1807. The bell of this school bears the following inscription: " Ad scholam discipulos voco."

696.

VIGILATE, QUIA NESCITIS DIEM NEQUE HORAM.

Matt., chap. xxv. ver. 13.

Watch, for ye know neither the day nor the hour.

In the Via San Vittore al Teatro, Milan. The dial is eight feet square, the gnomon a circular disk standing out from the wall by means of three iron rods.

697.

VIGILATE, QUIA NESCITIS HORAM.

Watch, for ye know not the hour.

The dial, defaced and without date, is painted between the windows of a house at Arles, having curious balconies; and which looks into a small square where the peasants on *fête* days dance their national Catalan dance in the white caps and *espartillos* that are still worn in the Eastern Pyrenees. For this Arles must not be confounded with Arles in Provence; but is a town with about 2,000 inhabitants, near the head of the valley of the Tech, thirty-nine kilometres from Perpignan, and it is surrounded by mountains, of which the Canigou towers highest. It has an ancient church with a cloister of great elegance and beauty, dating from the thirteenth century, and is about two or three hours distant from the Spanish frontier.

698.

VIRTUS AD ASTRA TENDIT, IN MORTEM TIMOR.

Courage strives towards the stars, fear to death.

This is on the Chateau of Oberhofen, which is situated on the Lake of Thun, and is a picturesque building, close to the water's edge, belonging to the Count Pourtalès.

699.

VITA FUGIT SICUT UMBRA.

1840. Z. G. F.

Life flies like a shadow.

At Vallouse (see No. 61); and also at Abriès, dated " 1841. S. P." The initials " Z. G. F." are those of Zerbola, G. F., who seems to have been a maker of dials. See No. 507. It is strange that Petrarch's line—

" La vita fugge e non s'arresta un ora "

has not been, so far as we know, used as a dial motto.

700.

VIVE HODIE.

Live to-day. ·

CRAS MINUS APTUS ERIT.

To-morrow will be less seasonable.

REMEMBER NOW THY CREATOR IN THE DAYS OF THY YOUTH.

These mottoes are on three dials which adorn three sides of the tower of the Lyme Cage, a building standing in Lyme Park, Disley, Cheshire. See Nos. 247, 444.

701.

VIVE MEMOR QUAM SIS AEVI BREVIS. 1767.

JOHN METCALFE, FECIT., CHURCHWARDEN. 1767.

Live mindful how short-lived thou art.

On a dial fixed outside the terrace walk at Wentworth Woodhouse, Yorkshire, the seat of Earl Fitzwilliam, K.G. It also appears on a dial attached to the glass house in Lord Fitzwilliam's garden, with " Lat. 53—28. Dec. W. 34° delineavit Johan. Metcalfe 1766." See No. 392. The same motto is on the church of Goosnargh-cum-Wittingham, Preston, Lancashire, with " C. Swainson M.A. Minister of Goosnargh " above the gnomon, and below it is " H. Porter of Westfield, delin. & Sculp: 1748. Lat. 53°—38 ". The line is taken from Horace, Sat. ii. 6, 97.

702.

VIVE MEMOR QUAM SIS BREVIS.
Live mindful how short (lived) thou art.

CITO PEDE PRAETERIT AETAS.
The age goes by with speedy foot.

On a horizontal dial-plate which stands on a short

pillar at Wigmore Grange, Herefordshire. Below the two mottoes a death's head and Time's scythe are respectively carved.

703.

VIVIT MEMORIA ET FUGIT HORA.
Memory lives and the hour flies.

On a house at Monthey, in Canton du Valais, Switzerland. The dial is very plain, and circular in form. The motto "*Lethi vive memor fugit hora.* 1764" (*Live mindful of Death, the hour flies*) is below a church clock in Venice.

"When Time who steals our years away
Shall steal our pleasures too,
The memory of the past will stay
And half our joys renew.

"Then talk no more of future gloom,
Our joys shall always last ;
For hope shall brighten days to come,
And memory gild the past ! "

T. MOORE.

704.

VIVITE, AIT, FUGIO.

Live ye, it says : I fly.

On a dial over the porch of Wrenbury Hall, near Nant-wich. This inscription is thus alluded to in a letter from Bishop Atterbury to Pope, dated Bromley, May 25, 1712 : " You know the motto of my sun-dial, *Vivite, ait, fugio.* I will, as far as I am able, follow its advice, and cut off all un-necessary avocations and amusements." In the same cor-respondence of the Bishop the following epigram occurs :—

"Vivite, ait, fugio.
Labentem tacito quisquis pede conspicis umbram,
Si sapis, haec audis : 'Vivite, nam fugio.'
Utilis est oculis, nec inutilis auribus umbra ;
Dum tacet, exclamat, 'Vivite, nam fugio.'"

Whoso on hushed foot mark'st the gliding shade,
If wise thou hearest, " Live ye, for I fly."
To eyes and ears the shadow lends its aid,
Silently crying, " Live ye, for I fly."

The dial was probably a mural one on the ancient moated palace of the Bishops of Rochester, at Bromley, which was pulled down by Bishop Thomas in 1774. The building which he substituted has ceased to be an episcopal residence.

705.

VIVITE, ECCE FUGIO. 1712.

Live ye, behold ! I fly.

On an octagonal stone dial fixed on the church tower of Kirkby Overblow, Yorkshire.

706.

VOICI VOTRE HEURE.

Behold your hour.

To be read near Geneva.

707.

VOLAT SINE MORA.

It flies without delay.

In the cloister of the Franciscan convent at Cimièz, Nice. See No. 112.

708.

VOLAT TEMPUS.

Time flies.

OH, EARLY PASSENGER, LOOK UP, BE WISE,
AND THINK HOW, NIGHT AND DAY, TIME EVER FLIES.

On the east dial on the pillar at Tytherton, Kellaways,
Wilts. The south face bears the following inscription :—

DUM TEMPUS HABEMUS OPEREMUR BONUM.
Whilst we have time, let us do good.

LIFE STEALS AWAY, O MAN THIS HOUR IS LENT THEE,
PATIENTLY WORK THE WORK OF HIM WHO SENT THEE.

On the west side is—

REDIBO, TV NVNQVAM.
I shall return, thou never.

HASTE, TRAVELLER, THE SUN IS SINKING NOW,
HE SHALL RETURN AGAIN, BUT NEVER THOU.

The Latin motto is in each case above the dial, the English
lines below. The dials are on three faces of a block sur-
mounting a stone pillar which stands on the bank of the
Avon, beside a bridge crossed by the road from Chippenham
to Tytherton, and in the parish of Tytherton Kellaways.

The dial pillar was erected in 1698 by the trustees of
Maud Heath's Causeway. About the year 1828 the Rev.
William Lisle Bowles, rector of the adjoining parish of
Bremhill, distrusting the power of the passers-by to under-
stand the Latin mottoes, obtained leave to engrave his own

poetical paraphrases in smaller letters below them. Mr. Bowles has given a slightly different version of the lines in the "History of Bremhill," and has perhaps improved them. We give them, however, as they stand on the dials.

709.

VOLVITUR IN PUNCTO
PUNTOQUE RESOLVITUR.

17 AETAS 44

Bruyere fecit.

(Time) passes in a moment,
And in a moment it is gone.

This motto, with its inconsistent spelling, is on a wooden dial-plate bought by Charles T. Gatty, at a sale at Sotheby's.

710.

VULNERANT OMNES, ULTIMA NECAT.

All (hours) wound, the last kills.

Painted, south declining east, on the church tower of Urugne, department Basses Pyrenées. The motto is in large capitals above the dial, which is placed below the open arch of the belfry.

Urugne is on the great western road leading from France into Spain, and is the last French post-station, having the wild irregular ridges of the Spanish mountains in full view. The dark Spanish-looking church has associations connected with the Peninsular War. The "Subaltern" gives an account of a night spent in it after the assault and capture of the village on the previous day, in November, 1813, when he and his men were cantoned in the church, whose thick walls were proof against the field artillery of the French. This village formed part of Marshal Soult's famous position in front of St. Jean de Luz. The same motto is on the Duomo, Grosseto.

At Cawder House, near Glasgow, there is a slightly different version—*Omnes vulnerant, ultima necat,* together with *Horas non numero nisi serenas,* and *Carpe diem.* This dial is dated 1698. See No. 388.

> " . . . Past hours
> If not by guilt, yet wound us by their flight."
>
>   YOUNG's *Night Thoughts.*

711.

WACHET; DENN IHR WISSET NICHT, UM WELCHE STUNDE EUER HERR KOMMEN WIRD.

Watch, for ye know not at what hour your Lord doth come.
        Matt. xxiv. 42.

At Erstfelden, near Altdorf, in the Canton Uri, there is a dial painted on the wall of a little village church. It is circular in form, with the face of the sun at the top, out of which comes the gnomon. A full-length skeleton stands on each side of the dial, like the supporter to an heraldic shield, and appears to hold up the plate. Beneath it are cross-bones, and the motto is above. Some words under the cross-bones are defaced and illegible.

712.

WAN ICH BIN EIN GESCHENCKH VOL,
SO ZAIG ICH DI STUNDT GER WOL;
BIN ICH ABER LEHR,
SO DIE ALS NIT MER.

> *When I am full,*
> *I show the hour;*
> *But when I am empty,*
> *I do so no more.*

On a goblet-shaped dial in the Nuremburg Museum; the inscription is engraved round the outside of the lip. The goblet is of silver or copper gilt. Probably the dial was originally accompanied by a compass, or had some directions for setting it, otherwise it is impossible to understand how it could "show the hour," whether full or empty.

713.

WATCH AND PRAY. 1735.

On the south wall of Alwalton Church, Huntingdonshire; and on the church porch of Terrington St. Clement, Norfolk, with the names of the churchwardens, "Mudd and Dewson", but no date.

714.

WATCH AND PRAY
TIME FLIES AWAY.

Over the door of a shop, Leighton Buzzard. The gnomon is surrounded with rays, and below is a small dim landscape view with trees and windmill.

715.

WATCH AND PRAY,
TIME HASTES AWAY.

Over a cottage at Barton, near Darlington ; also on the church porch of Llantiglos-by-Fowey, Cornwall; and on a horizontal dial in the churchyard of Westward, Cumberland.

716.

WATCH AND PRAY,
TIME HASTENS AWAY;
WHEN TIME IS DONE
ETERNITY COMES ON.

On a pillar dial in Mottram Churchyard, with the names of Joshua Andrews and James Goddard, churchwardens, 1811.

717.

WATCH AND PRAY,
TIME PASSETH AWAY LIKE A SHADOW.

On the church at Isleworth, which was built in 1705. The dial is quaint. Above it Time is represented as a bearded old man with wings, and he reclines on his back holding a scythe, the point of which touches a scroll at his feet, on which is written, "Watch and pray," whilst "Time passeth," &c., is on another scroll above the dial face, which half hides a radiated sun, and from this comes the gnomon. The dial is lineated, and the hours marked at several distant places, such as Jerusalem, Moscow, &c.

718.

WATCH AND PRAY

TIME STEALS AWAY.

J^{no} Berry fecit 1757.

Is on St. Peter's Church, Tawstock, Devon, over the south-west porch.

719.

WATCH FOR YE KNO NOT THE HOVRE.

1649.

On a stone with three faces, which was formerly attached to the wall of the south-west corner of St. Anne's Court, Dunbar. Two of the faces bore metal dial-plates, and the motto and date were carved on the third face. Miss Ritchie, of Barnlea, Dunbar, who has kindly contributed this motto, describes St. Anne's Court as a quaint mansion with two courtyards in front, and the side of one of these was formed by an old building supposed to have been part of the church of St. Anne's, built upon Dunbar Sands. According to the ancient rhyme :—

"St. Abb, St. Helen, and St. Bees
They a' built kirks which to be nearest the sea,
St. Abb's upon the Nabs, St. Helen's on the Lea ;
St. Ann's upon Dunbar Sands, stands nearest to the sea ! "

The church has long ceased to be used for worship ; the sea has made such inroads on the coast that it now washes the building at high tides, in spite of a stone bulwark. There is a tradition that the dial was originally on the church, and was removed from thence to the Court, when the former. was dismantled. Miss Ritchie's grandfather used to live at the Court, and she recollects when there was an old pulpit in the cellar. The property has now passed from her family into other hands, and the dial has been taken by her to Barnlea.

720.

WATCH, FOR YE KNOW NOT THE HOUR.

INSCRIBED 1862, M. G.

The fine old village church at Ecclesfield, in Yorkshire,

was externally rebuilt *circa* 1470. In the middle of the churchyard, on the south side, stands the broken shaft of a mortuary cross. Two stone steps form the pedestal which supports it, and it is surmounted by a small copper dial. On the upper step, around the shaft, the late Mrs. Alfred Gatty had the above motto engraved in 1862. It is also to be read on the porch of St. Margaret's Church, Ormsby, Norfolk.

721.

WATCH WEEL.

This, which is the heraldic motto of Sir Walter Scott, is

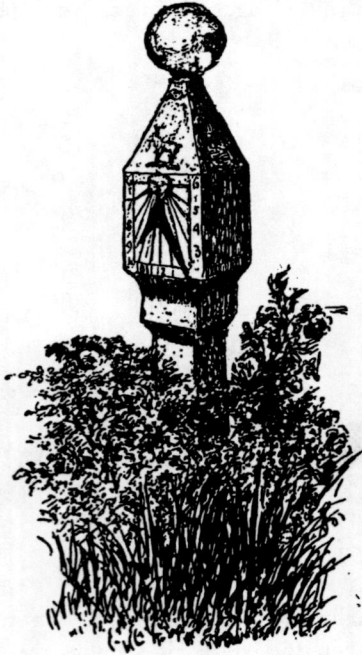

inscribed on a very graceful pillar dial, having four faces to the different points of the compass, which stood in a little shrubbery near the arch of the ruined abbey of Dryburgh, under which lie the mortal remains of the great romance writer, and those of Lady Scott. It is supposed that the date of the dial is 1640. The Haliburton arms and the initials "т. н." are carved on the eastern slope of the dial stone, and a corresponding shield with "ı. c." on the other. At the back is the motto *Fiducia constante.*

A tree which was blown down a few years ago unfortunately fell upon the dial stone, breaking the piece which supported the ball at the top. It has never been repaired, and the dial block now lies at the foot of its pillar, and amongst other stones collected from the ruins. The gnomons are gone, but the motto and hour lines can still be traced.

Dryburgh Abbey belonged to the Haliburton family before it came into the possession of the Earls of Buchan, and Robert Haliburton, grand-uncle of Sir Walter Scott, had settled it by will upon the poet's father, as heir in the maternal line. But this ancient patrimony was lost to the Scotts through Mr. Haliburton's commercial misadventures ; "and thus," wrote Sir Walter, in his brief autobiography, "we have nothing left of Dryburgh, although my father's maternal inheritance, but the right of stretching our bones where mine may perhaps be laid ere any eye but my own glances over these pages."

The collector (M. G.) sketched the dial on the 10th August, 1839, and thus wrote :—

" ' Watch weel,' lest thieves should enter while ye sleep—
But pray to God His favour to obtain :
Except the Lord Himself the city keep,
The careful watchman waketh but in vain."

722.

WE MAY NOT STAY. 1782.

On a dial over the south porch of Middleton Church, near Pickering.

723.

WE MUST AND SHALL ERE LONG DYALL.

On a brass dial-plate formerly belonging to the Rev. Vernon Yonge, and given by him to be placed in the garden of Blackden House, near Crewe, from whence it has unfortunately disappeared. It bore the date 1647, and at the four corners were quarterings of arms belonging to the Yonges of Charnes, Staffordshire, and the family motto, *Et servata fides perfectus amorque ditabunt.*

724.

WE RESEMBLE THE SHADOW. 1812.

On a large geographical dial of very elaborate workmanship, over the porch of Wragby Church, Yorkshire. The church stands within the walls of Nostel Park, near the site of the Priory.

725.

WE SHALL —— 1693. (*scil.* DIAL *i.e.* die-all).

This somewhat cumbrous joke is not uncommon. It may be read in Buxted Churchyard, near Uckfield, Sussex, where it is inscribed on an old and rather elaborately engraved dial. Also over the south porch of Bromsgrove

Church, in Worcestershire, is a dial inscribed *Wee shall* in old English characters.   At Kedleston, in Derbyshire, it is *We must;* and on a house at Easton, near Stamford, there is *Wee shall* —.   An old story connected with this quaint conceit is, that a certain pious cleric, who had seen the inscription "We must" on a sun-dial, and ascertained how the "die all" to conclude the sentence was obtained, ordered the words "we must" to be inscribed on the clock face of his church !

It is a very old witticism.   Silvanus Morgan finishes his work, "Horologiographia Optica," published in 1652, with these words: "So that as I began with the Diall of Life, So we shall Dye all.   For *Mors ultima linea.*"

726.

WE SHALL DIE ALL.

Over the door of Mr. Emmerson's house, Walgrave, Northamptonshire, the dial being probably of the last century. Another version of the motto—

WE MUST DIE ALL

is on the church porch, Writhlington, Somerset.

727.

WEN DAS SONNENS STÖCKLEIN RECHT SOL WEISEN
SO RICHT ES NICHT NAHE BEY EISSEN.

The style will not point right, I fear,
Should there be any iron near.

This is rather a motto for a compass than a dial, but it occurs on a cube-shaped portarium which combines both, and is in the British Museum.

728.

WHAT I SAY UNTO YOU I SAY UNTO ALL, WATCH.

From Mark xiii. 37, and inscribed on a horizontal dial in the grounds of Derryquin Castle, co. Kerry. The pillar which supports it has at one time formed the gnomon to a dial traced on the circular stone slab on which it stands, but this is now overgrown with grass. The plate has the engraver's name, John Milne, Kenmare, and was probably put up about 1870.

729.

WHEN THOU DOST LOOK UPON MY FACE,
   TO LEARN THE TIME OF DAY;
THINK HOW MY SHADOW KEEPS ITS PACE,
   AS THY LIFE FLIES AWAY.
TAKE, MORTAL, THIS ADVICE FROM ME
   AND SO RESOLVE TO SPEND
THY LIFE ON EARTH, THAT HEAVEN SHALL BE
   THY HOME WHEN TIME SHALL END.

Suggested by Mr. Harrison, Sheffield, as an inscription for a stone dial eighteen inches square, dated 1748, which he bought and placed in Garden Plot 59, Totley Brook Estate, Abbeydale, Sheffield, in 1877.

730.

WHERE NOW YOU STAND THE TIME TO SPY
WHO KNOWS HOW SOON YOU THERE MAY LIE,
BOTH TIME AND PLACE ARE MONITORY
THAT YOU AND THEY ARE TRANSITORY.
HEAVEN IS OUR TEMPLE, DEATH'S THE PORCH,
CHRIST IS THE WAY, HIS WORD OUR TORCH,
HERE LET US WALK WHILE WE HAVE LIGHT,
TOO LATE BEGINS OUR WORK AT NIGHT.

Formerly at Hadleigh, Suffolk (see No. 604).

731.

WHILST PHŒBUS ON ME SHINES
THEN VIEW MY SHADES AND LINES.

Formerly in the Isle of Man.   See No. 331.

732.

WHO DULY WEIGHS THE HOURS.   1715.

Is at Breage, in Cornwall, where Mrs. Godolphin was
buried.   This eminent lady, whose life was written by
John Evelyn, one of her most intimate friends, was a daughter
of Colonel Blagge, and born in 1652.   She became a maid
of honour to Queen Catherine at the court of Charles II.,
and in 1675 married Sidney, third son of Sir Francis Godolphin.   What especially distinguished her was her pious,
modest, and discreet character, whilst living at a court where
Christian virtues were strange.   She died in 1678, and was

buried at Breage, where her husband's family had been settled before the Conquest. Her surviving husband was created Earl of Godolphin, and through their grand-daughter they are ancestors of Godolphin Osborne and the Duke of Leeds.

733.

WITH WARNING HAND I MARK TIME'S RAPID FLIGHT
FROM LIFE'S GLAD MORNING TO ITS SOLEMN NIGHT;
YET, THROUGH THE DEAR GOD'S LOVE, I ALSO SHOW
THERE'S LIGHT ABOVE ME BY THE SHADE BELOW.

Inscription on a sun-dial for Dr. Henry J. Bowditch, written by John Greenleaf Whittier and published in the complete edition of his poems.

734.

WORK TO-DAY, AND PLAY TO-MORROW.

On Turner's Hospital, at Kirkleatham, near Redcar, Yorkshire. See also No. 138. Both the dials are plain in pattern, and circular.

735.

WORK WHILE IT IS DAY. Lat. 53' 28'.

J. S. 1849.

This sentiment is taken from St. John ix. 4, and is the motto on a dial placed by Mr. Joseph Sidebottom, on the south porch of Bredbury Church, Cheshire.

"Swift fly the hours and brief the time
For action or repose ;—

Fast flits this scene of woe and crime, .
And soon the whole shall close.
The evening shadows deeper fall
The daylight dies away,
Wake, slumberer, at the Master's call,
And work while it is day ! "
H. F. Lyte.

736.

YET A LITTLE WHILE IS THE LIGHT WITH YOU : WALK WHILE YE HAVE THE LIGHT. John xii. 35. 1671.

At Aynho.   See 136.

737.

YOU HAVE SEEN ME RISE
BUT MAY NOT SEE ME SET.

Is inscribed on a dial plate in St. John's Churchyard, Margate.   On the pedestal below is—

AB HOC MOMENTO PENDET AETERNITAS.

738.

YOU MAY WASTE, BUT CANNOT STOP ME.

Is painted on a board over the door of a chapel of ease in Chapel Place, near the Pantiles, Tunbridge Wells.   There is no date, but the maker's name is recorded, "Alexr. Rae fecit."

Richard II. thus soliloquizes in his dungeon in Pomfret Castle :

" I wasted time, and now doth time waste me.
For now hath time made me his numb'ring clock :
My thoughts are minutes ; and, with sighs, they jar
Their watches on to mine eyes, the outward watch,
Whereto my finger, like a dial's point,
Is pointing still, in cleansing them from tears."

SHAKESPEARE, Richard II., Act v. Sc. 5.

ADDENDA.

I.

AS A SERVANT EARNESTLY DESIRES THE SHADOW.

On Prince Albert Victor's dial at Edinburgh Exhibition, 1886. See No. 516.

II.

CARPE DIEM.

Seize the (present) moment.

At Cawder House, near Glasgow. See No. 710.

III.

DAY GIVES PLACE TO NIGHT; LIFE SOON ENDS IN DEATH; AND TIME WILL BE SWALLOWED UP IN VAST ETERNITY.

On a dial in the grounds of Amisfield, near Lochmaben, co. Dumfries. The plate is of metal, and is further in-

scribed, "This dial belongs to And. Cowan. J. W. fecit
1825."

IV.

DAY UNTO DAY UTTERETH SPEECH, AND NIGHT UNTO NIGHT SHOWETH KNOWLEDGE.

On a dial made by the late Henry Cadell, Esq., of Grange,
Borrowstounness, Linlithgowshire; dated 1856.

V.

EXPULSIS TENEBRIS RECREAT SPLENDORI-BUS ORBEM.

Dispelling the darkness, he revives the earth with his rays.

On the campanile at Sori, Riviera di Levante.

VI.

FUGIT IRREVOCABILE TEMPUS.

Time passes never to be recalled.

At Tesero, Val Fièmme, Tyrol.   See No. 165.

VII.

HORA PARS VITÆ.

An hour is a portion of life.

On the church of St. Nicholas, Skirbeck, co. Lincoln.

VIII.

IT IS A LIGHT THING FOR THE SHADOW TO GO
DOWN TEN DEGREES; NAY BUT LET THE SHADOW
RETURN BACKWARDS TEN DEGREES.

On a pillar-dial about five miles from Glasgow. See
No. xx.

IX.

LIGHT IS THE SHADOW OF GOD.

On Prince Albert Victor's dial at the Edinburgh Exhibition, 1886. See No. 516.

X.

MAN'S DAYS ARE AS A SHADOW THAT PASSETH AWAY.

On Prince Albert Victor's dial at the Edinburgh Exhibition, 1886. See No. 516.

XI.

SEGNANDO I PASSI AL SOL L'OMBRA FUGACE,
LA VITA TUA, MORTAL, MISURA E TACE.

As the sun's steps records the shadow fleet,
Thy life in silence, mortal, doth it mete.

On a house at Castellavazzo, near Longarone.

c c

XII.

SON SENZA SUON E SENZA VOCE ANCORA, OPUR SE LUCE IL SOL TI DICO L'ORA.

I have no sound, nor voice, yet by the light
Of sunbeams touched, I tell the hours aright.

At Vegliasco, near Alassio.

XIII.

TEMPORI PARE.

Obey time.

Formerly at Park Hill, near Oswestry.   See No. 423.

XIV.

TEMPUS FUGIT VIA.

Time flies on its way.

This motto, remarkable for the barbarity of its Latin, was seen some years ago on Haydor, or Heydour Church, co. Lincoln.

XV.

ΘΕΟΣ, DEUS, GOD.

On the S.W. corner of John Knox's house in Edinburgh, there is a curious piece of sculpture consisting of a man's figure kneeling on a stone base. Upon two sides of the stone there are dial faces. The man has a long curly beard, and in one hand holds a tablet, whilst with the other he points towards a carved sun on the wall above him. In the centre of this sun the name of GOD is inscribed in three languages. The figure seems to be intended for Moses. There are rays of flame round the dial faces, as well as round the sun.

XVI.

TORNA IL SOLE NON IL TEMPO.

The sun returns, but not so time.

On the wall of the cloister of S. Stefano, Belluno, now used as public offices. See No. 537.

XVII.

TUTTE LE COSE PERISCONO IO SONO IMMORTALE.

All things perish, I immortal am.

At Diano Castello, on the Riviera.

XVIII.

VIVO TRA VITI MA IL MIO CORE INGOMBRA TEMA DI SI SPARIR COME QUEST' OMBRA.

Midst vines I dwell, and yet my heart o'er weighed,
Fears that it too may vanish like this shade.

In the sacristy of the church of the Frari, at Venice, there is an old clock, having a frame elaborately carved with figures and devices. One of these represents a man in armour standing amidst vines, and holding a sundial, above which the foregoing motto is inscribed. The four corners of the clock represent Childhood, Youth, Manhood and Old Age, together with the four Seasons, and the four Winds, or cardinal points. The setting sun, and waning moon, a skeleton, an owl, and various other emblems are also represented, and an explanation of the carving written on parchment is affixed to the door. The frame was carved out of a single piece of cypress wood, by Francesco Pianta, A.D. 1500.

XIX.

WATCH AND PRAY
TYME IS SHORT,

A vertical dial on Yarrow Church, dated 1640, and bearing also the initials M. I. F. M. Described in " Reminiscences of Yarrow," by J. Russell, DD., page 166, (Blackwood and Son, 1886).

XX.

WE SPEND OUR YEARS AS A TALE THAT IS TOLD.

IT IS A LIGHT THING FOR THE SHADOW TO GO DOWN TEN DEGREES: NAY, BUT LET THE SHADOW RETURN BACKWARDS TEN DEGREES.

These texts from Psalm xc. 9, and 2 Kings xx, 10, are engraved on an elaborate pillar dial, nearly ten feet high, which was erected in 1840, about five miles from Glasgow.

It was designed and executed by a stone-mason named Alexander Fraser, whose name is carved on one of the steps at the base.

XXI.

WELL ARRANGED TIME IS THE SUREST SIGN OF A WELL ARRANGED MIND.

On Prince Albert Victor's dial at the Edinburgh Exhibition in 1886.   See No. 516.

FURTHER NOTES ON REMARKABLE SUN-DIALS.

ALTHOUGH it was the interest attached to sun-dial mottoes which gave rise to this collection, it was seen after a time that dials were interesting on their own account, from the variety and ingenuity of their structure ; and though no inelegance of form or poverty of material can render a beautiful motto insignificant, it is a fact that some of the finest and most curious dials are without mottoes. Of such of these as have not been noticed before, we think that a brief description will be acceptable.

Several specimens of Greek and Roman dials have been discovered of late years, and probably more exist than have come under our observation, or than we have space to chronicle. The hemicyclium mentioned by Vitruvius, and said to have been invented by Berosus, is perhaps the most usual form. It is best described as " an excavation, nearly spherical, in a square block of stone, within which the hour lines were traced, and having the anterior face sloped away from above, so as to give it a forward inclination adapted to the polar altitude of the place for which the dial was made." [1]

[1] Rich's " Dictionary of Antiquities."

The hours shown were those unequal ones into which the
day-time was divided by the Greeks, their length varying
according to the season of the year. There were usually
eleven hour-lines, five, that is, on each side of the mid-day
line, so that ten complete hours were marked ; the numbering beginning at the first hour after sunrise and ending at the
last before sunset. A small space, not wide enough for a full
hour, was left beyond these first and last lines, but for all
practical purposes ten hours were sufficient, as the times of
sunrise and sunset speak for themselves. These hour-lines
were crossed by three parallel arcs of a circle, one near the
gnomon marking the winter solstice, below this another arc
for the equinox, and, close to the outer edge, the third for
the summer solstice. The gnomon was placed upright on
the edge of the hollow, and was then bent at a right angle
over it, so that the horizontal portion projected as far as the
equinoctial line. The shadow passed along this line at all
hours of the day, on the 21st of March and 21st of September. It then gradually increased in length until at Midsummer it had reached the outer arc, when it began to recede,
and on the 21st of December, having dwindled to the shortest
possible measure, it passed along the line of a brief day literally
made up of " small hours." The position and bent form of
the gnomon, and the curve of the hollow, in connection with
the more vertical or more oblique position of the sun, effected
the shortening of the shadow in winter and its lengthening in
summer. Sometimes, as in the case of the dial found at Tusculum, and described by Zuzzeri and Martini, the angle at
which the front face was cut corresponded with the latitude
of the place for which the dial was made; at others, as
with a specimen found at Aquileia, to be noticed below, the
inclination was considerably less. In such cases a plane
drawn through the line of the summer solstice forms an angle

with the plane of the pedestal, and the number of degrees by which this exceeds a right angle should be added to the angle of inclination in order to find the correct latitude.[1]

As an illustration of this class of dial, we have given a sketch of a specimen which was found in 1852 near Alexandria, at the base of Cleopatra's Needle, by Mr. J. Scott

Tucker, and is now in the British Museum. It probably belongs to the Roman period. The dial is concave, and is hollowed out of a block of stone $16\frac{1}{2}$ inches in height, 17 in width, and 11 in depth. The corners have been broken away, but most of the hour-lines can be plainly seen, and the Greek letters which numbered them, as alluded to in Lucian's epigram (see Introduction, p. 10), ΑΒΓΔΕϚΖΗΘΙ.

These hour-lines are crossed with arcs marking the

---

[1] Dr. F. Kenner, " Römische Sonnenuhren aus Aquileia."

equinox and the summer and winter solstices. There is a large hole for a vertical gnomon, and the inclination of the face of the block appears to correspond with the latitude of Alexandria. The base, which slopes to the ground at a wide angle with the face, is cut in six small inclined steps. A very fine dial of the same kind, with a bust of Berosus on its base, found at Palestrina, is in the collection of sculpture at Ince Blundell, in Lancashire.

Besides a plain vertical slab on which eleven hour-lines are traced, the British Museum possesses a handsome semi-circular marble dial about 21 inches high, 18 in diameter at the upper part, and 14 at the base. It is hollowed to a greater depth than the Alexandrian dial, and lies more open to the sun. The back is globular, and the base slopes very slightly forward between two lions' heads which support the dial, and which each rest on a single foot, like the supports of a tripod table. This specimen belongs to the Townley collection. The hours are not numbered. A similar dial, almost cup-shaped, and with no forward inclination of the face, stands in the window of the same basement room. It is quite small, about 7 inches high and 5 deep, and only the equinoctial and hour-lines are marked. In both these dials the gnomon seems to have been placed horizontally; a furrow, in which the remains of metal is to be seen, taking the place of the deep hole where an upright rod could be fixed. This last little dial stands upon a small pillar.

The fine block of dials brought from Athens by Lord Elgin, now kept in the inscription-room of the British Museum, is figured in "Museum Marbles," Pt. IX. It is of white marble, the back is plain, while the front and sides consist of four dials engraved on vertical planes at angles with each other. In its original position it probably commanded four streets. One face bears the inscription :

ΦΑΙΔΡΟC: ΖΩΙΛΟΥ :

ΠΑΙΑΝΙΕΥC : ΕΠΟΙΕΙ

" Phædrus, son of Zoilus, a Pæanian, made this."

The last letter of the lower line is lost from the wearing away of the marble. The name of the architect, Phædrus, was found also upon the flight of steps leading up to the Dionysian theatre. He is thought to have lived in the second or third century A.D. From the shape of the letters it is evident that the dial cannot be of earlier date than the time of Hadrian.

The museum at Palermo also possesses an antique white marble dial with four faces.

Two semicircular dials, one of which was found at Ostia, are to be seen in the Vatican musem. Both are cut out of blocks of white marble. The larger of the two is about 8 inches high by 20 wide and 10 deep. It is divided into hour-spaces by eleven lines, and crossed by seven parallel arcs, between which the Latin names of the months are cut in Greek letters. A circle is described in the centre, and the first syllables of the zodiac signs are engraved beside it. Two diagonal lines cut the circle at the equinoxes, and are continued to the line of the summer solstice. Another dial of the same class is placed outside a window of the museum of the Capitol, and was found on the Via Flaminia in 1751. That discovered at Tusculum in 1741, near the site of Cicero's villa, has been frequently noticed and figured. In 1815 it was in the monastery of San Gregorio, and is said by Mr. Burn to be now in the Collegio Romano museum.[1]

A photograph of another specimen was exhibited at a meeting of the Society of Antiquaries in 1877. It was of white marble, and had been found at Aphrodisias, in the valley of the Meander, by Mr. Purser, who was making a railway there. The hours were numbered in Greek letters, and on the pedestal was an inscription in Greek, stating that the dial was dedicated to Marcus Aurelius Antoninus. It had probably belonged to the Temple of Aphrodite.

A description of a very perfectly preserved dial, discovered by M. Rayet at Heraclea (Latmos), was given in the "Globe" newspaper a few years ago. It was found in a building which probably served for the meetings of the Senate, and consisted of a block of marble so cut that one of its faces was parallel to the plane of the equator in the latitude of Heraclea. The actual dial was a semicircular hollow like those already described, the hour-lines being crossed by seven parallel arcs, each of which would be traversed by the shadow of the point of the gnomon when the sun was in the middle of one of the signs of the zodiac. A second dial was placed on the northern face of the block, and a Greek inscription beneath the principal dial stated that the instrument was dedicated to Ptolemy the king, by Apollonios son of Apollodotas, and constructed by Themistagoras of Alexandria, son of Meniskos. M. Rayet thought that the king here referred to Ptolemy Philadelphos, and that the dial probably dated from the early part of the 3rd century B.C. It is now in the Louvre.

[1] " Rome and the Campagna," 1873.

A Greek dial in the shape of a marble disc, once set vertically upon a pedestal from which it had been broken off, and marked with six hour-lines, was found in the island of Delos early in this century, and brought to Paris. M. Delambre published a description of it in 1814, when it had been placed in the Cabinet des Antiquités, and it is probably now to be found in the Louvre.

A curious pair of dials, the upper one shaped like a shield, the lower circular, but both probably hollowed out on the same plan as those already described, was found at Herculaneum, and is figured in the " British Cyclopædia." It may now be in the National Museum at Naples, which contains several interesting specimens of ancient dials. One of these has often been noticed. It was found at Herculaneum in 1754 and is of bronze faced with silver, shaped like a ham, and engraved on one side with seven lines enclosing spaces under which the Latin names of the months appear abbreviated. These are again divided into six irregular spaces by cross-lines for the hours, and a small gnomon, shaped like a tail, projects over one side ; the dial hangs from a small ring. It was for some time thought to be the only existing specimen of a portable Roman dial, but this is not the case ; for another was brought to light not long ago at Aquileia, near the Gulf of Trieste, and belongs to Dr. Gregorutti, of Baperiano. It is described, together with five other Roman dials, by Dr. Kenner, in an interesting paper already referred to.[1] This *viatorium* is of bronze, the size and shape of a penny, engraved on both sides, and the lines inlaid with silver. Two horizontal lines are drawn across the disc, one near the top and the other near the bottom. From the centre of the upper one seven lines diverge, four resting upon the lower horizontal line, and three others touching an oblique line at a

[1] " Römische Sonnenuhren aus Aquileia."

sharp angle with the horizontal one. The central and vertical line is the equinoctial, the outer one to the right for the summer, and that to the left for the winter solstice. Under the spaces enclosed by these lines the initials of the months are faintly marked, as in the ham dial :

IV . M . AP . M . FE . IA .
IV . N . SE . OC . N . DE .

The upright lines are crossed by others which show the hours of the day, and there is a hole for a little gnomon in the centre. This gnomon must have been bent at an angle corresponding with the complement of the latitude, so as to touch the point where the lines of the months part company. The instrument would be held in a vertical position. The letters R O. on the one side and R A. on the other, with a slight difference in the arrangement of lines, show that the dials were made to be used at Rome and Ravenna.

The other dials found at Aquileia are not less interesting, though four of them belong to the semicircular and concave form already noticed. The most perfect one, cut out of a block of grey limestone, measures 10 inches in height by $16\frac{1}{2}$ in width, and 15 in depth, and the hollow has a maximum depth of $9\frac{1}{2}$ inches. There are eleven hour-lines, crossed by the solstice and equinoctial arcs. The gnomon hole remains. The second specimen is cut with its pedestal out of a block about thirty-eight inches high, the pedestal being carved with acanthus and other designs. There could not have been more than seven hour-lines, and no place for the gnomon is visible, but the upper edges of the dial are broken away. These two dials formed part of the collection belonging to Dr. Zannini, which was bought in 1828 for the I. R. cabinet of coins and antiquities in Vienna.

A less ornamented block than the above, but hollowed

out in the same manner, is in the collection of the Baron
V. Ritter-Zahony, at Monastero near Aquileia, for the
latitude of which place it was evidently calculated. It has
nine hour-lines and would show the time from 8 a.m. to
4 p.m., the second and tenth hours of the ancients.

Another similar dial, of which a very small fragment remains, was found at Schloss Buttrio, near Udine; it is
mounted on a limestone pedestal, against which a half-
draped female figure is sculptured. The specimen is now in
the collection of Count Toppo.

The last of these discoveries was of a rarer kind, namely,
a horizontal dial, identical with the "disc in a plane" mentioned by Vitruvius. It is engraved on a stone table made of
slabs fastened together, 8 feet 3 inches long, and 3 feet
2 inches wide, with a raised border. This table stands on
two round stone columns, each 16 inches in diameter, and
22 and 25 inches in height respectively; the front pillar
being more deeply sunk in the ground than the other.
Certain flaws which mark the surface show where breakages
have been mended, evidently in Roman times, by iron
clamps set in lead. The dial is formed of eleven hour-lines
which spring from the line of the summer solstice, and are
continued, after being crossed by the equinoctial line, at
varying lengths to that of the winter solstice. The dial
being horizontal the long shadows of winter fell on the
outer line. The gnomon was placed, as usual, a little beyond
the summer solstice mark. The whole is enclosed in a
circle, which is divided into eight parts, marked with the
names of eight winds,

DESOLINUS EVRVS AVSTER AFRICVS FAONIVS AQVILO

SEPTENTRIO BOREAS

and "M. Antistivs . Evporus . fecit ." is also added. The surname of Euporus has often been found on the Aquileian remains.

As the names given to the winds are apt to vary, it is worth noting that Aquilo is here the north-west, and Boreas the north-east wind, according to the later custom; and contrary to the arrangement described by Vitruyius and Pliny, with whom Aquilo stands for the north-east wind. The Vatican wind-dial agrees with this latter plan and places Aquilo in the north-east, below the Greek word Boreas. Desolinus seems to be a local name for Solanus the the east wind, and Faonius a corruption of the Latin Favonius, the west. The word Bora is still used for the north-east wind, both in the neighbourhood of Trieste and all down the Adriatic. The strangest feature about the dial is that the mid-day line lies between Eurus and Aquilo, and points south-east and north-west, instead of due north and south.

The dial is placed at the north end of the table, not in the middle, owing probably to the position of neighbouring buildings. It seems to have been moved to avoid the shadow of a wall above, and set down with some inaccuracy, so that the exact time could no longer have been told.

At the three other sides, and fastened to the table, are stone benches, the one at the south end having a block of stone higher than the table placed upon it, with two little holes, partly filled with lead, where a weather-cock might have been fixed. The northern end of the table was left open to the approach of anyone who wished to know how the time went, without running the risk of standing in his own light.

This curious relic of Roman times was found about three feet below the surface of the ground in the Marigniane, or salt marshes, to the north-west of Aquileia. From other researches which have been made, it appears that a Circus formerly stood in this place, built probably towards the end of the time of the Republic, or beginning of the Empire. Two tablets, tickets for seats in the theatre, were found very near the dial table, with the names of the owners, and numbers of the seats, engraved on them. The style of the letters belongs to the above-named period. Aquileia was then a large city and a strong frontier fortress. The fact of its possessing a Circus, always a State institution, shows its importance. It was frequently visited by the emperors, beginning with Augustus. The dial, from the character of its inscription, has been assigned to the time of Commodus, and probably served to mark the time for the races, and other games in the Circus, until Attila swept down upon Italy and left Aquileia a heap of ruins.

Dr. Kenner considers this dial to be an example of the " lacunar " mentioned by Vitruvius, as well as of the " discus in planitia " ; and also judges it to be the earliest known specimen where the names of the winds are given in Latin.

A fragment of a very similar wind- and sun-dial was found in 1814 in the Vigna Cassini, near the Via Appia, Rome, and described by Signor Francesco Peter. It had been used as a gravestone in an Arenaria which formed part of the Catacombs of St. Calixtus. It was inscribed with the names of twelve winds in Greek, and being made of Pentilic marble, from quarries which belonged to Herod Atticus, Signor Peter concluded that it had belonged to his villa, which was little more than half a mile distant from the place where the dial was found. Another fragment of a horizontal dial, but without the winds, found at Tivoli in 1838, is likewise described in the " Atti dell' Accademia Romana."

One more ancient dial comes to us from Spain. It was discovered at Yecla, in the province of Alicante, and is now in the Archæological Museum, Madrid. A cast of it was exhibited in 1876 at South Kensington, in the Loan Collection of Scientific Instruments. It had once possessed a gnomon, but the dial when used had to be placed in the shade facing the north. "A small spherical concave mirror was placed at a short distance, which reflected the light of the sun upon the dial, and by that means projected the shadow of the needle marking the hours. At the base are inscriptions in Greek characters, but the language appears to be of the Semitic class." [1]

Whether the fragments of a small concave stone found at Hofen in Wurtemburg, and now preserved in the museum at Stuttgart, constitute a dial seems open to doubt. Portions of what may have been hour-lines, eleven in number, remain, and the words " IVNIVS TA—", the rest of the inscription, which went round the edge, being lost. The diameter is 8 inches, the height 3¾ inches. It is described and figured in the "Jahrbüchern der Alterthums freunde im Rheinlande" (b. iv., Bonn, 1844), but how it was fixed, or where the gnomon was placed is not shown. Hofen was once a Roman settlement, and coins of Antoninus Pius, Hadrian, Aurelius, Septimus Severus and Trajan were found near this little relic.

The hour-lines on the octagonal " Tower of the Winds " at Athens can still be discerned, and a gnomon appears to have been recently placed above each dial, so that the hours of the day may be told as of yore. The tower was built by the astronomer Andronicus of Cyrrha, and is forty-four feet in height, and covered by a conical roof of white marble slabs. The eight sides of the tower face the cardinal and intermediate points of the compass ; and figures representing

[1] Catalogue of the Loan Collection, 1876.

the winds are carved upon them. The hour-lines are engraved below these figures. On the central point of the roof a bronze Triton holding a wand, was formerly fixed and served as a weathercock.

Another ancient dial, of Pentilic marble, is inlaid in the wall of Cimon, near the theatre of Dionysius.

Dr. Clarke, who travelled in Greece in 1802, described a vertical dial on the wall of the church at Orchomenes, which has also been figured in Dodwell's " Greece." It was cut in a semicircle on a large marble slab, the eleven hour-lines having the numbers (in Greek letters) beneath them. A representation of a goose, a bird sacred to the sun, was placed in each of the lower corners. The church was built on the site of the ancient Temple of the Graces.

A dial resembling this one was found at Herculaneum, and a woodcut given in the "Literary Gazette" for 1823. The day was divided into twelve hour-spaces.

The Crusaders appear to have destroyed a very remarkable dial at the taking of Constantinople by Baldwin, Count of Flanders, A.D. 1205. Nicetas thus describes it :—"In the Hippodrome was placed the brazen eagle, the work of Apollonius Tyaneus, who, when visiting Byzantium, had been asked for a charm against the venomous bites of the serpents which invested the place. For this purpose he employed all his natural skill, with the devil for his coadjutor, and elevated upon a column a brazen eagle. The wings of the bird were expanded for flight; but a serpent in his talons, twining around him, impeded his soaring. The head of the reptile seemed approaching the wings to inflict a deadly bite; but the crooked points of the talons kept him harmless; and instead of struggling with the bird, he was compelled to droop his head, and his breath and his venom expired together. The eagle was looking proudly, and almost crowing out

'Victory!' and for the joy of his eye one might suppose that he intended to transport the dead body of the reptile through the air. Forgetful of his circling spires, and no longer venomous, the serpent remained as a warning to his species, and seemed to bid them betake themselves to their hiding-places. But the figure of the eagle was more admirable still, for it served as a dial; the horary divisions of the day were marked by lines inscribed on its wings; these were easily discernible by the skilful observer, when the sun's rays were not interrupted by clouds." [1]

The small stone sun-dial described and figured in the "Archæological Journal" (xxi. 262), and which is now in the museum at Dover, is thought to belong to the Roman period. It was found, as were other Roman relics, on the site of the disused church of St. Martin's-le-Grand, in 1862. The church was founded by Wictred, King of Kent, between 693-725, and was not disused till 1545. The dial is described as a cube of fine grained oolite, $4\frac{1}{4}$ inches each way, and may possibly have been placed on a small column. There are dials of various forms, heart-shaped, triangular, and oblong, cut in the stone on the four sides, and these were apparently made for Lat. 47°, some degrees south of Dover.

It is possible that another stone cube of seven or eight inches, now in the Taunton Museum, may belong also to Roman times, as it was found in Wigborough, Somerset, near a Roman camp. There are concave dials on three sides, and a horizontal one at the top; the lines in the hollows have been painted probably in later times.

But we have lingered long enough over these foreign relics, and must turn to those which are of more special interest to us, as they help to illustrate the history of our own land.

[1] Clarke's "Travels," vol. vi., p. 434, app. ii., 1818, from a MS. in the Bodleian Library, translated for Dr. Clarke by the Rev. S. Browne.

The Anglo-Saxon dials alluded to in the Introduction deserve to be more fully noticed. They are to be found in several English counties, but the Yorkshire specimens are, on account of their inscriptions, by far the most interesting and valuable. The earliest of these is to be seen at old Byland, a village in the Hambleton Hills, where in later times, a band of Cistercian monks settled themselves, and when after a few years sojourn they removed into more fertile plains and built the beautiful Abbey which is now in ruins, they called its name Byland, in remembrance of the old home they had left. But the dial at Old Byland had marked time for nearly three hundred years before the first Cistercian set foot in Ryedale. It has now been built upside down into the wall of the church tower, and the inscription is hard to decipher. Semi-circular in form, and traced on a vertical plane, this dial divides the day into ten portions. The noonday hour-line is crossed at the end, as are those on either side of it, and two of the others—viz., at the beginning of the third and ninth hours. It is thought to be the work of a Dane of the ninth century, and is thus inscribed :—

+ SVMARLETHAN . HVSCARL . ME . FECIT.

(Sumarlethi's huscarl made me.)

The outer circle is ornamented with the *mæander* pattern.

Over the south door of Weaverthorpe church, in the East Riding of Yorkshire, there is a small dial of similar shape, only that here the half circle is divided into twelve spaces, every alternate line being crossed. The inscription is incomplete :—

+ IN HONORE SCE ANDREAE APOSTOLI HEREBERTVS
WINTONIE
HOC MONASTERIVM FECIT IN TEMPORE REGN—

The unfinished name is thought to be that of Regnald II., to whom in 942 King Eadmund stood godfather. A portion of an inscription above this one remains, and has been read as "OSCETULI ARCHEPISCOPI." Oscetul was raised to the See of York after A.D. 952, and having been Bishop of Dorchester, was probably well acquainted with Ethelwold,

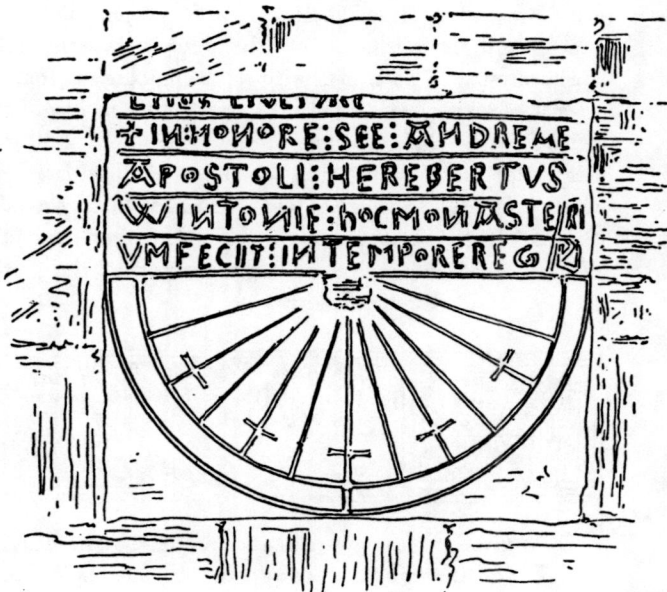

afterwards Bishop of Winchester, and a great restorer of monasteries. This would account for the transference of Herebert from Winchester to Weaverthorpe, and for the association of his name with the building of this monastery, of which he was probably the abbot. If the Danes spared the building, in all likelihood the Normans did not, for Domesday records Weaverthorpe as "Waste."

A longer and more precise inscription over the south door of the ancient church at Kirkdale, near Kirkby Moorside, tells the history of a singularly perfect dial. A great part of the church is ante-Norman, and the dial must have been placed in its present position when the church was restored by Orm, as recorded below. It is projected for a south aspect, and the position over the door is the same as that at Bishopstone. The stone, with its accompanying inscriptions, measures seven feet in width by nearly two in height; in the centre is the dial, the five greater hour-lines indicating the central points of each "tide," being marked with a cross, and the space between them halved by smaller lines, thus dividing the day into eight portions, the whole enclosed in a half circle. The index line for the beginning of the first tide of day, $7\frac{1}{2}$ a.m., is marked with a $\times$.

The inscription is given as interpreted by the Rev. D. H. Haigh, and the contractions supplied in smaller letters:—

╈ ORM GAMALSVNA BOHTE SanCtuS GREGORIVS MINSTER THONNE HIT WÆS AL TOBROCAN AND TOFALAN AND HE HIT LET MACAN NEWAN FROM GRVNDE CHRistE AND SanCtuS GREGORIVS IN EADWARD DAGVM CyniNG AND iN

TOSTI DAGVM EORL.

╋ THIS IS DÆGES SOLMERCA ÆT ILCVM TIDE

AND HAWARTH ME WROHTE AND BRAND PRæposituS.

Trans. Orm Gamalson bought S. Gregory's monastery when it was all utterly broken and fallen, and he let it to be made anew from the ground to Christ and S. Gregory in Edward's days the King and in Tosti's days the Earl.

> This is the day's sunmarker at every tide
> And Hawarth me made and Brand Provost.

It will be noticed that the fylfot is marked on this dial in two places.

The date of this rebuilding of the monastery may probably be fixed between 1063, the year in which Orm's father, Gamal Ormson, was treacherously murdered by Earl Tosti, and 1065, when the latter was deposed and banished. It is possible that this Provost (or Prior) Brand is the same who was elected Abbot of Peterborough in 1066, and Hawarth may have been his superior, and abbot of the newly restored monastery at Kirkdale. Tosti was made Earl of Northumberland in 1056, on the death of Siward, and was slain at the battle of Stamford Bridge, 1066. Orm, the founder of the " Minster," is named in Doomsday book as holding the manor of Chirche bi (Kirkby) under Hugh Fitzbaldric ; and there is the further entry, " Ibi P'b'r et Eccl'a." (" There is a priest and a church.")

The dial at Kirkdale is in good preservation. It is fortunately protected from the weather by a modern porch, on the front of which another sun-dial is placed, a simple slab of wood, and with no motto.

Orm's younger brother Gamal is mentioned in Doomsday as the holder of Michel-Edestun, or Great Edstone, two miles from Kirkby Moorside, and this church also possesses a Saxon dial. The arrangement of the hour lines is the same as at Kirkdale, the slab is 3 feet 11 inches long, and 1 foot 7½ inches in height. Over the semi-circular plane are the words, partly mutilated, "ORLOGIVM VIATORVM," or the " time-teller for wayfarers," and on one side a half-finished inscription, " + LOTHAN ME WROHTE A— " ("Lothan made me"). The name of Lothan is only known as that of a Dane who ravaged Kent and Essex in the year 1048, together with Osgod, who had been banished from England in 1046, and whose flight and outlawry he may have shared.

The dial in the south wall of the nave of Aldbrough Church, in Holderness, is of a different order. It is circular, and is divided into eight equal parts, with a hole in the centre for the style. In one of these divisions is a fylfot, or svastika, as on the Kirkdale dial, but here marking the beginning of the first tide, 7.30 a.m. The inscription is on the outer circle, and runs as follows :—

+ VLF HET ÆRIERAN CYRICE FOR HANVM AND FOR GVNWARA SAVLA.

(Ulf bade arrear church for poor (or for himself) and for Gunware (her) soul.)

It is not unlikely that this was Ulf Thoraldsen, who gave his lands to the Minster at York, and whose horn is still preserved there amongst the treasures of the church. The inscription is a curious instance of a mixed dialect, old English and Scandinavian. The dial is $15\frac{1}{2}$ inches in diameter.

The other early dials found in Yorkshire are not inscribed. One is horizontal, like that of Aldbrough, and divided into eighths. It is about ten inches in diameter, and was discovered on a gate-post at Mouse house on Elmley Moor. Another is built into the wall of the church at Sinnington. It has the remains of an inscription of which two words alone can be deciphered, MERGEN ÆFERN (morning, evening) ; it is divided into eight, and sub-divided into sixteen spaces. This is also the case with a dial at Lockton, near Pickering, cut on the rounded end of a rough block of stone, and now built into the wall of a cottage.

Of three curious little dials on the church at Kirkburn, one has apparently been lost during a restoration. The two that remain are both circular, with half of the circle sub-divided, one into ten spaces, the other into twelve.

At Swillington a specimen of the decimal division of time (as at Old Byland) is found on a dial built into the wall of the church, which itself belongs to the fourteenth century. It was evidently a horizontal dial, " and designed to show seven equal tenths of day-night, with the spaces below the equi-noctial line equally trithed, and to be used in a latitude where the sun rises at midsummer at 3.36 a.m., which is almost exactly the case at Swillington."

In the south wall of Carnaby Church, near Bridlington, there is an ancient stone dial face, on which the remains of twenty-four radii can be traced. On the south wall of Speeton Church there is also a rude stone which may possibly have been a dial.

A roughly-executed dial at Marton-cum-Grafton, now built into the wall of the vestry, is probably also of early date. A fragment of another, beside one of the windows in the church of Kirkby Moorside, which has suffered much from being chiselled all over at the restoration of the church, shows, as at Weaverthorpe, a division of the day into six portions.

The church of Lastingham, a very early foundation, bears the traces of a dial on its wall, and the little old church beside Bolton Castle in Wensleydale, has one upon its south buttress. The lines of this are irregular, but holes neatly drilled at equal distances mark the hours. On the porch of Kirkby Malzeard Church there is an old dial much worn, which formerly told the time from 5 a.m. to 7 p.m. Others

have been found at Bulmer; on a buttress of the south aisle of
Kirklington Church ; and near the priest's door at Burneston.
These only differ from the modern dials in bearing no
numerals ; but there is a large dial cut on the wall of the
church of Appleton-le-Wiske with the hours marked in
Roman characters.

The Rev. J. T. Fowler notices several Yorkshire dials in
the " Yorkshire Archæological Journal," vol. ix., pts. 34 and
35, and adds, that he found so many in Holderness that they
cannot be so uncommon as has been supposed. The church of
Monk Fryston, near South Milford, has one on a stone worked
in as a corner-stone of the south aisle, and the circle of which
is only about 4¼ inches in diameter. Burton Agnes church
has two, one somewhat irregularly divided, and the other
extending over three stones, telling the hours from 9 a.m. to
7 p.m., and marked by Roman numerals, some of which
have disappeared. At Skipsea there is " a very distinctly
marked dial, the radius about a span, the lower half of the
circle divided by thirteen radii into six spaces, the fourth and
seventh line prolonged, and with cross-bars, apparently to
mark 9 a.m. and noon ; the 11 a.m. line lengthened, but
without a cross-bar. At the same church I saw another
similarly divided, but not so large or so deeply cut, another
smaller still, unequally divided into twelve portions below the
horizontal line, and seven above, and there were traces of
three others. At Armthorpe, near Doncaster, there are two
dials close together on the face of an ashlar block, one somewhat larger than the other, and the two circles in contact.
Each has a central hole for a gnomon, and radiating lines
ending in little holes, disposed somewhat irregularly, but
apparently meant to indicate twelve or thirteen day hours.
These circular dials may be of any date, but are probably
mediæval. In Colsterworth Church, near Grantham, is pre-

served a semi-circular dial, with radiating lines, said to have
been cut by Sir Isaac Newton when a boy."

At Knook Church, Wilts, the western cap of the south
door is formed out of a Saxon dial. It is quadrant-shaped,
divided into eight spaces, and the "day mark" which showed
the change from morning to full day stands between the first
and second radii.

Three early dials of small size have been found in the
county of Durham; one horizontal, divided into eighths, and
cut on a slab of red sandstone, is in the choir of St. Cuthberts,
Darlington; another, a vertical dial, is in the wall of a Norman church at Pillington, and shows six divisions of the day.
A third specimen is in the little pre-Conquest church of
Escombe.

Two small specimens of circular horizontal dials have been discovered at Bottesford, in Lincolnshire. These are divided into twenty-four parts, twelve of which, the day hours, are again halved.

A dial somewhat resembling these is built into a buttress on the south side of the church at Higham Ferrars, Northamptonshire, near the priest's door (see fig., p. 412). It is about eleven inches in diameter, and is now placed sixteen feet from the ground. It has apparently been a horizontal dial, the hole for the style is in the centre, and there are twenty lines radiating from it, and two spaces between each group of ten

lines which would have contained four more, thus making the complete number of twenty-four. Possibly these last may have been defaced by time. Two small circular dials, with the twelve hours marked upon the lower half, are in the walls of Castlethorpe Church, apparently coeval with the building, which is perpendicular in style.

Several rough specimens of early dials come to us from Northamptonshire. There is one on the old Saxon tower of Barnack church, the upper half of which has a floreated pattern, the lower half is plain. The dial is circular, and there are no lines or figures remaining. At Ecton, on the east side of the present porch (see fig. above), there is a stone with a circular dial cut on it. This is divided into twelve spaces, and then sub-divided by small lines, and in the centre a deep hole for the gnomon.

A curious circular dial, built into the south wall of St. Nicholas Church, Potterspury, shows what appear to be two sets of lines cut at different times, possibly when the dial was turned from a vertical to a horizontal position, and long before it was placed where it now is (see fig. below). The smaller lines divide half the circle into thirteen spaces, the larger and

deeper ones into ten. Four of these last project beyond the circle, and are crossed, and possibly two others may have been treated in like manner, but the stone has been cut away for the splay of the window. These crossed lines are placed in the same position as on the dial at Old Byland. It would seem as if this one also belonged to the same period or people where or with whom the decimal division of time was in use. It may afterwards have been marked to show twenty-four hours, and placed horizontally, and then put in an upright position when used in the building of the church. And yet there is no especial look of antiquity about this dial stone, which is not more weather-worn than the mouldings of the window beside it. There are several other rough little dials in the walls of St. Nicholas, Potterspury. The date of the

building is uncertain, the oldest part may belong to the reign of Henry III., when mention is made of a church at Potterspury. "A priest" alone is named in Domesday Book.

At Grafton Regis three out of the four dials would seem

to be older than the present church. Two of them are circular (see figs. above), about nine inches in diameter, and of these one is built upside down into the side of a window, and the other on the west side of the porch. Both appear to divide the day into eight equal spaces, but in the porch dial the

earlier and later hours of the day are wanting.   Three lines
to the right and two to the left of the twelve o'clock hour-
line are marked, other spaces between them are nearly equal.
In the first named dial the circle is imperfect, and only the
hours from six a.m. to three p.m. are marked.   A third
specimen, beside one of the windows in the south wall of the
nave, consists of two incomplete circles of holes, with a large
hole in the middle (see fig. below).   The inner half circle
would seem to mark the division of time according to the
octaval system ; the outer one is irregular, and the holes are

not all of the same size and do not correspond with those on
the inner line, and the arc itself is imperfect.

Of the other small dials scratched or cut on the stones of
Grafton Church as on that of Potterspury, and on the tower of
Earls Barton, it is needless to speak.   It is evident that such
rough timekeepers were very commonly made and used in
early times, and that these should, in the fourteenth century,
have been looked upon as nothing better than stones for
building, probably shows that more accurate dials had taken
their place.   Great Linford, Bucks, has several close beside
the priest's door, but so scattered about that they could not
all possibly have told the time at once, and irregular both as

to lines and holes. Sherrington Church, in the same neighbourhood has three, one with the remains of Roman numerals.
Whaddon also possesses three, and the parish church of Tow-
cester one of fair size on the south-west corner of the south
aisle. Loughton Church has a dial seven inches in diameter,
divided into twenty-four hour spaces, on a buttress of the
south aisle which is of perpendicular architecture. Binsey
Church, Oxon, an early English building, has two, one on
the buttress near the priest's door, and the other on the porch.
Blakesley Church, Northants, has also a dial of this kind on

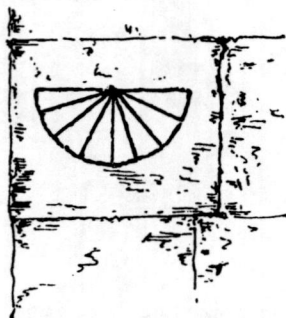

HARDINGHAM.

a south buttress ; and Caythorpe Church, Lincolnshire, on
the porch.

A sketch of an ancient circular stone dial on the south
face of the nave of Bricet Church, Suffolk, is given by Mr.
Syce Cuming, in the "Journal of the British Archæological
Association," Sept., 1873. The dial measures fifteen inches
across, one of the hour-lines terminating in a cross botonée,
another having a tripartite end. Mr. Cuming assigns it to
the eleventh century, Bricet Church having been founded in
1096. On the outside of Hales Church, Norfolk, no less
than five small dials have recently been observed by the Rev.

E E

G. J. Chester ; and he also found one at Sporle, in the same
county, built into a buttress of the church.

Through the kindness of Mr. J. Park Harrison, we are
able to add some notes on the dials which he has visited.
One on a stone in the porch buttress of Hardingham Church,
Norfolk (p. 417), is a plain semicircle, divided into eight
equal spaces ; another is at Daglingworth, Gloucestershire ;

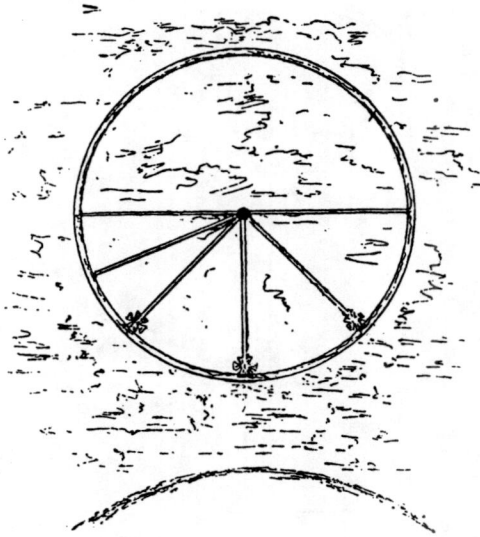

and three small ones at South Cerney, in the same county.
That at Daglingworth is circular, about ten inches in diameter, and the lower half divided into four equal spaces.
The mid-day line and those on each side showing the middle
of the first and third tides of day are crossed.   There is also
a line subdividing the first division, and so marking the beginning of the first tide of day, 7.30 a.m.   The dial appears
to be in *situ* though covered by a porch of apparently almost

contemporary date, and is in perfect preservation. At South Cerney also, a church of very early date, three dials are built into the south buttress of the tower, and are formed by circles of dots without any connecting lines; two of them are divided into day and night hours, and would therefore seem

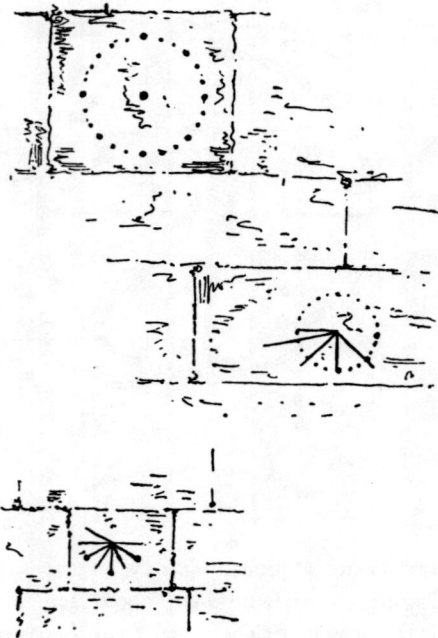

once to have been horizontal. The third dial is divided into six day spaces, with a supernumerary line sloping upwards to the left. In the uppermost dial, midnight and three o'clock a.m. are marked by larger holes than the rest. This dial has suffered the most from the weather.

It is worth noticing that the Daglingworth dial is a dis-

tinct specimen of the octaval system, according to which the
Angles and Norsemen divided time, and that Daglingworth
was within the kingdom of Mercia.

A curious projecting stone in the south wall of Stoke
d'Abernon Church, Surrey, placed nearly above the old south
door, has a dial cut upon it. The edges are broken away, the
lines so placed as to divide the morning hours into four fairly
equal spaces, the afternoon into three unequal parts. Part of
the church dates back to Saxon times, and there are Roman
bricks worked into the wall near the dial.

There are two Saxon dials in the church of Uphill, near
Weston-super-Mare, which have been described by the Rev.
G. J. Chester as follows : " This church (Uphill) which
occupies a commanding position on a grassy hill overlooking
the Bristol Channel, has now for some years been abandoned
so far as public worship is concerned, a new church having
been erected in a far less picturesque position below. The
chancel of the old church has, however, been preserved as a
burial-chapel, and the tower still holds the bells. The nave
has been unroofed, and lies open to the weather. The lower

part of the tower, which is central in position, is of Norman character, and has on its southern side a small and narrow round-headed window, apparently of Norman date. Worked into this window, and forming its top, is a more ancient stone,

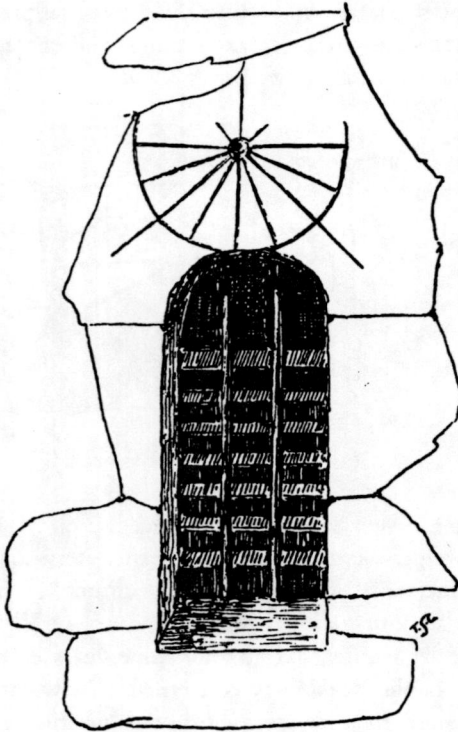

which bears upon it a sun-dial, possibly of the Saxon period. The semi-circle of this dial seems to be divided into seven spaces, but two vertical lines divide the upper half of the dial into three irregular divisions. A small hole drilled in the

face of the dial on the left side seems to indicate that the
gnomon had a support.

"The south doorway of the nave at Uphill is of very early
character, and although I am not confident that it has not
been altered at some later period, it also, may I think, be of

pre-Norman date. The tympanum is formed of a single
block of limestone incised with a circle, the centre of which
contains a kind of maltese cross. On the right of this are
the radii of a second sun-dial, similar in character to that on
the tower."

At the ancient little church of Brympton, county Somerset, there are traces of two dials on stones which have been fastened into the walls of the building ; and at Tarrant-Rushton, county Dorset, a similar dial face was found in the

BISHOPSTONE.

church wall when the plaster was removed during the course of restoration.

One of the most perfect specimens of an early dial is at Bishopstone, in Sussex. It is placed over the church porch, and is inscribed with the name " EADRIC." The stone is rounded at the top, and ornamented with the *mæander*, or Greek fret ; the hour lines are thirteen in number, *i.e.*, five principal lines crossed at the end, and dividing the day into the usual four parts, and each of these parts divided again into three, thus marking twelve hours in the day according to Roman usage, combined with the four tydes of the octaval system. Eadric, a prince of the South Saxons, son of Egbert, King of Kent, was living in A.D. 685, the last year of Wilfrith's stay in Sussex, and it may be his name which is here inscribed. Another dial at Warnford, Hants, may with certainty be assigned to this time. This is a plain double circle, the lower half divided into four spaces, and is cut on a square stone with foliated ornaments in the four corners. An inscription in Warnford Church tells us of the foundation of the building by Wilfrith, cir. 681, as of its subsequent restoration by Adam de Porter. A similar dial belonging to the same period is in the south wall of Corhampton Church, and another on St. Michael's, Winchester, may also be of the same date. This differs from the former ones in that the lower half of the circle is unequally divided, two divisions of the morning hours being each subdivided by three, while the afternoon spaces are only halved.

Another relic of Wilfrith's time may be seen on the fine old cross at Bewcastle, Cumberland, which is thought to mark the grave of King Alcfrith of Northumbria. It bears on its south side, in the midst of a sculptured scroll pattern, a semi-circular dial with lines which mark the four parts of the day, subdivided by others showing the intermediate hours, thus making twelve, as as Bishopstone. The Runic inscription on the cross states that it was " set by Hwœtred, after Alcfrith sometime king and son of Oswi, in the first year of the king of this realm Ecgfrith " (A.D. 670). Alcfrith's death probably took place in 665 or 666. He was made King of Deira by his father Oswy, and being a sincere Christian, greatly helped the evangelization of Northumbria and Mercia. He chose Wilfrith for his friend and chaplain, and aided him in his endeavours to bring the customs of the Northumbrian Church into conformity with those of Augustine's followers, and consequently of western Christendom generally. On the great question of Easter, the victory won by Wilfrith's party over the Scottish Bishops at Whitby was partly due to the influence exercised by Alcfrith over his father, Oswy. It is interesting to find these traces of the life's work of the great Northumbrian bishop upon these dial stones, alike in his southern mission field of Sussex as in the northern kingdom of his early friend.

The following notes on Ancient Dials in Cumberland we owe to the kindness of the Rev. W. S. Calverley, Vicar of Aspatria, and shall be given in his own words :—

"At Isel Church (St. Michael's), near Cockermouth, there are four dials: three of these are placed one above another in the west jamb of a decorated chancel window on the south side, close to a walled-up priest's doorway. The upper one is five inches in diameter, it has the whole twenty-four divisions of day-night, and reminds one of the Bottesford dial, Lincolnshire, figured at p. 79, 'Yorkshire Sun-dials,' by the Rev. D. H. Haigh. A Roman capital N is cut on the east side of the dial just above the horizontal diameter, and another much disfigured N appears just below the horizontal line.

"Below this dial is another of the same diameter, but only marking the hours betwixt 9 a.m. and 1 p.m. I tested the dials on St. Michael's day, 1883.

"The third and lowest dial has the greater part of the day hours marked (from 7 a.m. to 3 p.m.) with one line above the horizontal diameter to the east, and a nail stump where the upper N appears in the topmost dial.

"All have holes in the centre, and the lowest one still retains some of the iron of the gnomon. Diameter, $6\frac{1}{4}$ inches.

"On the east jamb of the Norman south main entrance,

now covered in by a rude porch, is another dial, seven inches in diameter, similar to the second, described above.

"This is the finest and most interesting set of dials I know, but I should think those in the chancel window jamb are not in their original position ; they were first noticed by me after the late restoration of the church.

" Similar dials to the last described are found on either side of the Norman south entrance, now covered by an early English porch, of Dearham Church, near Maryport, on the east side of Newton Arlosh Church door, and on the west side of the Norman south entrance of Milburn Church, Westmoreland, where there are two placed one above the other, the upper one being wrong side up.[1] I have also discovered a similar dial in the inside of Torpenhow Church, Cumberland. It is built into the south wall of the south aisle, between the two square windows, having evidently been placed there at some enlargement of the church. The aisle is Norman, possibly the dial belonged to a pre-Norman church, as I believe the majority of these dials must have done.

"At Caldbeck Church, Cumberland (see p. 428), I discovered on Aug. 23, 1883, the finest specimen of a dial, having all the day hours marked like the Kirkburn one, figured in Mr. Haigh's paper, that is, having a nearly horizontal diameter to the circle and the lower half equally divided into hours. This dial is built into the south wall of the chancel, east of the lintel of the priest's doorway. It is seven inches in diameter, the circle deeply cut, and part of the old iron gnomon remains in the centre wedged with lead and nails. The upper half of the circle is plain, the lower half is divided into sixteen divisions by seventeen round pops drilled into the stone where the division lines from the centre touch the circle. At the third pop below the horizontal line is a mark outside the circle in the same position as that of the lower N in the Isel dial. The nearly perpendicular mid-day line is continued beyond the circle and ends in a cross. This dial has been removed from some other place, and put here when the lancet window was restored.

" A similar dial, with twelve day hours marked, is now on

---

[1] A third and larger dial, measuring sixteen inches by fourteen, is on the south side of the chancel, about eight feet from the ground.

the south face of the buttress at the south-west angle of
Bolton Church, Westmorland."

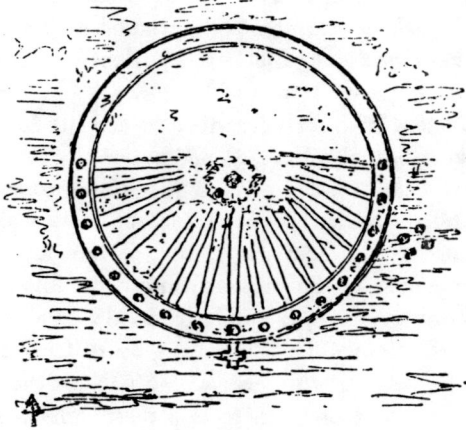

CALDBECK.

Mr. Calverley also mentions as a possible dial, a stone
built into the wall of Kirk Oswald Church; it is divided into
spaces, but the number of divisions—fifteen—can hardly be
accounted for. (Transactions of the Cumberland Archæological Society, Art. xxi.)

A Saxon Psalter in the British Museum has a sketch of a
horologium, in which the arrangement of hour-lines corresponds pretty nearly with the dial at Bishopstone. The horizontal six o'clock line is wanting, the hour-lines being carried much farther back than a real dial would allow of, but
the noon-day line projects beyond the circle, and is crossed,
as are the lines for the third and ninth hours, the hours being
counted and marked both in Roman letters and figures, from
6 a.m., the first hour. On the inner circle the fylfot occurs
at two distinct places. The MS. is of the eleventh century,
" Liber Psaltorum cum versione Saxonica," Tib. c. vi. Bibl.
Cotton.

It is worth noting that directions for the construction of sun-dials are given in one of the Ven. Bede's scientific works, e.g., "To make a dial of metal or wood with six sides, each with a gnomon." ("Libellus de Mensura Horologii, op. Colon, 1612," tom. ii., p. 392.)

The ancient Irish dials described by the late Mr. Du Noyer ("Archæo. Journal," No. 99), and noticed by the Rev. D. H. Haigh, are chiefly found on upright stones placed erect on the ground. One in the graveyard of Innishcaltra, Lough Derg, consists of a semi-circle divided into four equal parts with a large hole for the gnomon; another at Kilcummin, near Killala, county Mayo, is similarly divided, and both are assigned to the time of St. Cummin, Abbot of Innishcaltra and Bishop of Clonfert, who died A.D. 661. In the churchyard of Saul, county Down, there is an escutcheon-shaped dial carved on a headstone with lines also marking the octaval division of time, the equinoctial line alone being wanting; and at Kilmakedar, county Kerry, another, more ornamented but of the same class, in shape somewhat resembling a horse-shoe, and resting on a massive stone shaft, is assigned to a later date.

A semi-circular dial on a tall slab of stone on the southeast side of the old church of Clone, county Wexford, which dates from the thirteenth century, is marked according to the twelve hour system with the exception of the early morning hours, where one line marking 7.30 does duty for 7 and 8 a.m. In the churchyard of Kells, county Meath, a dial which may have been intended to serve both in a horizontal and an upright position, is engraved on a rough slab now serving as a headstone. It is divided into twenty-four hours, the lines which divide the circle into four parts projecting beyond it and terminating in ornamental crosses, while the letter R, in sixteenth century character, is carved at its side.

Mr. Haigh also describes the curious portable dial first noticed by Mr. Du Noyer, which was turned up by the plough within the old fortress of Cleobury Mortimer, in Shropshire. It is of shell limestone, and is pierced through from edge to edge as if intended to be worn strung upon a cord. With it were two beads, with Runic inscriptions, evidently intended to hang on the same string on each side of the dial. The dial itself is pierced by a centre hole, from which the hour-lines diverge to the outer circle. These are placed so as to divide the day-night into ten divisions, those in the lower half of the circle being halved, as at Swillington and Old Byland. Seven little holes pierced through the stone below the circle forming an arc, and one outside of this, are thought to represent, from their position, a crescent of stars opposite the constellation of the Great Bear (Woden's or Ceorl's Wain), which in its turn is shown by six stars at the end of the stone. The dial measures about $3\frac{1}{2}$ inches by $3\frac{1}{4}$ inches. Professor Stephens suggests as an interpretation of the Runic, " *Let the* CLAW (*pointer*) EYE (*show you*)," and assigns the dial to the sixth century. It may have been made by Jutes or Goths.

Professor Stephens mentions one other dial with Runes which has come under his notice, but a comparatively modern one, being dated 1754: " It is of simple marble, nearly a foot square, and was found near Norrkoping, in Sweden, about 1876. A line of modern Runic runs round all the four edges, and gives a rule how to arrange the gnomon in leap year. I described it in Swedish (with chemotype illustrations) in Mänadsblad, Stockholm, 1877."—Stephens' " Old Northern Runic Monuments," vol. iii., p. 163.

Another portable dial, made of soft sandstone with a large hole in the centre, was found in the moat of Stokesay Castle,

Shropshire. There are six conical holes round the edge, arranged so as to mark six out of the eight tides of the day, the introduction of the earliest one, 3 a.m., showing that the maker must have been a man who had lived in a latitude as high as 60° N., probably in Norway, and so was used to early sunrises. It is a rough little instrument, and is thought to belong to the earliest times of the Teutonic settlements in Britain.

On Linlithgow Church, N.B., there is a stone built into the outer south wall, on a level with the capitals of the porch pillars. It is engraved with six radii, and is evidently a dial face of very ancient date.

This slight sketch of early dials may serve to show how large a field still remains for the explorer. Whether the presence of these little stones, built carelessly into churches by no means modern, may throw any light upon the settlements of different tribes known by their different method of marking the day-night, or upon church or monastic founda-tions, archæologists and historians may hereafter determine. Some explanation, too, of various crosses which mark some of the lines is much to be desired. It is certainly possible in some cases that the crossed lines mark the canonical hours, as well as the central points of the four tides of the day. Prime, Tierce, Sext, Nones, and Vespers might very well be indi-cated by the monastic sun-dial, more especially as Durandus (Rationale Divisiorem Officiorum), writing in the thirteenth century, states that the " Horologium, by means of which the hours are read, teacheth the diligence that should be in priests to observe at the proper time the canonical hours, as he saith, ' Seven times a day do I praise Thee.' "

The mode of obtaining the shadow within a hollow, which was practised by the Greek dial makers, has been commonly used by more modern workers. There is a fine specimen of this kind of dial near the side entrance to Madeley Hall, Shropshire.

No history attaches to the dial, but the mansion was formerly the country house of the Prior of Wenlock Abbey. This remarkable dial is in form a solid cube of stone, standing on four low feet, and elevated on a circular platform of steps. In three of the sides is a concave circle, which is bordered by

smaller hollows, round, triangular, and diamond-shaped, and these equally serve to indicate the hour at one time of day or another. The top is convex. The instrument can also be used for finding the position of the moon in relation to the planets.

Perhaps one of the most elaborate, complicated, and beautiful dials in the world, is that of Buen Retiro, Churriana, near Malaga, in Spain, which is made of white marble, includes three stages in its construction, and is so carved and diversified

in shape, especially in the upper part, that it contains 150
dials in all. The upper face includes a star, and there is
another below, also a cross, which is inclined and covered
with dials; and beneath them are engraved the two castles
and lion, " Castilla y Leon," the royal badge of Spain. The
sides of this front are hollowed and lineated, after the manner
of the Greek or Assyrian model. On one side of the middle
stage is a shell carved, which contains a dial, and another is
beside it ; and so ingeniously are the angles cut throughout
this piece of machinery, that they do not seem to be indicated
on the surface, but dials exist wherever there is room to
scratch a line. The step on which the whole rests is formed
of thin flat bricks, the pavement being black and white. It
stands beside a stone tank, on a terrace which faces a lovely
view over a fruitful plain and distance. The neighbouring
hills glow in the sunlight, the sombre cypress trees cast their
gloom around ; and the melancholy glance of Time seems to
be present, throwing its shade over its own fleeting footsteps,
as these are expressed by the many gnomons on this remarkable instrument.

The white marble of the structure strongly contrasts with
the dark sad green of the funereal trees ; and as among the
devices cut in the sides of this structure are the cockle-shell
or scallop of the pilgrim, the star of hope, and the Cross of
Christian faith, in contrast with the ducal crown, the cardinal's
hat, and the kingly quarterings,—enough, and more than
enough, is suggested for serious meditation to anyone who
visits this curious time-reckoner.

A small dial, cut on the same principle as that at Malaga,
is in the Museum at Clermont-Ferrand, in Auvergne. It is
made of white marble, but the lower half has been coloured a
brick red, with a star painted upon it. The top is a hollow
globe, set, as it were, in a cup of larger size, upon the rim of

F F

which the hours are marked by the shadow of a gnomon. On the pedestal are various hollows and curves, as well as flat and perpendicular surfaces, on each of which one or more dials are traced, to the number of about thirty. The whole block is not more than a foot and a half high, and is said to date from the sixteenth century. It was found at the Château of Tournouelles in Auvergne.

The vertical dial of white marble, which projects from the façade of the Church of Santa Maria Novella at Florence, bears the following inscription :—"Cosm. Med. magn. Etr. dux, nobilium artium studiosus, astronomiæ studiosis dedit, anno D. MDLXXII. *Cosmo Medici, the Grand Duke of Etruria, a student of the ennobling arts, gave this to the students of astronomy*, A.D. 1572. The dial was the work of Fra Ignazio Danti of the Dominicans, to which order the Church and Monastery belonged. On the other side of the slab may be seen the "armilia di Tolomeo"—*sphere of Ptolemy*—for observing the ingress of the sun into the first point of Aries.

The Church of Santa Maria Novella is the one which Michael Angelo called "his Bride." A clock in one of the transepts bears the following inscription :—

Sic fluit occulte, sic multos decipit ætas ;
Sic venit ad finem quidquid in orbe manet.
Heu ! heu ! præteritum non est revocabile tempus ;
Heu ! proprius tacito mors venit ipsa pede.

So flows the age unperceived, so it deceives many ;
So comes to an end whatever remains in the world.
Alas, alas, the time past is not to be recalled ;
Alas, death itself comes nearer with silent foot.

Scotland is very rich in elaborate dials, most of which were erected during the seventeenth century. Queen Mary's dial at Holyrood must first be mentioned. This stands in the gardens of the palace, and consists of a column mounted on three steps, and crowned by a block of stone cut into many planes (as may be seen in the figure), and on these planes the concave dial faces are engraved. The dial was thought to have belonged to Mary Queen of Scots, but the accounts in the Register Office show that the Queen after whom it was named was Henrietta Maria. It was presented to her by Charles I., who in 1633 paid the sum of " £408. 15. 6 Scots. to John Mylne, Maisonne, for the working and

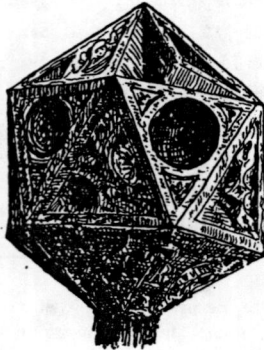

the hewing of the dyell." The Holyrood dial was described and figured in the " Proceedings of the Edinburgh Architectural Association," vol. iii., Sessions 1880-82. The plates show that the panels between the dial faces are decorated with the royal arms and initials " c. r. m. r. and c. p."; figures of St. Andrew and St. George also appear, and the rose and thistle, in various forms.

There is an interesting dial at Glamis Castle, near Forfar, the residence of the Earl of Strathmore; where, we are told, " the Chevalier slept in 1715, and had above eighty beds made for himself and his retinue." Here was the castle, by inheritance, of Macbeth—

1st Witch. All hail, Macbeth ! hail to thee, thane of Glamis !
Macbeth. Stay, you imperfect speakers, tell me more.
By Sinel's death, I know I am thane of Glamis.

This pillar dial is supposed to have been made about the beginning of the seventeenth century. It stands on steps, and above its base are four lions erect, and back to back, each holding in his paws a shield, on which is a dial face. The names of months and days are engraved below. These figures support a further structure, and a large block at the top is cut into eighty triangular planes on which gnomons are fixed. The pillar terminates in a coronet. The name and arms of the Strathmore family account for the introduction of the lions.

There are two large dials in the grounds of Kelburne

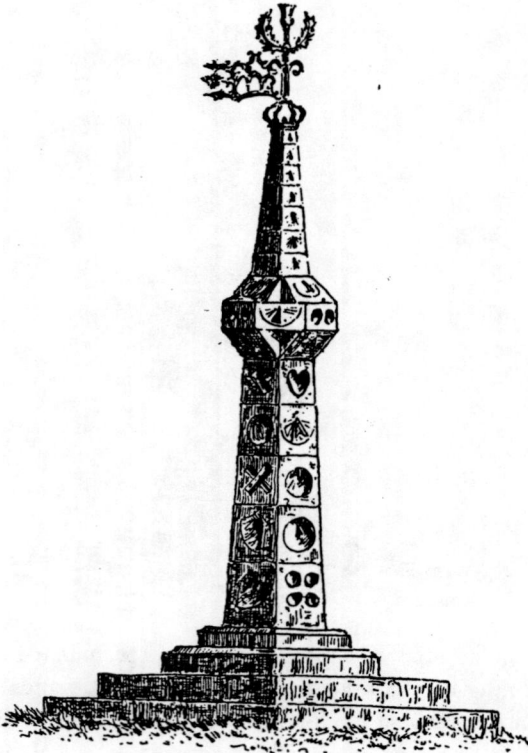

Castle, Ayrshire, the seat of Lord Glasgow. The one of which we give a figure is 10 feet 4 inches high; it is a four-sided column, tapering towards she top, and crowned with a vane, on which the initials of David, Earl of Glasgow, and those of his wife are entwined. The whole column is covered with variously-shaped sinkings, heart, cross, and shell shaped, besides the usual vertical planes for the gnomon. It is dated 1707. The second dial is similar in construction, but it is crowned with a simple stone ball at the top. The column is 10 feet high, and stands in a stone basin full of water. Its sides are also covered with concave and vertical dial faces.

A column of the same character, but rather simpler in its decorations, stands in a cottage garden in Dalmeny Park, Linlithgowshire, not far from the ruined castle and gardens of Baronbough, to which it probably belonged.

At Barnton, near Edinburgh, there are two more of these fine pillar dials, one of them is exactly like the figure given of the Kelburne dial, and it is dated 1692. The column of the second is more elaborately decorated with armorial bearings and other designs, and its eight dial faces are vertical.

At Tongue (Lord Reay), there is a four-sided column dial, with an almost innumerable number of faces. It is 7 feet 4 inches high, and dated 1714. There is a smaller specimen at Auchenbowie, near Stirling.

At Ellon Castle, Aberdeenshire, there is also a pillar dial, set on three steps and crowned by a ball, and similar dials are said to be at Pitmedden, and at Turner Hall, in the same neighbourhood. At Rubislaw Den, near Aberdeen, there is one which has been for several generations in the possession of the family of Skene of Rubislaw ; and ancient dials are further reported to exist at Mellestains, near Kelso; at Bemersyde, near Dryburgh ; at Inch House; at Meggetland ; at Woodhouselee ; and at Carberry Tower, the four last-named places being in the neighbourhood of Edinburgh.

There is a fine and elaborate dial at Cramond House, near Edinburgh ; and one of more solid structure at Midmar

Castle, Aberdeenshire; the latter closely resembles the Holyrood dial.

At Mount Melville, St. Andrews, there is another fine
specimen, like the Holyrood one. It is a stone pillar 7
feet 5 inches high, mounted on three steps. The shaft of
the pillar is octagonal, and this, as well as the capital, and
the block which forms the top, are covered with dial faces.
There were seventy originally, but the gnomons of some of
them are now worn away. There are eight devices carved
on the lower part of the shaft, a rose, a thistle, a fleur-de-lis,
a shamrock, and other things which cannot now be easily
identified. The dial has been brought to its present position
from some other spot. A somewhat similar dial is said to
exist at Craignethan Castle, Lanarkshire; and there is one
also at Melville House, Fifeshire, which stands on three
steps, and has many faces on the block which crowns the
pillar. It apparently dates from the seventeenth century,
but was only erected at Melville House about the year 1862.
It previously stood at Balgonie, Fifeshire, but the owner of
the estate sold it, and brought the dial to Melville House,
which was also his property.

In the gardens of Warriston, near Edinburgh, there is
another fine specimen of the Holyrood type. This probably
belonged to Warriston House, which is now destroyed, and
the gardens are included within the extended boundary of
Edinburgh. The fine pillar of the market cross at Inver-
keithing, Fifeshire, is surmounted by a unicorn, sejant and
collared, supporting a shield, thereon the cross of St. Andrew;
and below this is a vertical dial face.

At Dunglass, Berwickshire, there is a column of square
pillars, surmounted by a widely spread capital, and on the top
of this is a square block of stone bearing four vertical dial
faces.

At Pitreavie, Fifeshire, is another square pillar, decorated with armorial shields, and dated 1644; at the top is a block elaborately carved into dial faces.

Another very elaborate dial, bearing thirty-three gnomons, is at Crámond, near Edinburgh. One of the faces is dated 1732, and bears the name of " Sir Rob. Dickson." On another face is inscribed, " Ach. Handasyde, fecit." The same Handasyde made the dial on Inveresk Church, which is mentioned under the motto *Sic transit gloria mundi*.

There is a legend that the dial at Cramond was brought to that place from Lauriston Castle, which is two miles distant. A few years ago it was seen by Mr. Thomas Ross, broken into three or four pieces, but he called the attention of the Committee of the Edinburgh Exhibition (1886) to the fact, and the dial was borrowed from the owner for exhibition, and put into repair. The ball which now surmounts the top has been recently placed there.

In the garden at Calder House, Midlothian, there is a pillar dial of solid character, the upper part of which is an inclined plane, cut into semi-circular faces, and bearing concave ones on its sides.

A dial of the same quaint character now stands in the garden at Rucklaw near Prestonkirk. This place has been in the possession of the family of Sydserff since 1537. The dial is not dated, but appears to be very ancient; it was thrown aside at one time, but replaced in its present position by the great grandfather of the present owner. The pillar is of grey stone and 6 feet in height; it has about thirty-five dial faces. There is a second dial in the same garden, but this is of later construction, its pillar is of red sandstone, and bears a horizontal dial face of white marble.

In the grounds of Kilmarten, in Glen Urquhart, Invernesshire, there is a dial 5 feet high, consisting of a square block of stone resting on four marble balls. The face is of copper, and has engraved on one side the Ogilvy crest and motto *Alma fide.* It was set up at Coniemony, in Glen Urquhart in 1840, by Thomas Ogilvy, Esq., and removed to its present place when that estate was sold.

There are pillar dials also at Craigmillar; and at Leuchars; the latter is a modern one, and was designed by Lady John Scott, who also gave the pattern for the one at Cawston, which is figured in our frontispiece.

The dial at Pinkie House, Musselburgh, is supposed to have been put up by Alexander Seton, Earl of Dunfermline, who died there in 1622. It rests on a wall, and is four-sided, a carved pinnacle rises above the block, and bears a weather-cock.

There is a sun-dial in the garden at Northbar, near Erskine. It consists of a female figure carved in stone, bearing a dial on her head. The date upon it is 1679, and there are the initials of Donald Mac Gilchrist, to whom the place once belonged. At Polton, near Edinburgh, there are two dials probably of late seventeenth century date. One shows a figure of Time in relief, winged, holding a scythe, and supporting a globe on his knee; a square dial face is below. The other is a fragment; on a square base rests an hexagonally carved stone : on the faces of both there have been dials; but how the structure terminated is not known.

The pillar at Skibo Castle, Sutherland, is of simpler character than some of the preceding ones; it stands about three feet high. The block of dials faces the four points of the compass; on the north and south sides the dials are simply vertical, while on the east and west, and on the top, they are concave or angular. It is not dated, but must be very ancient. Skibo was originally the palace of the Bishops of Sutherland and Caithness.

A pillar crowned with a block curiously cut into dial faces, once stood in the former Zoological Gardens at Edinburgh. It is figured in "Chambers' Cyclopædia" (p. 531).

Another pillar dial is stated to have been at Heriot's Hospital.

At Bowland, near Galashiels, there are two solid stone posts to what had once been a gateway entrance, and on the tapering top of each is a globe, round which the hours are figured, whilst the gnomon is an iron rod pointing from the north pole.

One of the most remarkable dials in Scotland still remains to be described. It stands upon the terrace of Dundas Castle, Linlithgowshire, and consists of a fountain built in castellated form ; the top is reached by a flight of steps, and on this is a pedestal elaborately decorated with the heads of goddesses, and crowned by a block of stone which is cut into many dial faces. The sides of the fountain are also elaborately decorated, and round them runs a Latin inscription, of which the following translation was given in "Summer Life on Land and Water at South Queensferry," by W. W. Fyfe :—

"See, read, think, and attend.
Through rocks and crags by pipes we lead these streams of water,
That the parched garden may be moistened by the spring.
Forbear to do harm therefore to the fountain and garden which thou
        seest ;
Nor yet shouldst thou incline to injure the signs of the dial,
View and with grateful eyes enjoy these hours, and the garden.
And to the flowers may eager thirst be allayed by the fountain.
In the year of human salvation 1623."

Below this inscription there is a further one, of which we again quote Mr. Fyfe's translation :—

"Sir Walter Dundas, in the year of our Lord 1623, and sixty-first of his own age, erected and adorned, as an ornament of his country and family, sacred to the memory of himself, and as a future memorial of his posterity, as also an amusing recreation for friends, guests, and visitors, this fountain in the form of a castle, this dial with its retinue of goddesses, and this garden with its buildings, walls, and quadrangular walks, surrounded with stones, piled on high, rocks having been on all sides deeply cut out, which inconveniently covered the ground. 'Whoever thou art, who comest hither, we, so many half-fiendish spectres, are placed here lately by order, expressly for bugbears to the bad, so that the hideous show their visages, lest any meddling evil-disposed person, should put forth his hand on the dial or garden. We warn robbers to depart, burglars to desist, nothing here is prey for plunder ! For the pleasure and enjoyment of spectators are all these placed here : but we, who rather laugh with joyous front to a free sight, we bid frankly the kind and welcome friends of the host. Boldly use every freedom with the master, the dial, the garden, and with the garden-beds and couches—him for friendship and conversation, them for the recreation of the mind and thought. With ordinary things to content us here, is to be even with others, we envy not their better things." The " fiends " alluded to are faces carved in medallions round the lower part of the fountain.

We have only space to briefly record some of the simpler forms of dials which exist on many interesting buildings in Scotland. There is one on a buttress near the south door of Melrose Abbey, dated 1661. The little village of Newstead, near Melrose, has small pairs of vertical dials of grey stone projecting from the walls of several of the older cottages ; one of these is dated 1751. There are similar ones, only of larger size, on the towers and on the inner court of Heriot's Hospital, Edinburgh, twenty-two dials in all.

Innes House, Morayshire, which was built between 1640

and 1653 from the plans given by William Aytonne, "maister maissoun at Herriotts," has a couple of the like dials on its walls.

On a modern house in the street of Elie, Fifeshire, a very fine old doorway has been placed; it is dated 1682, and bears an armonial shield and other decorations, crowned at the top of the archway by a block of stone cut into various dial faces. A similar block rests on the head of a lion, who is seated, with a fox on each side, above the gateway of Waygateshaw, a mansion house near Lanark. The gateway leads into the courtyard of the house; possibly the lion and foxes have been brought from some other place.

At Grangepans, Linlithgowshire, there are two dials on the corners of the gables of the house. It is dated 1564.

On the gable of an old house in Clackmannan there is a curious vertical dial, oval in shape. At Crichton House, Midlothian, there is a horizontal specimen attached to the sill of a window. At Aberdour Castle, Fifeshire, there is one having a circular face, decorated with a sun, attached to an angle of the building.

At Balcomie Castle, Fifeshire, a small dial is singularly placed in the arch spandril of a fine gateway leading into the courtyard. Over the arch there are three large panels which contain escutcheons, "those in the centre panel being the arms and supporters of the Learmonths of Balcomie, with a motto, which seems to read 'Solis Feintis,' and the date 1660. The panel on the left hand contains the same arms .... with the initials of John Learmonth, and on the scroll above, the motto 'Sans Feintise.' The remaining panel .... contains the arms and initials of Elizabeth Myreton, of Randerston, wife of John Learmonth, with the motto 'Advysedlie.' On the frieze running along the top of the gateway is the inscription, ' THE . LORD . BVLD . THE . HOUSE . THEY LABOVR, IN-VAINE . THAT . BVILD . IT.' " [1]

On Hatton House, Midlothian, there are two dials, one of which bears the date 1675, and the initials E. M. On Pinkie House, Midlothian ; Fountain Hall, Haddington- shire ; Peffer Mill, near Edinburgh ; and Troquair, near Peebles, there are also vertical dials. At Keely Castle, Fife, there is one on the garden wall. On Prestonpans Church there is one at an angle of the wall, having three faces. At Northfield, near Prestonpans, which is the ancient seat of the Marjoribanks, there is a dial bearing the date 1647, and the initials G. M. and M. B. Over the front door of the house there is the date 1611, and a shield of arms, with the initials J. M. and M. S., which are those of Joseph Ma- joribanks, and his wife Marion Simson. Below the shield, and just above the doorway, runs the text, EXCEPT THE LORD BVLD IN WANE BVLDS MAN.

At Drummond Castle, near Crieff, there is a dial dated 1630, and bearing an inscription in Latin, consisting of five stanzas. This information reached us too late for the dial to be inserted in its proper place amongst those with mottoes.

There is a curiously shaped dial on the corner of the south wall of Oldhamstocks Church, near Cockburnspath ; and a still more singular specimen on Corstorphine Church near Edinburgh. This is a square block of stone, with four dial faces, set angle-wise on a buttress of the building, and there are six other buttresses crowned with imitation dials, similar in shape to the real one, but these are set with their sides parallel to the building. On the wall, close to the real dial, is a shield bearing three hunter's horns stringed—the arms of Forrester. The church is supposed to be of fifteenth cen-

---

[1] Castellated and Domestic Architecture of Scotland," vol. ii., 356.

tury date, but the dials are evidently of sixteenth century work.

On Belmont Lodge, Edinburgh ; and on King's College, Aberdeen, there are dials in similar positions to the one at Corstorphine.

On an old house in Lord Street, Rochdale, Lancashire— which is said to have been the ancient manor house of the Byron family—there is a vertical dial bearing two dates, 1521 and 1620; the latter probably refers to a time when it was restored. It has apparently undergone several restorations. This is the oldest dated dial of which we know. There is one at Warwick, dated 1556 (see No. 215), and another near Oswestry, dated 1578 (see No. 423), and in the churchyard of St. Anne's, Woodplumpton, there is one without a motto, dated 1598.

There are two curious old dials standing in Elmley Castle Churchyard, near Pershore, Worcestershire. One of which is placed on the eastern side of the burial ground ; the stone of this is 1 foot 10 inches square, and is bevelled off at the shoulder, where it is surmounted by a globular-shaped top, that is covered with sinkings of various forms—hexagonal, pentagonal, heart-shaped, but chiefly circular. All of these are much weather-beaten and worn. In several of the indentations there remains a thin iron rod, which was the original gnomon ; but many of these rods are beaten flat upon the stone. The whole height of the dial, not much exceeding three feet and a half, has caused it to be within reach of children, who have loosened the globular top; and it now revolves, when pushed, on the iron spindle in the centre, which holds it to the lower stone. On the flat surfaces of the stone the former existence of twelve gnomons may be traced by the remains of the lead with which they were fixed. Across two of the hemispherical sinkings an iron rod is extended diagonally; and two other sinkings contain thin metal gnomons, which are still tolerably perfect. When an examination and sketch of this dial were made, about nine inches of soil had to be cleared away from the base.

The other dial stands near the north-west angle of the churchyard, and is erected on a portion of the base and one of the steps of the old mortuary Cross. On this foundation there are six courses of stone masonry, rising to 2 feet 6 inches in height; and above them is reared a stone, so similar in size and shape to the dial already described, that one cannot help supposing they originally formed one structure. Three of these sides are marked with variously-shaped sinkings; and on the north side is a large shield, bearing the arms of Savage, with numerous quarterings. The manor of Elmley was granted by Henry VIII. to Christopher Savage, and this family has held property in the parish until within the last few years. There can be no doubt that this dial was put up at the cost of one of the name. At the top is a more modern four-faced dial, about ten inches square, sloped above like a house roof, which tells the hours in the ordinary way.

In William Leybourne's "Tractates," published in 1682, is an account of the marvellous pyramidical dial, set up in 1669, by order of Charles II. in the Privy Garden, and facing the Banquetting House, at Whitehall. It stood on a stone pedestal and consisted of six pieces, in the form of tables or hollow globes, placed one above another standing on iron supporters, and lessening in size as they neared the top. The inventor was the Rev. Francis Hall, alias Lyne, a Jesuit and professor of mathematics at Liège, where he had previously erected a similar collection of dials, reported in 1703 to be "shamefully gone to decay." This pyramid is said to have contained no less than 271 different dials: some showing the hours according to the Jewish, Babylonian, Italian, and astronomical ways of counting: others making the shadow of the hour lines fall upon the stile as well as the usual reverse of this; and others displaying things pertaining to astronomy, geography, astrology, &c. The four elements of fire, air, water, and earth, were also represented; and there were portraits on glass of the king, the two queens (the mother and wife of Charles II.), the Duke of York and Prince Rupert. Father Lyne wrote a description of his work, and illustrated it with seventy-three plates. The cost of this royal toy must have been enormous, for Mr. Timbs says that, "about 1710, William Allingham, a mathematician in Cannon Row, asked £500 to repair this dial: it was last seen by Vertue at Buckingham House," from whence it was sold.

By the inventor's own showing, the whole construction must have been rather what we may call trumpery; without any grace in the design, and though displaying great ingenuity, in faulty taste. It could not have been qualified to resist the weather—to which to be of any use it must have been constantly exposed—for he complains, "that the Diall, for want of a cover, was much endamaged by the snow lying long frozen upon it; and that unless a cover were provided (of which he saw little hope) another, or two such tempestuous winters would utterly deface it." The rough illustrations to the "Brief Explication of the Pyramidicall Diall set up in his Majesty's Privy Garden at Whitehall, July 24, 1669," are quite sufficient to reconcile us to the loss of this extraordinary conceit.

In "Anecdotes of Painting in England," it is related of the eminent sculptor, Nicolas Stone, under the date 1619, that he made a dial at St. James', the king finding stone and workmanship only, for which he received £6 13s. 4d. "And in 1622," Stone says, "I made the great diall in the privy garden at Whitehall, for the which I had £46, and in that year, 1622, I made a dial for my Lord Brooke, in Holbourn, for the which I had £8 10s." Also for Sir John Daves, at Chelsea, he made a dial, and two statues of an old man and a woman, for which he received £7 a-piece.

The Privy Garden dials, executed by Stone, were, however, designed by Mr. Edmund Gunter, Professor of Astronomy at Gresham College, who, in 1624, published a description and use of the same, which he dedicates to King James, praying him to accept these poor fruits of his younger studies when he was His Majesty's Scholar in Westminster and Christchurch. The stone, he says, was the same size as that which stood in the same place before, only that was of Caen stone, and this of one entire stone from Purbeck quarry. The base, a square of more than $4\frac{1}{2}$ feet, the height $3\frac{1}{3}$, and wrought with the like planes and concaves as the former, but many lines different, and such as were not in before.

There were five dials described upon the upper part, four in the four corners, and one, the great horizontal concave, in the middle.

The four sides of the stone were turned to account as well as the top. The south side had one great vertical dial, two equinoctial dials, "whereon the sun never shineth but in winter," one vertical concave in the middle, two declining dials on either side of this concave, two small Polar concaves, and two irregular dials with three styles in each dial. On the north side of the stone the lines were drawn so as to answer to those on the south side ; and the east and west sides, which had each four great dials, were also made to correspond. There were besides four triangular dials at the four corners, inclining to the horizon. Latin verses explaining the lines and their colours were inscribed in each of the larger dials.

This fine and curious work was defaced in the reign of Charles II. by a drunken nobleman of the Court, on which occurrence Andrew Marvell wrote :—

> " For a dial the place is too unsecure,
>   Since the Privy Garden could not it defend :
> And so near to the Court they will never endure
>   Any monument how they their time may misspend."

The fancy of Charles I. for sun-dials was well known. Mr. Oughtred, the mathematician, on being asked by Elias Allen, one of the King's servants, to advise him as to a suitable New Year's gift for his Majesty, replied that he had " heard that his Majesty delighted much in the great concave dial at Whitehall, and what fitter instrument could he have than my horizontal, which was the very same represented in flat." Horace Walpole (" Anecdotes of Painting ") also gives a copy of a bill of John de Critz, serjeant painter to his Majesty, wherein the colouring of a dial opposite some part of the King and Queen's lodging is described at length.

" For several times oyling and laying with fayre white a stone for a sundyall . . . . the lines thereof being drawn in several colours, the letters directing to the howers guilded with fine gould, as also the glorie, and a scrowle guilded with fine gould where the numbers and figures specifying the planetary howers are inscribed ; likewise certaine letters drawne in black, informing in what part of the compasses the sun at any time there shining shall be resident, the whole works being circumferenced with a fret painted in manner of a stone one, the compleat measure of the whole being six foot." This same Critz repaired pictures by Palma and Titian, and yet was not above painting the royal barge and coach.

To the great Fire of London (1666) we probably owe the destruction of Dr. Donne's sun-dial, which he put at the

Deanery of St. Paul's, and of which he makes mention in his will :—

"My will is that the four large pictures of the four Great Prophets which hang in the hall, and that large picture of ancient church work in the lobby, and whatever else I have placed in the chapel (except that wheel of Deskes which at this time stands there) shall remain in those places, as also the marble table sonnedyal and pictures which I have placed in the garden, and an inventory thereof to be made and the things to continue always in the house as they are." All are gone now, the Deanery was swept away by the fire, and not a vestige of Dr. Donne's legacies remain.

In Joseph Moxon's "Tutor to Astronomie and Geographie," published in 1659, there are full directions for making sun-dials of various kinds, and amongst them a "Dyal upon a solid Ball or Globe, that shall shew the Hours of the Day without a gnomon." The equinoctial or middle line of this globe must be divided into twelve equal parts, and marked with two sets of figures from 1 to 12 ; and the globe then elevated according to the Latitude of the place, with one 12 set to the north, and the other to the south. When the sun shines, the hour is indicated where the shadowed and the illuminated parts meet. "A Dyal of this sort," we are told, "was made by Mr. John Leek, and set up on a composite Columne at Leaden Hall Corner, London, in the mayoralty of Sir John Dethick, Knight." The column was adorned with four statues of women in caps and kirtles, and also formed the centre of a fountain. It was erected in 1655.[1]

The figure of this "pretty piece of Ingeniety," given in Chambers' "Book of Days," is copied from Moxon's work. The same writer gives an example of a glass globe dial borne

[1] Sir John Dethick's pillar and fountain was reproduced in "Old London," in the Health Exhibition, 1884.

on the shoulders of Atlas, which stood in the garden of Robert Titchborn, once Lord Mayor of London.

Another London dial in the form of a cross stood at the south corner of Middle Moorfield, by Moorgate, and is described as an iron sun-dial " fixed on a stone fastened in the ground with this inscription thereon : —' This dial was placed here as a Boundary of the Parish of St. Stephen, Coleman Street, in the memorable year 1706, in the 9th year of the glorious reign of our most gracious Sovereign, whom God long preserve.' "

The old pillar dial in Kensington Palace Gardens has also been spoken of as " once of great renown," but it has been removed, and only the name " Dial Walk " shows where it once stood.

Covent Garden was originally the Convent Garden belonging to the Abbey of Westminster ; and when, in 1631, Francis, Earl of Bedford, to whom the property belonged, had the present square formed, it was laid out by Inigo Jones, but not completed. The piazza ran along the whole north and north-east sides, the church of St. Paul was on the west, and on the south was the garden wall of Bedford House, under the overhanging trees of which a few temporary stalls were set up at market times. The square was gravelled over, and in the centre was erected, in 1668, a Corinthian column surmounted by a block of stone with four faces and a dial on each, and the whole crowned by a globe supported on four scrolls. The churchwardens' accounts of St. Paul's record some of these items :—

		£	s.	d.
Dec. 7, 1668.	Received of the Right Honourable the Earl of Bedford as a gratuity towards the erecting of yᵉ column . . .	20	o	o
— —	Received from the Honourable Sʳ Charles Cotterill, Master of the Ceremonys, as a gift towards the said column . .	10	o	o

April 29, 1669.	Received from the Right Honourable the Lord Denzil Holles as a present towards the erecting of the aforesaid column .	£	s.	d.
		10	0	0
27 Nov. 1668.	For drawing a Modell of the Column to be presented to the Vestry . . .	0	10	0
2 Dec. 1668.	To Mr Wainwright for 4 gnomons .	0	8	6

The column was raised on six steps of black marble, and there old women sold barley broth and milk porridge. A brochure, " The humours of Covent Garden," 1738, describes the scene :—

> " High in the midst of this most happy land,
> A well built marble pyramid doth stand,
> By which spectators know the time o' the day,
> From beams reflecting of the solar ray ;
> The basis with ascending steps is graced,
> Around whose area cleanly matrons placed,
> Vend their most wholesome food, by nature good,
> To cheer the spirits and enrich the blood."

The pillar figures in Hogarth's print of " Rich's glory, or, his triumphal entry into Covent Garden," published in 1732, and also in engravings of the " Covent Garden Morning Frolic," by Boitard, 1747, where it is represented as surrounded by the tiled roof of a market shed, and with the market women clustering about the steps. It was probably taken away when the present market was built.

The column in the centre of Lincoln's Inn New Square, designed by Inigo Jones, also supported a sun-dial, and was made a centre for a fountain, the water spouting out of triton shells held by four boyish figures, and falling into a basin at the foot of the pillar. The square block of stone on which the dials were traced was crowned by a pinnacle. It is possible that the motto quoted by Charles Leadbitter (" Art of Dialling "), as at Lincoln's Inn, " Let your light so shine before men," belonged to this dial. The column is represented in an engraving of the New Square by Nichols, 1730, and was not removed until the year 1817, when it was taken away to make room for a gas-lamp!

The "Seven Dials," which gave their name to a district in the parish of St. Giles-in-the-Fields, were, curiously enough,

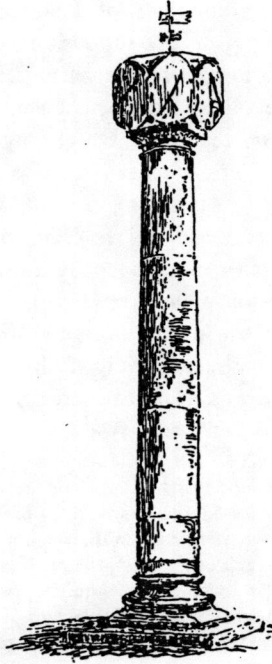

only six in number. They formed the six faces of a block of stone which crowned a Doric column, and each dial fronted one of the streets which met in the open space where the pillar stood. Two of these streets opened into one angle, so that the seven formed an irregular star as described by John Evelyn :—" I went," he says, 5th Oct., 1694, " to

see the building near St. Giles, where seven streets make a
star from a Doric pillar placed in the middle of a circular
area, said to be built by Mr. Neale, introducer of the late
lotteries."

Cunningham's "Handbook of London" says, "It was
removed in July 1773, on the supposition that a considerable
sum of money was lodged at the base. But the search was
ineffectual." The old column spent some years in a stone-
mason's yard, and in 1822 was bought by the inhabitants of
Weybridge, and set up on the Green as a memorial to the
Duchess of York.

It is mounted on a pedestal, and crowned by a curiously
inartistic object, a pinnacle capped by a ducal coronet, while
the block of stone on which the six dials can still be traced
by the holes where the gnomons were fixed, lies embedded
in the ground near the adjoining "Ship" Inn, after being
for many years used as a mounting-block.

In Gay's "Trivia" we read :—

> "Where famed St. Giles' ancient limits spread,
> An in-railed column rears its lofty head :
> Here to seven streets seven dials count the day,
> And from each other catch the circling ray ;
> How oft the peasant with enquiring face,
> Bewilder'd trudges on from place to place ;
> He dwells on every sign with stupid gaze,
> Enters the narrow alley's doubtful maze,
> Tries every winding court and street in vain,
> And doubles o'er his weary steps again."

A print of 1725 shows a sun-dial on the wall of Coney
Court, Gray's Inn ; and one of 1715 gives us two on the
tower of St. Clement Danes' Church, dated 1678. One
alone remains. The old church of St. Martin's-in-the-Fields,
pulled down and rebuilt about 1721, had a dial on its west

side, and also on the south side of the tower. That on the church of St. Sepulchre's still exists.

At one time there were three dials on the cupola of the Guildhall, as is shown by an old view of the building, reproduced in Mr. J. E. Price's "Descriptive Account of the Guildhall of the City of London." It is supposed that they were placed there at the close of the seventeenth, or very early in the eighteenth century. Another dial appears on one of the buttresses in the same engraving.

The sun-dial erected at the expense of Queen Caroline, wife of George II., on Richmond Green, has probably passed away. It was standing in 1776, and was said to be " affixed in a pretty taste and encompassed with seats."

A window dial, formerly in the church of All Hallows Staining, Mark Lane, and put up by Isaac Oliver, in 1664, is noticed in the " Universal Museum," 1762, but even then there was " scarcely any part of the painted glass remaining." In Lambeth Palace such a dial still exists, with the fly painted on it. It is thought to have been removed from the Presence Chamber to its present place in a window of the Lollard's Tower.

In the small garden of Clement's Inn, Strand, there was, until March, 1884, the life-size figure of a Moor, kneeling and supporting a sun-dial on his head. Peter Cunningham, in his " Handbook of London," says, " it was brought from Italy, and presented to the Inn by Holles, Earl of Clare, but when or by what Earl no one has told us." There were four Earls of Clare of the Holles family : John, Lord Houghton, created 1624, died 1637 ; John, succeeded 1637, died 1665 ; Gilbert, succeeded 1665, died 1689 ; John, succeeded 1689, created Duke of Newcastle, 1694. It was probably the second Earl, who was the great builder and improver of the neighbourhood, and erected Clare Market, which is called a

" new market," by James Howell, in his " Londonopolis,"
1657. He says, " there is, towards Drury Lane, a new
market called Clare Market; " and the founder of this new
market may have been the person who placed the figure with
the dial in the little courtyard of Clement's Inn. It is of
bronze, but having been covered with black paint, some wag
stuck on it the following lines :—

> " In vain poor sable son of woe,
>   Thou seek'st the tender tear:
> From thee in vain with pangs they flow,
>   For mercy dwells not here.
> From Cannibals thou fled'st in vain ;
>   Lawyers less quarter give,
> The first wón't eat you till you're slain,
>   The last will do't alive."

In 1884, this dial passed into private hands through a sale
of the property of the Inn, but two years later it was presented to the Society of the Inner Temple, and has been
placed in the gardens on the terrace facing the Thames Em-
bankment. The date inscribed on the dial plate is 1731.

Few sun-dials are of greater historical interest than that
which bears on its side the name of the celebrated Anne
Clifford, Countess of Pembroke, the able and excellent
lady who could discourse on every subject "from pre-
destination to slea silk," the last of the great house of Clifford, who fought in the courts for her vast estates with the
tenacity, and ruled them with the wisdom of a Maria Theresa,
raising also her castles from their ruins, repairing the churches,
building again, as the inscriptions state, the old waste places.
Amongst the monuments which she reared, this pillar by the
wayside between Brougham and Appleby still records her
name. It is octagonal, surmounted by a square block, bearing dials on two of its sides; on the remaining two are the

arms of Vipont (who brought the estate of Brougham into the Clifford family), and those of Clifford impaling Russell, surmounted by an earl's coronet, and also the following inscription :—

THIS PILLAR WAS ERECTED, ANNO 1656,
BY THE RIGHT HON. ANN COUNTESSE DOWAGER OF
PEMBROKE, AND SOLE HEIR OF THE RIGHT
HONOURABLE GEORGE, EARL OF CUMBERLAND, ETC.,
FOR A MEMORIAL OF HER LAST PARTING IN THIS PLACE
WITH HER GOOD AND PIOUS MOTHER, THE RIGHT HONOURABLE
MARGARET COUNTESS DOWAGER OF CUMBERLAND,
THE SECOND OF APRIL, 1616. IN MEMORY WHEREOF
SHE ALSO LEFT AN ANNUITY OF FOUR POUNDS,
TO BE DISTRIBUTED TO THE POOR WITHIN THIS
PARISH OF BROUGHAM, EVERY SECOND DAY OF APRIL,
FOR EVER UPON THIS STONE TABLE.
LAUS DEO.

The stone table for the alms stands at the foot of the pillar, an engraving of which may be seen in Pennant's " Journey to Alston Moor," 1801. See No. 460.

A handsome stone with concave and angular dials described upon it, still stands in the garden of the old manor house at Upton, Northamptonshire. Its dimensions are 5 feet 10 inches in height, and 3 feet $4\frac{1}{2}$ inches at the base moulding. An engraving as well as a description of this dial may be found in Gibson and Gough's " Castor," and in the " Bibliotica Topographia Britanica," vol. x., 1795. It is thought to belong to the time of Charles I. or II., and may possibly have been put up by Thomas Dove, Bishop of Peterborough, who bought part of the Upton property, and died in 1630, or by his son Sir William Dove, who lived at the manor house, and rebuilt part of the chapel.

Dials in former days must very frequently have adorned the walls or the gardens of gentlemen's houses. In old engravings they are as often to be seen on the manor house as on the church. From both these positions they have in many cases been removed. There is, however, a solid square stone dial at Guiting Grange, Gloucestershire, dated 1634. At Sudeley Castle (J. C. Dent, Esq.) there are two dials : one inside the court, and nearly over the entrance archway; the other, much worn, on the battlement above the principal entrance. Both are supposed to be as old as the castle itself. A curious and picturesque many-sided dial which stands on a shaft with steps, stands in the garden of Heslington Hall, near York, and harmonizes well with the architecture of the house, and the quaintly cut yew trees near it. There is, however, no date upon the dial.

The Queen of Bohemia's dial at Heidelberg deserves a passing mention. It is a small white marble pillar with four claws for its base, and is kept in the castle as one of the memorials of the Electress Elizabeth.

A very handsome dial stands in the Earl of Derby's park at Knowsley, mounted on three steps, with four eagles supporting the dials which face the four points of the compass, and which are crowned by a globe. The eagles are, no doubt, appropriate to the crest of the eagle and child which belongs to the Stanley family. Another fine dial of this kind is in the park at Blenheim.

At Walton Hall, Wakefield, a picturesque pillar of dials, made in 1813 by George Boulby, a working mason, was bought by Mr. Waterton, and set up near the house. It is "composed of twenty equilateral triangles, so disposed as to form a similar number of dials."

The account elsewhere given of John Howard's wish to have a sun-dial placed over his grave, which he expressed as he lay on his death-bed at Cherson, in the south of Russia, was not fulfilled after his interment. He was buried at the spot he had selected, near the village of Dauphigny, about five versts north of Cherson, and a little eastward from the road to Nicholaif. His friend, Admiral Priestman, read the burial service over his remains, and Dr. Clarke, in his "Travels in Russia," in 1800, says, "a monument was afterwards erected over him. This, instead of the sun-dial he requested, consisted of a brick pyramid, or obelisk, surrounded by stone posts and chains. The posts and chains began to disappear before our arrival; and when Mr. Heber made the sketch, the obelisk alone remained in the midst of a bleak and desolate plain."

In Dr. Henderson's "Researches and Travels in Russia," in 1821-2, an account is given of what he justly calls a "cenotaph." This was subsequently built near the gate of the town of Cherson, beside the Russian cemetery. He says it is of white freestone, about 30 feet in height, surrounded by a wall of the same stone, 7 feet high by 200 in circumference. On the pedestal is a Russian inscription of the following import: "Howard, died 20 January, 1790, aged 65." Towards the summit of the pillar there is a sun-dial, but the only divisions of time exhibited are the hours from ten to two. The sketch of this cenotaph gives a structure in form not unlike a windmill without its sails: the numerals are about one-third from the top. It was built by order of the Emperor Alexander, in honour of the devoted philanthropist, whose last wishes were thus gracefully remembered, though the sun-dial was not on the grave. Dr. Clarke could not have seen this building, since Alexander did not begin to reign till 1801.

This, and the dial captured on a gun at Kelbouroun Spit (No. 214), are the only Russian specimens recorded in this collection; and excepting the one at Norrkoping, mentioned by Professor Stephens, we have none to record from northern Europe. But probably the sun-dial is as much at home in

the churchyards of Sweden as in those of Britain, for Bishop
Tegner refers to it as a familiar object.

" Even the dial, that stood on a hillock among the departed
(There full a hundred years had it stood), was embellished with blossoms,
Like to the patriarch hoary, the sage of his kith and his hamlet,
Who on his birthday is crowned by children and children's children,
So stood the ancient prophet, and mute with his pencil of iron
Marked on the tablet of stone, and measured the time and its changes,
While all around at his feet an eternity slumbered in quiet."
        Children of the Lord's Supper. (LONGFELLOW's Trans.)

So far as we have seen, the dials which are commonest in
Germany are those painted on the walls of houses. Nuremburg possesses several, Munich also, though not many of
them have mottoes. The artistic taste and religious feeling of
the Tyrol and the Salzkammergut shows itself in associating
their dials with figures of the Virgin and Child, and in one
instance, on a church near Brixen the Virgin appears with
the Infant Saviour and attendant cherubs in a vision to St.
Francis and St. Dominic, whose figures are represented
below. (See next page.)

M. Delambre (" Astronomie au 18ième siècle ") describes
a curious and ancient sun-dial in the churchyard of Brou,
near Bourg. It had no gnomon, but the person who
desired to know the time could, by placing himself at
a certain point, and with his back to the sun, see his own
shadow fall upon the hour which he wished to ascertain.
Another equally ingenious contrivance was set up at Besançon
by a councillor named Bigot, and was placed under cover.
When the sun was hidden, nothing could be seen but the
figure of an angel pointing towards some unknown object,
but in sunshine a luminous and movable dial became visible,
and the hour of the day was indicated by the shadow of the
angel's finger. At Bedos de Celles a point of light is thrown

upon the hour-line of a vertical dial, by means of a round piece of metal with a hole in the middle supported by three iron rods. The meridian line in the pavements of S. Petronio, Bologna, and Milan Cathedral show in like manner the hour

BRIXEN.

of noon by a ray of light which falls upon them through a small hole in the roof.

In the Duke of Newcastle's garden at Clumber, betwixt the house and a fine marble fountain that was brought from Italy, is a pedestal, on which are two iron hoops, about a yard in diameter, placed transversely one inside the other, with a rod across the middle. In the centre of this is a knob, which, when the sun shines, throws its shade on the figures that are marked in gold within the hoops, and thus a very elegant dial is produced.

The great equatorial dial at Delhi, constructed in A.D. 1724 by Jey Singh, Rajah of Jeypore, called by him the prince of dials, and one of the most marvellous specimens in the world, almost defies description. We are told (Murray's " Handbook to Bengal," p. 133) that the dimensions of the gnomon are as follows :—

		ft.	in.
Length of hypothenuse .	. .	118	5
„ base .	. . .	104	0
„ perpendicular	. .	56	7

The gnomon is of solid masonry edged with marble, and the shadow is thrown upon a graduated circle, also of marble.

" At a short distance, nearly in front of the great dial, is another building in somewhat better preservation ; it is also a sun-dial, or rather several dials, combined in one building. In the centre is a staircase leading to the top, and its side-walls form gnomons to concentric semi-circles, having a certain inclination to the horizon, and they represent meridians removed by a certain angle from the meridian of the observatory, the outer walls form gnomons to graduated quadrants, one to the east and the other to the west, a wall connects the four gnomons, and on its north face is described a large quadrilateral semi-circle for taking altitudes of the celestial bodies."

The inventor of these and other wonderful constructions was a Rajpoot prince, and one of the Satraps of Aurungzebe ; celebrated as an engineer, a mathematician, and an astronomer. He erected observatories at Delhi, Benares, Muttra, Ujani, and Jeypore, the city which he founded, and over which he ruled. It is said that the Emperor gave him the title of Sawai = "one and a quarter," to show that he was a quarter more excellent than any of his contemporaries. He arranged a series of astronomical tables, and hearing from a Portuguese missionary of the European discoveries, he dispatched an embassy to King John of Portugal, who in return sent him a *savant*, Xavier da Silva. Jey Singh thus became acquainted with the tables of De la Hire, published in 1702, and found the more advanced European knowledge of great service to his own calculations. The dial at Benares is on the same principle as that at Delhi.

The cross at Chichester, used as a market house, was erected in the fifteenth century by Bishop Edward Story, and repaired in the reign of Charles II. It formerly presented four faces with dials to principal streets of the city, but these have now given place to a clock. The cross at Taunton, which likewise bore dials, was taken down in 1715; that of Oakham, in Rutlandshire, similarly adorned, so far as we know, still stands. At Woodstock, a plain pillar bearing a square block on which a single dial fronts the south, and surrounded by the roof of the market house, is shown in an engraving of 1777, in Grose's "Antiquarian Repertory." At Martock, Somerset, a tall fluted column surmounted by four dials, with a ball and vane, stands on an ancient base. Bromborough Cross, in Cheshire, has been restored, and the dials removed; this has also been the case at Doncaster; and at St. Mary's, Cheltenham, a pinnacle has been put into the dial's place. At Saintsbury, Gloucestershire; Backwell, Kenn, Queen's Charlton, and Chelvey, Somerset, these picturesque monuments are, we trust, still to be found. At Ashleworth churchyard, in Gloucestershire, the shaft of an old cross, 5 feet high, likewise supports a block of dials (p. 465). Geddington Cross is said to have borne sun-dials, as well as the Queen's

Cross at Northampton ; and Tottenham High Cross, after being rebuilt in 1600 by Dean Wood, had two stone dials placed on its south and west sides, one of which remained till 1809.

At Biddulph, in Staffordshire, there is a fine old dial, four-

square, and mounted on a well-proportioned shaft, to all appearance like that of a churchyard cross, but that the dials seem to be as old as the shaft. It is thought to date from the sixteenth century. A dial of this kind was put up a few years ago at Henbury, Gloucestershire, with a drinking-fountain at its base, and it is a great ornament to the village.

The market cross at Carlisle was erected in 1682, and

consists of an Ionic column, rising from the centre of a flight of six circular steps. It is surmounted by a square block of stone bearing four faces, on each of which a sun-dial is traced; and is crowned with a lion bearing the Corporation arms. Above the capital of the column is the inscription, "Joseph Reed, Maior, 1682."

Steeple Ashton, Wilts, also owns a cross, of which probably only the original steps remain, and which now consists of a pillar bearing four vertical dials, and supported on a large square base. It is about 20 feet high, and is thus inscribed, "T. S. Repaired in 1785, and in 1826. Founded in 1071. Rebuilt 1679. Repaired in 1714." The dials probably date from the rebuilding.[1]

Four cathedral dials have already been noticed in the collection of mottoes. There was formerly one on Bristol Cathedral; and in 1794 on the south aisle of the Collegiate Church (now Cathedral) of Manchester. There is still a horizontal dial in the last-named churchyard, but so closely imprisoned by heavy iron railings that it is practically useless. And yet the Dean and Chapter might remember that

> " A prison is a house of care,
> A place where none can thrive "—

not even a sun-dial!

In Drake's "Eboracum," B. ii. ch. 2, we read "Over the doors of the south entrance of York Minster, by the care of the same Dean (Henry Finch, 1702-1728), was also placed a handsome dial, both horary and solar, on each side of which two images beat the quarters on two small bells. This, in 1750, gave place to a clock, which has been recently removed and placed inside the cathedral near the south aisle. (See No. 3).

---

[1] It is engraved in "The Antiquarian Cabinet," vol. vii., 1819.

A dial still remains on the walls of St. George's Chapel, Windsor; and there is one on Ripon Minster; and another on Merton College, Oxford, which is dated 1622.

None of the English cathedral dials are as beautiful as those of Chartres, and of Laon, where in each case an angel, eccle-

siastically draped, is represented as holding a large semi-circular dial. The one at Chartres, is dated 1578. Falaise Cathedral has also a dial, but a plain one; and there is a nearly illegible one on the south side of Amiens Cathedral. The tower of the ruined Abbey Church of Jumiéges still boasts a dial, and there is a curious one on the church of Caudebec, where the hour of noon alone is marked.

At the Château of Josselin, in Brittany, there is a picturesque semi-circular dial perched on a buttress, a human head and shoulders carved in stone, with the dial upon its breast. The date below is 1578. There is a stone dial surmounted by the crown of Spain on the cathedral of Burgos, it may be seen from the cloisters.

On one of the buttresses of Bolton Abbey there is a dial with the date 1646.

When the Cathedral of St. Paul's was rebuilt it would seem that clocks were beginning to supplant sun-dials. The tower of old St. Paul's had borne, as we learn from Mr. Charles Knight's "London," "a goodly dial, made with all the splendour that might be, with its angel pointing to the hour both of the day and night," but in the new building the "clock chamber" became an important place. Sir Christopher Wren had, nevertheless, in early days, interested himself in the subject; he designed, it is said, the sun-dial on All Soul's College, Oxford; and in Evelyn's diary we find reference made to him as well as to another Oxford mathematician, Bishop Wilkins. In 1654, while at Oxford, Evelyn dined "with the universally curious Dr. Wilkins, at Wadham College. He was the first who showed me the transparent apiaries which he had built like castles and palaces, and so ordered them one upon another as to take the honey without destroying the bees. These were adorned with a variety of dials, little statues, vanes, &c., and he was so aboundantly civil, finding me pleased with them, to present me with one of ye hives which he had empty, and which I afterwards had in my garden at Sayes Court, where it continued many years, and which his Majestie came on purpose to see and contemplate with much satisfaction. He had above, in his lodgings and gallery, a variety of shadows, dyals, perspectives, and many other artificial, mathematical, and magical curiosities, a way-wiser, a thermometer, a monstrous magnet, conic and other sections, a ballance on a demi arch, most of them of his owne and that prodigious young scholar, Mr. Ch^r Wren."

Dr. Wilkins apparently left no tangible record of his pursuits at Wadham, but Wren's dial remains at Oxford; there is also one on the wall of the Peckwater Quadrangle, Christ Church, and another on the north side of Quad. No. 1, Brasenose. But a far older dial than these is known to have once existed in the churchyard of St. Mary's, Oxford. In the " Annals of Oxford," by Anthony à Wood, it is said, when referring to the condemnation of Luther's doctrines in 1521, that "Cardinal Wolsey wrote to the University of Oxford to appoint certain men to enquire into Luther's opinions, and a convocation was held at the cardinal's house, at which the doctrine was condemned, and a 'testimony' of this was sent to Oxford and fastened on the dial in St. Mary's churchyard by Nicholas Kratzer,[1] the maker and contriver thereof . . ." The figure of this cylinder is preserved by Loggan in his " Oxonia Illustrata," plate xi. It seems to have been about 6 or 7 feet high, and was placed upon the churchyard wall. The lower part was round, the upper part had four square faces on which were dials ; it terminated in a pyramid surmounted by a ball and cross. Another writer says that it was made in 1517, at the command of Henry VIII. Mr. Henry Cotton who wrote about it to " Notes and Queries," in 1857, remarked that the churchyard wall was practically removed in 1744, but he thought there still remained a mark near the eastern end of it, where the column had stood, facing High Street.

Kratzer also erected a dial in the garden of Corpus Christi College, which was figured and described with the St. Mary's

[1] See p. 25, Introduction.

one, in a MS. preserved in the College Library, by Robert Hegge. No. xl. "Codex. Chartaceous," 4to.

Among the entries in the college books of Gonville and Caius College, Cambridge, 1576, there is a notice of a pillar which formerly stood in the courtyard, whereon was a "stone of marvellous workmanship containing in itself sixty dials, made by Theodorus Haveas of Cleves, a famous artist, and notable exponent of architecture, blazoned with the arms of the nobles who then died in the college, and dedicated by him as a memorial of his good-will to the college. On the summit of this stone is placed a winnowing fan placed like a Pegasus." The pillar was standing when Loggan's views of the colleges were taken (pub. 1688), but the dials were gone. There are notices of repairs made to several other dials in the same college, the last in 1696. There were "globe dials," a "concave dial," and six dials on the gate in Caius Court. All were probably removed early in the eighteenth century, as were the dials at Trinity College, Christ's, St. John's, Jesus, and Pembroke College, those on the last named building having been set up in 1552.

It is with regret that we part with the tradition that the fine and elaborate dial on the walls of Queen's College was placed there by Sir Isaac Newton, but the college books show that it was put up in 1733, five years after the great astronomer's death, to replace one made in 1642.

It is impossible to mention a tenth part of the ordinary dials without mottoes, even of those which have been seen and taken note of. Many localities where they may abound have either never been visited or very slightly touched upon. Even in respect of English churches the record is very partial, and of churchyards even more so. Thanks to the late Mr. Ladbroke, who published sketches of all or nearly all the churches of Norfolk, the dials of that county have been more completely noted than those of any other. But many of the dials which appear in his drawings have since disappeared. They have become decayed, and have not been replaced. Dials are wont to cling to certain neighbourhoods. They are plentiful in some districts of Yorkshire, other parts of the county are entirely without them. Next to Norfolk and Yorkshire, Cornwall and Devon have contributed the most largely to this work. Dorsetshire has dials, but not many mottoes. A village in the county of Durham, Hurworth, is noticed by Mr. Howitt in his " Visits to Remarkable Places," as " distinguished by the greatest number of sun-dials on the points of its houses of perhaps any village in the kingdom." These are due to William Emmerson, " a rough fellow, but one of the first mathematicians of his age," who was born at Hurworth, and died there in 1782. His works include a book on "Geography, Navigation and Dialling," published in 1750.

The church of Hartburn (p. 472), in Northumberland, has a curious stone cut with concave dials on its south porch; and at Whitton Shields, in Northumberland, there is a graceful cross dial, not a very common form, though there are modern specimens in other places. We have a sketch of one which stands on a pillar at Staverton Vicarage, Gloucestershire, where it was removed from King's Hill, near Dursley, by the Rev. T. Parnell. Leadbitter (" Mechanick Art of Dialling"), writing in 1737, considers the one at Little Moorfields the only cross dial in England, but he may have been mistaken.

Amongst the various devices for supporting a horizontal dial, that of placing it on the shoulders or in the hands of a figure has been more than once noticed. Mr. Syer Cuming regrets the destruction, not many years ago, of a boldly sculptured figured of Atlas resting on one knee, and bearing a spherical dial which stood in the grounds of Gloucester House,

Walworth, the attitude being that of the statue which once supported on its head the hemicyclium at Ravenna. We have also heard of a Ring dial borne on the head of a stone figure of Atlas, at Oakley Park, Shropshire, the only specimen of a Ring dial in such a position with which we are acquainted. At Flaxley Abbey, Gloucestershire, on the lawn, a curious

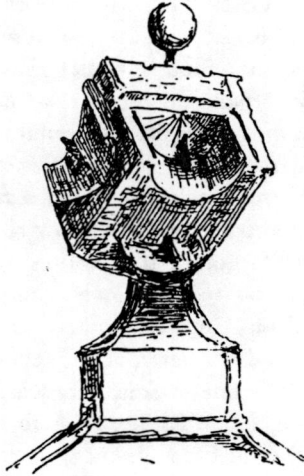

HARTBURN, NORTHUMBERLAND.

leaden figure of Time kneeling holds a sun-dial on his head. It is said to be about two hundred years old.

In Bradbourne Churchyard, Derbyshire, there is a dial mounted on a stone column with a circular base of three steps, and having a stone cap on which certain regimental badges are engraved, showing that the dial was set up by Captain Thomas Buckstone, who fought at the battle of Culloden in 1745. The face and gnomon are made of brass. In the garden at Bradbourne Hall, the ancient seat of the Buckstone family, there is another dial, entirely made of stone, except the gnomon. This is dated 1740, and is the work of the same maker as that in the churchyard.

At St. Mary's, the largest of the Scilly Isles, and near the fort called "Star Castle" (if we remember the spot where we sketched it), is an old cannon stuck upwards in the ground, and over its mouth a dial plate is fixed. What storms must have broken upon it in that tempestuous region! What hurricanes must have blown around! What dark nights covered it! and yet, whenever the sun shines, and cheerfully as if no disturbance ever reached it, the dial face becomes bright again, and the gnomon sends its shadow round the plate.

Nor will it be forgotten that a sun-dial, moss-grown and weather-beaten, stood in the lonely churchyard, and beside the ruined chapel on Conan side, near Cromarty Frith, and appealed to the mind and heart, at once thoughtful and poetic, of a journeyman stone-mason, afterwards well-known in other walks of life, Hugh Miller. "A few broken walls rose on the highest peak of the eminence, the slope was occupied by little mossy hillocks, and sorely lichened tombstones that mark the ancient graveyard, and among the tombs immediately beside the ruin there stood a rustic dial, with its iron gnomon worn to an oxydized film and green with weather stains and moss. And around this little lonely yard sprang the young wood, but just open enough towards the west to admit in slant lines along the tombstones and the ruins, the red light of the setting sun."

The thoughts suggested by this scene were embodied in his "Lines to a Sun-dial in a Churchyard":—

* * * *

"Grey dial-stone, I fain would know
 What motive placed thee here,
Where sadness heaves the frequent sigh
 And drops the frequent tear.

Like thy carved plain, grey dial-stone
　　Grief's weary mourners be :
Dark sorrow metes out time to them,
　　Dark shade metes time to thee.

　　　*　　　　*　　　　*　　　　*

" Grey dial-stone, while yet thy shade
　　Points out those hours are mine,—
While yet at every morn I rise,
　　And rest at day's decline,
Would that the SUN that formed thine,
　　His bright rays beamed on me,
That I, wise for the final day,
　　Might measure time, like thee ! "

The Museum at Taunton contains a curious old dial, which was found in the centre of a wall attached to Wigborough House, Somerset. It is a stone cube of seven or eight inches, without a gnomon, the shadows being cast by the angles of the stone into the hollows, which are lineated.

The making of dials was formerly reckoned a necessary qualification for masons, when they probably depended less than now on the architect for designs ; and they certainly showed both invention and skill. The lineating of the dial plate was a matter of science, to which the highest mathematician of his day sometimes gave his attention. The engraver's art was next called into use ; and some existing plates of bronze or copper exhibit great care and beauty of execution. Thus, in the garden of Babworth Hall, Notts, there is a finely executed plate on a stone pedestal. It was placed there some time ago by the late owner (H. Bridgeman Simpson, Esq.), after removal from his estate at Stoke Hall, Derbyshire ; and so perfect is the elaborated engraving, showing the months of the year as well as the hours of the day, that even a thought has arisen of turning it into a letter-weight for the library table

A finely-worked dial plate at Staverton Court, Gloucester-shire, has the arms of Sir William Strachen, Bart., engraved upon it, and bears the name of "Thomas Wright, Instrument maker to his Majesty George II.," the mathematician before alluded to.

A curious specimen of a dial drawn on the ceiling of a room, existed till about twenty years ago, in an old house at Market Overton, in Rutlandshire, a village where the grandmother of Sir Isaac Newton lived. It was thought that the mullion of the window served as the gnomon, and cast its shadow upon the ceiling, but it is more probable that the sunlight was reflected there by a piece of looking-glass.

At Canons Ashby, in Northamptonshire, the seat of Sir Henry Dryden, Bart., there is a brass dial-plate mounted upon a stone pedestal, which stands in the formal garden laid out in 1700 by Edward Dryden. The Dryden crest is engraved upon the face.

During the reign of Queen Anne there was a dial-maker of some note, living in London, named Edmund Culpepper, and we have received descriptions of two of his portable dials from Albert Hartshorne, Esq., F.S.A. The first of these is mounted in the ivory handle of a walking stick, which combines also a telescope and a stiletto blade to screw on the ferule end. Within the viatorium is inscribed " Edmund Culpepper at ye Cross Daggers in Moore-fields, Londini fecit 1700." the cross daggers being represented by signs, not words.

The second dial is enclosed in a round ivory box, with brass fittings, about 2¼ inches in diameter. The gnomon is on a hinge, and can be erected at will. The instrument includes a compass on which " E. C. fecit 1701 " is engraved, whilst on the dial there are the same words as those in the walking stick.

Both of these dials belonged to John Postlethwayt, chief master of St. Pauls' School, who died 1713. It is interesting to note that at Lewaigue House, in the parish of Maughold, Isle of Man, there is a dial, with a fine brass face about 8 inches square, on which is engraved " Ed^m Culpeper fecit. 1666."* Perhaps the same dial-maker is not likely to have worked for thirty-five years, but the Culpeppers may have been a race of dialists, and the two Edmunds father and son. (See No. 566.)

Ring and pocket dials were common in the seventeenth century, and even later. The ring dial, of which an illustration is given, belongs to Mrs. Dent, of Sudeley Castle, and

was found at Kemerton Court, Gloucestershire. The small piece of projecting brass, with a hole in it, slides in a groove, and acts the part of a gnomon. The small ring is for suspending it in the sun's light, with the side having the sliding hole offered to the sun, whereby a ray falls on the numbers inside the ring, and declares the hour. Such instruments may have been used for astrological purposes. They used to be made in great numbers at Sheffield.[1]

---

[1] Ring-dials have been frequently noticed by archæologists, and specimens of them are to be found in more than one museum. References to existing ones may be found in the " Reliquary," vol. ii., " Transactions of the Society of Antiquaries," iv., Series 2 ; " Archæological Journal," xxvi. ; " Journal of British Archæological Association," xix. ; Montgomeryshire Collections," xv., &c.

It has been often thought that a ring dial was the article alluded to in " As You Like It " (Act ii., Scene vii.), where Jacques tells us that his motley fool

> " Drew a dial from his poke ;
> And looking on it with lack-lustre eye,
> Says, very wisely, " It is ten o'clock."

In parts of Italy and Tyrol these dials are still carried about by the shepherds. Walter White ("Holidays in

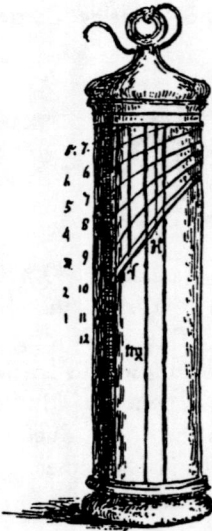

ULMER'S DIAL.　　　　PYRENEAN DIAL.

Tyrol ") mentions them as in use about Paneveggio, and a few months ago a specimen was bought in Primiero. It happened to be the last in the shop, but the shopkeeper said they were frequently demanded by purchasers.

There is however, a simpler form of dial described in an

old volume (" De Horologiis ") by John Conrad Ulmer, dated
MDLVI., which may have been the common pocket-dial of
Shakespeare's time.   It is almost identical in form with the
instrument now in use amongst the peasants of the Pyrenees,
as may be seen by the accompanying figures.   The Pyrenean
dial consists of a small cylinder, made of boxwood, and not
larger in size than a pocket-knife.   The top of it can be drawn
out, when a small blade turning on a pin forms a gnomon,
which can be adjusted to the lines, figures, and initials of the
month that are carved in the wood.   It will tell the time

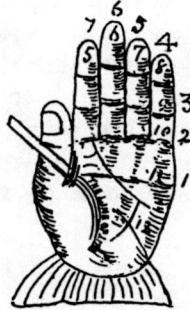

within five minutes.   Ulmer's book contains three woodcuts
of the pocket-dial; and it only differs from the Pyrenean one
in giving the signs of the zodiac instead of the initials of the
months.[1]

Directions for a still simpler dial, called the " Shepherd's
Kalender, or the Countryman's " companion, are given in a
work "sold by Edw. Midwinter at the Looking glass, on
London Bridge."

[1] A similar dial made in ivory is in the Museo Correr, at Venice,
dated " Anno D[ni] 1638 Fr. Clement. Ven[l] Sac[s] Cap[t] F." There is also
one in the Nuremburg Museum, dated 1556.

" To tell what is a Clock (when the Sun Shines) by one's hand.

"Take a small streight stick of about four inches long, and hold it between the Forer Finger, and the Thumb of the left hand, and turn about towards the Sun till the Shadow of the Ball of the Thumb touch the line of Life, and then the Shadow of the Stick will appear on that part of the Hand, which tells the Right Hour of the Day."

There are several specimens of pocket-dials with compasses, of various shapes and workmanship, in the British Museum. The museum of Edinburgh possesses a round one, which was presented by J. Johnstone, Esq.; and also a small circular silver dial, found in the ruins of an old house at Carnwath. Small ivory portariums, combining dial and compass, were much made at Nuremburg in the sixteenth and seventeenth centuries, and are not unfrequently to be met with.

The Rev. J. Stacye, Governor and Chaplain of the Shrewsbury Hospital, Sheffield, has in his possession a very elaborately worked silver pocket dial with compass, which is of French manufacture, the maker's name being Sautout Choiz, of Paris.

A specimen of a portable dial with compass was found in 1871, near the ruins of Pipewell Abbey, Northamptonshire.

The dial plate was set on a hinge, and when lifted up was supported by a small cross, which also acted as a gnomon. In the hollow of the box was a metal plate, to which a steel or iron magnet had been attached, and on this was stamped the head of a bishop, with the letters "S. D.," which have been thought to signify St. Dunstan, the patron saint of metal workers.

Another kind of ring dial, or dial ring, is described in " De Symbolis Heroicis " (Antwerp, 1634), by Silvestro Petro Sancta, of the Society of Jesus. This is a finger ring, the bezel of which, bisected, contained the hours ; a magnetic needle was placed in the centre, so as to regulate the position of the dial, while the shadow was thrown by a pointer fixed to its setting. It was in fact but a miniature edition of the ordinary portarium, and when not in use was concealed by the jewel of the ring, which closed upon the dial like the lid upon a watch.

Though the construction of complicated dials requires the skill of the mathematician, and the adornment of them might employ an artist, there is no doubt that the making and setting of a simple dial is no more than what any intelligent workman can accomplish. A gentleman whose name has been frequently mentioned in these pages as having put up several sun-dials on his estate, had the work done by two intelligent masons, who by the help of the Encyclopedia learnt all that was necessary for the setting of the dials ; the chief requisites being a candle, a piece of string, and the North Star. Some forty or fifty years ago this same gentleman sent for a well-known dialler in the district of Craven, in Yorkshire, to put up a dial on the village inn, he himself having painted on the sign board the portraits of the Queen and Prince Albert. It was election time, and there were fears that the man was about to give his vote to the enemy.

He was captured at a public house, driven up to the squire's door late one evening, and duly instructed in what was required of him.   As for the dial, he was willing to go to work at once and take his measurements.   The squire remonstrated, it was a dark night, there was no moon.   "Nay, nay," said the old fellow with more knowledge, looking up at the stars, "it's a gran' neet."   "What d'ye want then?"   "Eh, I wants nout but a cannel and a bit o' band."   With these materials the party proceeded to the village and the measurements were duly taken.   The order was, however, a long time in being carried out, as the old man was better at promises than performances, and the work was put off from month to month.   At last, in reply to a remonstrance, the gentleman received the following letter.

—— —— 1843.

"DEAR SIR,
        "Ever since I have imbrased every applicable opportunity possible for a complition, and yet after all defeated! if I could possess you (but I have treated you so) we will let alone fixing a time, the model will take two or three days yet to finish it, you need not be afraid of any preposterous executions (because it might fright Her Majesties Horses as her Royal Highness and her consort Prince will ride over every day [1]) though I could like somewhat handsome with regard to its perspicuous situation, and a little towards a melioration of my conduct towards you.

        "I have for the present resolved it the most extant job I have on hand, if I am well shall not delay another hour till it be finished, but every process requires its own time, say two days to finish the Model, 1 day in casting, when I take it to Keighley (on my way to Wilsden to see my sister whom I've anxiously expected) then its to paint and Gild but I must be

[1] Alluding to the portraits on the signboard.

I I

over at K—— in the meantime but cannot with any pro-
priety fix a day yet.

"Dear Sir,

"Your humble servant,

—— ——"

The dial was finished and brought in course of time, and
fixed up on the village inn where it still remains, and has the
honour of being noticed in "Murray's Handbook."

Amongst the eminent men who have paid respect to the
sun-dial may be reckoned George Stephenson, the great railway engineer, who set his son Robert (still a boy at school)
the task of making a dial to be placed over their cottage door
at West Moor, near Newcastle. Father and son together got
a stone, which they hewed, carved, and polished; and, with
the aid of "Ferguson's Astronomy," they found out the
method of making the necessary calculations to adapt the dial
to the latitude of Killingworth. The dial, with the gnomon
coming from the sun's face, and dated "August 11th,
MDCCCXVI," may still be seen over the entrance to the
humble early home of these distinguished men. Let us then
venture to hope that the healthy taste of the Stephensons,
who by their inventive genius have contributed more than
any other men to disturb society in its old stationary customs,
may plead in favour of the sun-dial—its preservation and its
continued use.

> "'Tis an old dial, dark with many a stain,
>   In summer crown'd with drifting orchard bloom,
> Trick'd in the autumn with the yellow rain,
>   And white in winter like a marble tomb;
> And round about its grey time-eaten brow,
>   Lean letters speak—a worn and shatter'd row—
> 'I am a shade; a shadow too art thou:
>   I mark the Time: say, Gossip, dost thou soe?'"

In taking leave of the reader, we will quote a line from Dante's " Paradiso," which is well fitted for a dial motto, and not inappropriate to the action of bidding farewell :—

" PENSA, CHE QUESTO DÌ MAI NON RAGGIORNA."

Stone formerly the Seven Dials.
Weybridge 1864.

NON REGO NISI REGAR.

APPENDIX

ON THE

CONSTRUCTION OF SUN-DIALS.

BY

W. R.

CONTENTS.

ON THE CONSTRUCTION OF SUN-DIALS.

IN this short chapter I shall confine myself, as far as may be, to the mechanical construction of sun-dials. Those who wish to understand the theory may refer to any encyclopædia, and almost all works on astronomy have something to say on the subject. The student who will take the trouble to master thus the whole subject will not fail to find it at once interesting and highly instructive. I can recommend the following works, viz. :—

"Elementary Lessons in Astronomy," by J. Norman Lockyer, published by Macmillan and Co., 1877.

"Clocks, Watches and Bells," by Edmund Beckett Denison, published by John Weale, 1860. This work contains an account of the Dipleidoscope, invented by J. M. Bloxam, by which form of sun-dial Mr. Dent, the maker of the Westminster clock, used to rate his chronometer.

"Dialling," by William Leybourn, published by A. and J. Churchill, 1700. This is the most exhaustive work which I know on sun-dials of every form and shape.

"Treatise on Dialling," by Peter Nicholson, published in Newcastle-on-Tyne, 1833. This last is perhaps the clearest work of all on the construction of sun-dials, but it requires some patience to master the author's method of projection.

Sun-dials may be either *fixed* or *portable*. For the latter I would refer the student to the new edition of the " Encyclopædia Britannica."

Fixed sun-dials may be in any plane. That is to say, the dial itself may be *horizontal* or sloping (usually called *inclining*), or *vertical*, as on the wall of a house, in which case they may face in any direction, and if not facing due south they are usually called *declining*, or the dial may be spherical or cylindrical and either convex or concave.

Again a dial may either be opaque, as is usually the case, or the shadow may be cast upon a window of ground glass. This latter type is called *refractive*, and it is a singularly elegant form, having the advantage, very suited to our climate, of being observable from indoors, and the shadow of the gnomon will appear to go round the same way as the hands of a clock, instead of the reverse way, as must be the case in a wall sun-dial.

A further variety of sun-dials are those called *reflective*. In the numbers of " Aunt Judy's Magazine " for March and April, 1878, there is a charming account of how Sir Isaac Newton placed a mirror on the floor of his room which reflected the sun's rays on to the ceiling, upon which the hour lines were traced.

I propose to explain the way to construct two kinds of sun-dials only, viz., *horizontal* dials and *wall* dials, the latter facing to any point of the compass between due west and due east.

The gnomon, or stile of the sun-dial, must always be parallel to the polar axis of the earth. Strictly speaking there should be a correction for the slight angle due to the distance from the earth's centre, but the distance of the earth from the sun is so great that this may in practice be disregarded. Otherwise expressed, the gnomon must always point to the pole star, or to speak again more precisely, to the centre round which the pole star appears to revolve.

The simplest form of a sun-dial is a watch face marked to twenty-four hours, *i.e.*, twelve and twelve hours, with a wire passed through the centre hole. Stretch the wire so as to point to the pole star and place the mark for XII or noon at the bottom, and you have a complete but inconvenient form of sun-dial; inconvenient because the shadow would sometimes fall on the upper and sometimes on the lower face.

Another simple form is a concave half cylinder or half sphere, with a wire stretched down the middle, and on the surface where the cylinder (or sphere) has been cut in two, the hour lines will be at equal distances of fifteen degrees apart. This form of dial will, however, evidently only show the time between VI a.m. and VI p.m.

In a horizontal dial, the angle of the gnomon will always be equal to the latitude of the place. In a vertical sun-dial facing due south, it will equal the complement of the latitude, or in other words it will equal 90° minus the latitude, *i.e.*, what is left of a right angle after deducting the angle of the latitude. The woodcut, Fig. 1, will make this clear to anyone having the least knowledge of geometry.

Let E E be the equator of the earth.

C P the polar axis,

L the position of the sun-dial on the earth's surface.

The angle, E C L, will be the latitude of the place.

The level of the earth's surface, and of the horizontal dial at L will be the line, T P, which is a tangent to C L, the radius.

The line A L G will be the gnomon, parallel to C P, the polar axis.

It is evident that the angle G L P, the angle of the gnomon, is equal to the angle E C L, which is the latitude. *Q.E.D.*

Also, the line V L will represent a wall dial, and since the angle V L P is a right angle, the angle V L G will be the complement of the angle G L P.

But the angle G L P is equal to the latitude, therefore the angle of the gnomon in a wall dial is the complement of the latitude. *Q.E.D.*

How to set off a given angle.—The best way to set off

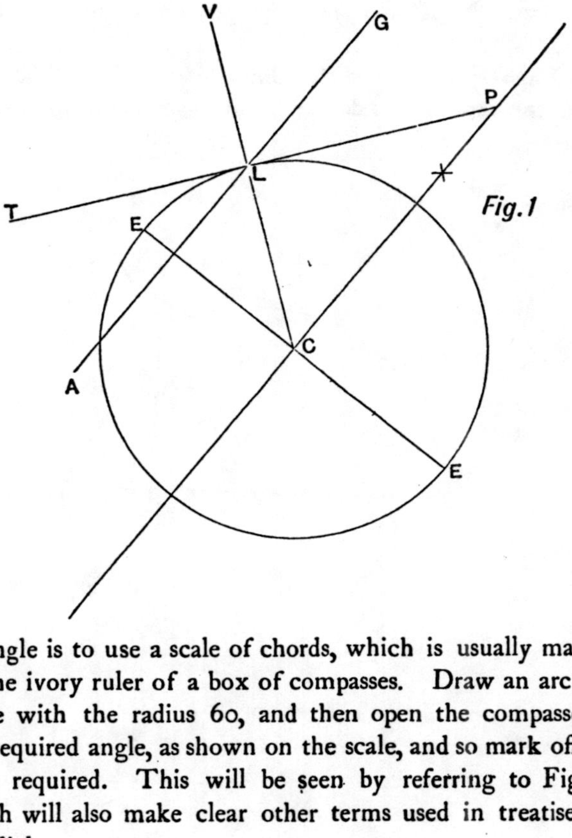

Fig.1

an angle is to use a scale of chords, which is usually marked on the ivory ruler of a box of compasses. Draw an arc of a circle with the radius 60, and then open the compasses to the required angle, as shown on the scale, and so mark off the scale required. This will be seen by referring to Fig. 2, which will also make clear other terms used in treatises on sun-dials.

From the centre, C, describe a circle with the radius of 60 on the scale of chords.

From the end of the diameter at D, measure off with the same radius, D X, and draw C X S.

Draw N X and D S perpendicular to the diameter *d* D.

Then X D is called the Chord of the Arc of 60 degrees, and the chord of 60 degrees is always equal to the radius.

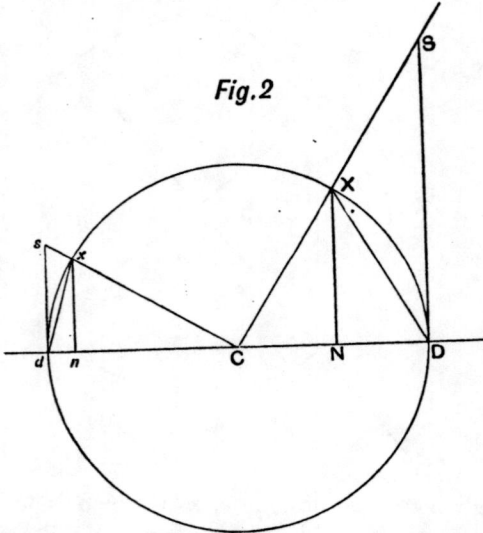

Fig.2

D S is called the Tangent of 60 degrees.

N X is called the Sine of 60 degrees, and

C S is called the Secant of 60 degrees.

All these scales are marked on the ivory ruler in a box of instruments, and the seller of them will explain how to use them.

There is also another Scale, called the Scale of Half Tangents, but it would be more correct to call it the Scale of Tangents of half the angle.

On the left side of the centre in Fig. 2 the small italic letters indicate the chord, &c., for 30 degrees, thus :—

xd is called the Chord of the Arc of 30 degrees.

ds is called the Tangent of 30 degrees.

nx is called the Sine of 30 degrees.

Cs is called the Secant of 30 degrees.

It is evident that the angle may be set off by either of the three Scales of Chords, of Tangents, or of Sines, but the Scale of Chords is the most convenient. All are more accurate than the brass semicircle sometimes called a protractor.

To construct a Horizontal Sun-dial for the latitude of 54 *degrees.* Plate I., Fig. 3.—Draw a square or rectangle, as shown in Fig. 3, and down the centre draw a perpendicular line P S. On the left of this draw a parallel line, and make its distance from P S equal to the thickness of the gnomon. This double line is called the substile (or substyle). In all horizontal dials, and in all wall dials which face due south, the substile will be perpendicular, and the vi o'clock hour line will be horizontal or at right angles with the substile.

At any convenient point draw the horizontal line vi O vi, cutting the substile in O.

Draw O F, making the angle xii O F equal to the latitude or 54 degrees.

Draw xii F perpendicular to O F.

Make xii P equal to xii F.

Extend the top line on each side as shown.

The angle of an hour is 15 degrees. Draw lines P 1, P 2, P 3, P 4, and P 5 so that the angles at P are each 15 degrees.

Then the true hour lines of the dial will be drawn from O to the points 1, 2, 3, 4, and 5. The VI o'clock line will be horizontal as already drawn, and the hours before VI a.m. and after VI p.m. will be continuations of the hour lines above the VI o'clock lines, taking care to allow for the thickness of the gnomon.

If the dial be divided into half and quarter hours, or into minutes, the angles must be correctly set off at P.

The gnomon will be a right-angled triangle, having one angle of 54 degrees at O, and placed on the substile O XII.

Plate I., Fig. 4.—Another method is as follows, and for the sake of clearness in this and in the subsequent examples I assume the gnomon to have no thickness.

Describe a circle N E S W, and draw the lines N S perpendicular, and E W horizontal.

From S, set off by the Scale of Chords, the arc S a equal to the latitude or 54 degrees, and from W set off the arc W b also 54 degrees.

Join E a and E b, cutting N S in P and in Æ.

Describe the arc of a circle W Æ E. This may be done by trial or from the centre C, making Æ C equal to the Secant of 36 degrees, for 36 is the complement of 54. That is to say, 36 + 54 = 90 degrees.

Divide the semicircle W N E into arcs of 15 degrees each at the points 7, 8, 9, 10, 11, and 1, 2, 3, 4, 5.

From O draw O 8, cutting the arc W Æ E in 8_1.

From P draw P 8_1 x, cutting the circle N E S W in x.

Draw VIII X O VIII, which will be the VIII o'clock hour-line.

The other hour-lines will be drawn by the same method.

The gnomon will be a right angled triangle, having one

angle of 54 degrees, and placed on the substile N O, with the 54 degree angle at O.

It is advisable to use both methods so as to correct any error.

To construct a Wall Sun-dial, facing due South, for the latitude of 54 degrees, the above methods may be followed, the only difference being that the *complement of the latitude* must be taken in every case in lieu of the latitude, that is (in our example) 36 in lieu of 54 degrees. (Plate I., Figs. 3 and 4.)

Similarly the Secant of 54 degrees must be taken instead of the Secant of 36 degrees.

If a horizontal and a wall dial be drawn, the one on the bottom and the other on the side of the inside of a box, the gnomon will be common to both, and the hour-lines of the respective dials will join where the bottom and the side of the box meet.

To construct a Wall Sun-dial for the latitude of 54 degrees, declining from the South towards the West 30 degrees. Plate II., Fig. 5.—Draw a horizontal line H T.

From any point A in this line draw a line A S, making the angle T A S equal to 30 degrees.

If the dial had been declining towards the East this line A S would be drawn to the left instead of to the right.

Draw A Z perpendicular to H T, and A C perpendicular to A S.

Make A C the xii o'clock or meridian line of a horizontal dial, and draw its hour-lines, C i, C ii, C iii, &c., and C xi, C x, C ix, &c., as explained *ante.*

Draw C P, cutting A S in P, and H T in B, and make the angle A C P equal to the latitude or 54 degrees.

Make A Z equal to A P. Then is Z the centre of the

declining dial, and lines drawn from Z to I, II, III, &c., will be the true hour-lines of the declining dial.

To find the position of the substile, draw B G perpendicular to H T, and cutting A S in G.

Make A R equal to B G, and join Z R. Then will Z R be the position of the substile.

From R draw R Q perpendicular to Z R, and make R Q equal to A B.

The angle R Z Q will be the angle of the gnomon.

Plate II., Fig. 6.—Another method is as follows, and let us in this case take a wall sun-dial declining 30 degrees from the south towards the *East*.

Upon C as a centre, with the radius C A, describe the quadrant A X Q, and with the same radius from A (which shall be the centre of the dial) describe the arc C L, and with the Scale of Chords make the arc C L equal to 36 degrees, the complement of the latitude, and draw the horizontal line R C Q.

Draw A L D, cutting R Q in D.

Cut off from Q to A the arc Q X equal to 30 degrees, the declination of the dial.

Join X C, prolonging the line down to S.

From the centre C with the radius C D describe the arc D S.

Draw S R perpendicular to R D.

Make C Y equal to S R, and join A Y.

Then will A Y be the position of the substile.

Through Y draw the long line G Y P M perpendicular to A Y.

Make Y G equal to C R, and join A G.

Then will the angle Y A G be the angle of the gnomon.

From Y draw Y *g* perpendicular to A G, and make Y O equal to Y *g*.

Then will o be the centre of the equinoctial circle. Draw one half of this circle with any radius from F to F, making F F parallel to G Y P.

Draw o P 12, cutting the equinoctial circle in 12.

From 12 lay off arcs of 15 degrees each, as at 1, 2, 3, &c., and 11, 10, 9, &c.

From o draw lines o 1, o 2, &c., and o 11, o 10, &c., cutting the line G Y P M in I. II., &c., and XI., X., &c.

Then the true hour lines will be drawn from A to I., II., &c., and to XI., X., IX., &c.

Trigonometrical Calculations. There are various other methods of delineating sun-dials, but I think that those which I have given are the simplest. It can never be amiss, however, to check the geometrical or projective methods by trigonometrical calculations which are fully explained and illustrated in Leybourn's work.

Equation of Time. A sun-dial will only agree with the clock on four days in the year.

There are two reasons for the two not agreeing. One is that we divide the year into 365 days, whereas there are really about 365¼ days in the twelvemonth.

The other is due to the revolution of the earth round the sun.

Both subjects are very clearly explained in Denison's work on " Clocks, Watches, and Bells," in which work the author gives a table of the Equation of Time. In the Nautical Almanack, and in many other almanacks, the number of minutes and seconds which must be added to or deducted from sun-dial time (called apparent time), are given for every day in the year.

It is always well to engrave such a table (more or less in extenso) on the sun-dial itself, unless it is graphically shown by a curve, as I shall now proceed to describe.

To construct a sundial which at noon on each day of the year shall show true mean time. Plate III., Figs. 7 and 8.—Let GW (Fig. 7) be the face in section of a wall sun-dial, and GP the gnomon thereof.

When the sun at noon on the 21st of June is high in the

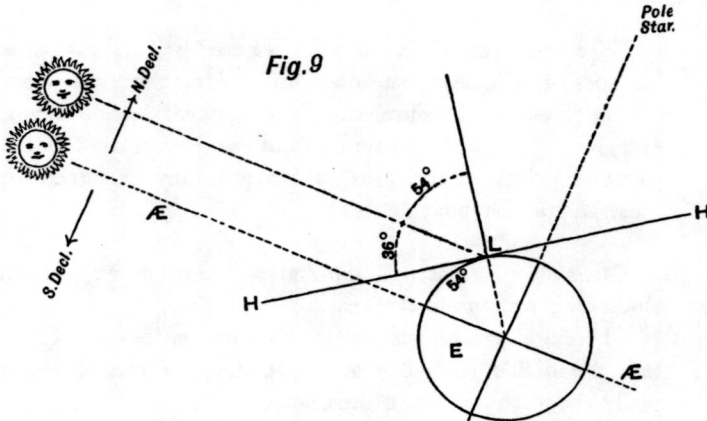

Fig. 9

heavens, as at S_1, it will cast the shadow of P on the dial at s_1.

In the Spring or Autumn, when the sun is at S_2, it will cast P's shadow at s_2.

When the sun is on the horizon, as at S_3, it will cast the shadow of P horizontally to s_3.

Now, in the Nautical Almanack will be found a table of the sun's apparent declinations, which means the distance of the sun at noon for each day of the year north or south of the heaven's equator. See Fig. 9.

K K

Let E be the earth, and ÆÆ the line of the equator extended to the heavens.

Through L draw a tangent H H, which will represent the horizon at the latitude L, say 54 degrees north.

Inasmuch as, on account of its great distance from the earth, a line drawn from the sun to L will be practically parallel to the line drawn from the sun to the centre of the earth, the sun when on the celestial equator will at L appear to be 36 degrees above the horizon. But 36 degrees is the co-latitude.

Wherefore the altitude of the sun at noon above the horizon can be ascertained for any day in the year by adding to the co-latitude of the place the north declination or subtracting the south declination respeectively, as the cas may be.

Plate III., Fig. 7.—Construct a table of altitudes as above, and make Ps_3 equal to 60 degrees on your scale of chords.

Set off from s_3 to w, by the scale of signs, the distances $s_3 s_2, —s_3 s_1, —$&c.

Or, set the angles off along the arc by the scale of chords.

Plate III., Fig. 8.—Having now ascertained the vertical height of the shadow of P for every day in the year, transfer them to the face of the dial, and write the dates opposite each line.

From the table of the equation of time set off the number of minutes and seconds on the right or the left of the meridian line according as they have to be added or subtracted, and you will have a series of points forming a curve like a figure of eight.

If the above is done with accuracy when the shadow of P falls on the curve, you will not only have the true mean time (subject only to the slight error for Leap year, which will average only about $\frac{1}{4}$ minute), but you will have the day of the month as well.

By the true mean time I mean the mean or clock time for the longitude of the place. If it is desired to show Greenwich clock time you must move the figure of eight to the right or to the left, as the case may be, or otherwise state on the sun-dial how many minutes the place is before or after Greenwich time. This latter will probably be considered the better plan.

Such a sun-dial as the above is of real value in country places. There is a fine example on the Guard House at the Palace of the Prince of Monaco, and there the end of the gnomon is flattened out to a disc with a hole in the centre having knife edges, and when I saw it the bright sun of Italy cast a clear spot of light about the size of a shilling on the lines of the curve, which, as well as the hour lines, were about $\frac{3}{4}$ inch broad. The sun-dial itself must have been 12 or 14 feet high.

On the size, the material, and the fabrication of sun-dials.— I sometimes think that when our architects are fain to put in a blank window to relieve part of the wall of a house, they might give us a sun-dial of large dimensions in place thereof. A sun-dial can hardly be too large, and it might very well cover the whole end of a barn, or even of a house.

If made of small size as is usual in England, the best material for horizontal dials is brass, and for wall dials slate, or marble, or granite.

In all cases the dial itself, or a full-sized model, should be made first in the workshop.

To orient a sun-dial.—It will be useless to make a dial accurately, unless it be truly placed as regards the points of compass.

I recommend the following procedure in fixing a horizontal dial.

First consult a large Ordnance map (scale of an acre to a square inch), and place your dial approximately due north and south. Then level it by means of a spirit level.

Correct the line of the gnomon both by a compass and by the sun at noon, as rectified for the equation of time.

Then at the distance of some three or four yards north of the dial drive two long poles into the ground with a cross-piece at the top, like a tall Greek letter Π. The like, but not so tall, to the south of the dial.

Hang both north and south plummet lines, and during the day make the two lines and the gnomon in one line.

Ask any astronomical friend, or any ship's captain, at what hour the pole star crosses the meridian, at that hour get the two plummet lines in a line with the pole star. Be careful in doing this to move the one as much to the right as the other to the left, for otherwise the gnomon will not be in the same line.

Having got the plummet lines true to the pole star, it will not be difficult in the morning to adjust the gnomon.

For a wall declining dial the plan will be similar, but it will be necessary for one pair of the poles to project above the eaves. The other must be at some distance from the wall, but it need not go above the eaves.

A proper template of thin wood must be made and taken into the workshop. From this the angle can be accurately set off.

I shall be much gratified if this appendix to the work of Miss Horatia K. F. Gatty adds to its value. If any youthful reader will take the trouble to construct a sun-dial he will find that it will teach him more astronomy than a course of popular lectures could afford him, and he will almost surely be led to study further the mysteries of the great firmament on high, and in so doing he will every year of his life more and more marvel at the extent of the Divine power and wisdom, and be prepared hereafter, when we shall no longer see only as through a glass darkly, to truly enjoy that fuller knowledge which will be one of the joys which an infinite Love destines for us above.

On a tomb in Westminster Abbey you may read—

> "Man's life is measured by the workes, not dayes,
> No slothful age, but active youth hath prayse."

which suggested the following lines in a lady's album :—

> Our neighbours of a southern clime,
> forgetting the true gauge of Time,
> in their bright tongue have coined the phrase
> (suggestive of luxurious ways)
> of "dolce far niente."
>
> But "carpe diem" is the rule,
> which we, dear friend, were taught at school ;
> each day more swiftly fleets away,
> the gnomon's shadow will not stay,
> "old Time is still a-flying" !
>
> But oh ! we need not fear his flight,
> each day is long if spent aright,
> that year is long where much is wrought,
> 'tis sloth alone we count as nought,
> the cypher of existence.
>
> The keen steel blade may wear away,
> but rust more surely brings decay ;
> ah ! then of cankering sloth beware,
> bright be thy steel with work and wear,
> its temper true and trusty.

Then should our mortal foe appear
and from thy life cut half its years,
say not that shortened is that life,
say rather ended is the strife ;—
beyond the grave thy resting.

W. R.

Newcastle-on-Tyne,
December, 1887.

ERRATUM.

P. 238, line 12 from below, *for* St. Bunyan *read* St. Buryan.

PLATE I.

Fig. 3.

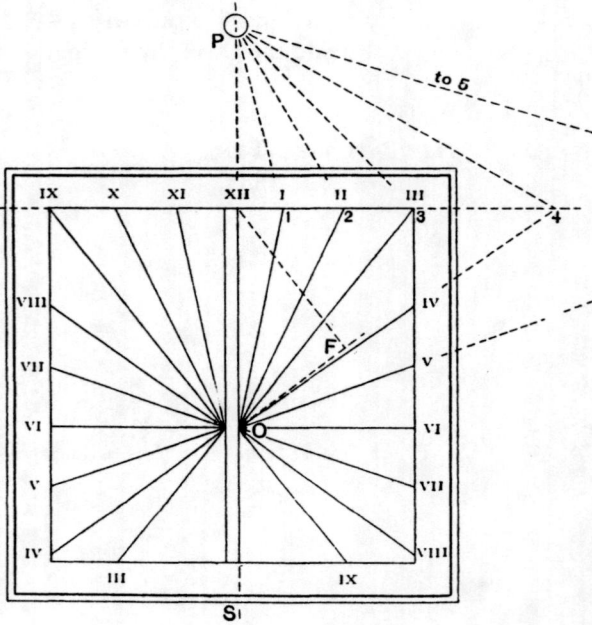

Fig. 4.

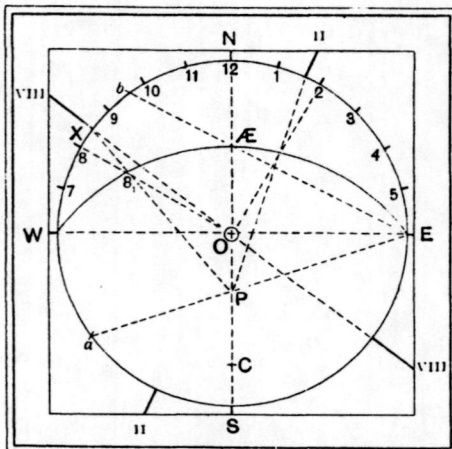

PLATE II.

Fig.5. West

Fig.6. East

WALL DECLINING.

PLATE III.

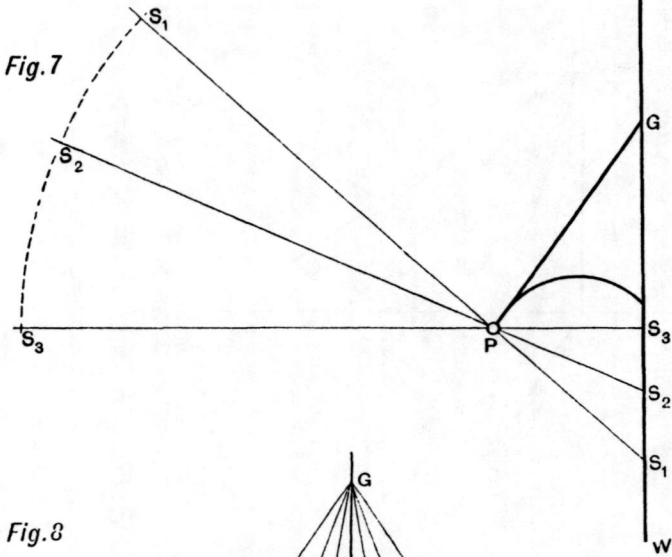

Fig.7

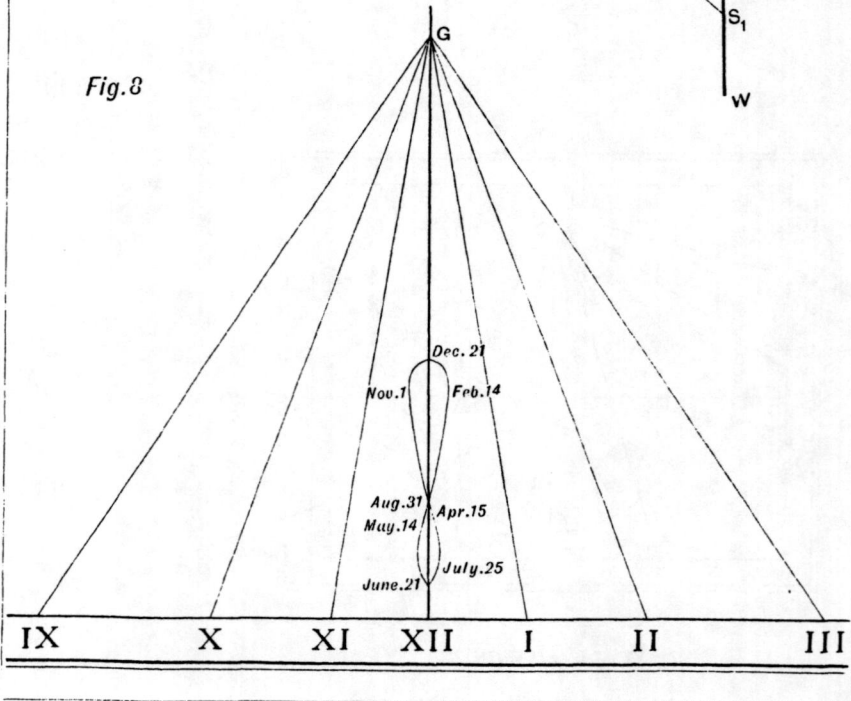

Fig.8

INDEX TO DIALS WITH MOTTOES.

The References are to the Numbers of the Dial Mottoes.

INDEX TO INTRODUCTION AND
FURTHER NOTES.

The References are to the Numbers of the Pages.

Chiswick Press

PRINTED BY CHARLES WHITTINGHAM AND CO.
TOOKS COURT, CHANCERY LANE, LONDON, E.C.

Printed in the United States
96263LV00002B/127/A

9 780548 135648